Volker Thomas, PhD
Terri A. Karis, PhD
Joseph L. Wetchler, PhD
Editors

Clinical Issues with Interracial Couples: Theories and Research

Clinical Issues with Interracial Couples: Theories and Research has been co-published simultaneously as *Journal of Couple & Relationship Therapy*, Volume 2, Numbers 2/3 2003.

Pre-publication REVIEWS, COMMENTARIES, EVALUATIONS . . .

" A USEFUL TEXT IN FAMILY SYSTEMS AND THERAPY COURSES. . . . A very useful, and even necessary, text for clinicians who do couples work and will increasingly be dealing with cross-cultural and interracial couples. The complexity of intimacy, race, and socialization are successfully tackled. I liked that the authors allowed the resilience of these couples to come through while showing them and their families as ordinary people. "

Maria P. P. Root, PhD
Psychologist,
Seattle, Washington

More pre-publication
REVIEWS, COMMENTARIES, EVALUATIONS . . .

"**V**ERY TIMELY AND INNO-
VATIVE. . . . A LANDMARK
IN THE LITERATURE. . . . Cap-
tures the real-life stories and
diversity of interracial couples—
complete with empirical data
to further our knowledge and
understanding of an important but often neglected area
in couple and family therapy.
The book is rich in both content and context. . . . WILL
GREATLY ENHANCE PRACTI-
tioners' and students' cultural awareness and sensitivity and overall as-
sessment/treatment skills related
to working with interracial couples.
We will rely on this book in our
program for years to come."

Marlene F. Watson, PhD
*Director, Programs in Couple
and Family Therapy
College of Nursing and Health
Professions*

The Haworth Press, Inc.

Clinical Issues with Interracial Couples: Theories and Research

Clinical Issues with Interracial Couples: Theories and Research has been co-published simultaneously as *Journal of Couple & Relationship Therapy*, Volume 2, Numbers 2/3 2003.

The *Journal of Couple & Relationship Therapy* Monographic "Separates"
(formerly the *Journal of Couples Therapy* series)*

Below is a list of "separates," which in serials librarianship means a special issue simultaneously published as a special journal issue or double-issue *and* as a "separate" hardbound monograph. (This is a format which we also call a "DocuSerial.")

"Separates" are published because specialized libraries or professionals may wish to purchase a specific thematic issue by itself in a format which can be separately cataloged and shelved, as opposed to purchasing the journal on an on-going basis. Faculty members may also more easily consider a "separate" for classroom adoption.

"Separates" are carefully classified separately with the major book jobbers so that the journal tie-in can be noted on new book order slips to avoid duplicate purchasing.

You may wish to visit Haworth's website at . . .

http://www.HaworthPress.com

. . . to search our online catalog for complete tables of contents of these separates and related publications.

You may also call 1-800-HAWORTH (outside US/Canada: 607-722-5857), or Fax 1-800-895-0582 (outside US/Canada: 607-771-0012), or e-mail at:

docdelivery@haworthpress.com

Clinical Issues with Interracial Couples: Theories and Research, edited by Volker Thomas, PhD, Terri A. Karis, PhD, and Joseph L. Wetchler, PhD (Vol. 2, No. 2/3, 2003). *"A USEFUL TEXT IN FAMILY SYSTEMS AND THERAPY COURSES. . . . A very useful, and even necessary, text for clinicians who do couples work and will increasingly be dealing with cross-cultural and interracial couples." (Maria P. P. Root, PhD, Psychologist, Seattle, Washington)*

Couples, Intimacy Issues, and Addiction, edited by Barbara Jo Brothers, MSW, BCD, CGP (Vol. 10, No. 3/4, 2001).* *"A much needed and insightful book for those who already work with couples, and a marvelous addition to the library of any new therapist just venturing into the field of couples therapy. This book opens windows to explore, with respect and understanding, the many ways of partnering." (Mary Ellen O'Hare-Lavin, PhD, Clinical Psychologist, Private Practice; Adjunct Faculty, Oakton Community College, Des Plaines, Illinois)*

Couples and Body Therapy, edited by Barbara Jo Brothers, MSW, BCD, CGP (Vol. 10, No. 2, 2001).* *"A wonderful revisiting and blending of two significant fields. Once digested, one wonders how the therapist can focus on the couple without addressing the bodies they inhabit." (Cindy Ashkins, PhD, LCSW, LMT, Couples Psychotherapist and Licensed Bodyworker in Private Practice, Metairie, North Carolina)*

The Abuse of Men: Trauma Begets Trauma, edited by Barbara Jo Brothers, MSW, BCSW (Vol. 10, No. 1, 2001).* *"Addresses a topic that has been neglected. . . . This book is unique in adopting a systematic perspective that focuses not solely on the males who have been abused but also on their partners and family members. . . . Gives detailed and specific directions for intervening with couples who have experienced multiple traumas." (Joseph A. Micucci, PhD, Associate Professor of Psychology, Chestnut Hill College, Pennsylvania)*

The Personhood of the Therapist, edited by Barbara Jo Brothers, MSW, BCSW (Vol. 9, No. 3/4, 2000).* *Through suggestions, techniques, examples, and case studies, this book will help you develop a great sense of openness about yourself and your feelings, enabling you to offer clients more effective services.*

Couples Connecting: Prerequisites of Intimacy, edited by Barbara Jo Brothers, MSW, BCSW (Vol. 9, No. 1/2, 2000).* *"Brothers views marriage as an ideal context for the psychological and spiritual evolution of human beings, and invites therapists to reflect on the role they can play in facilitating this. Readers are sure to recognize their clients among the examples given and to return to their work with a renewed vision of the possibilities for growth and change." (Eleanor D.*

Macklin, PhD, Emeritus Professor and former Director of the Marriage and Family Therapy program, Syracuse University, New York)

Couples Therapy in Managed Care: Facing the Crisis, edited by Barbara Jo Brothers, MSW, BCSW (Vol. 8, No. 3/4, 1999).* *Provides social workers, psychologists, and counselors with an overview of the negative effects of the managed care industry on the quality of mental health care. Within this book, you will discover the paradoxes that occur with the mixing of business principles and service principles and find valuable suggestions on how you can creatively cope within the managed care context. With* Couples Therapy in Managed Care, *you will learn how you can remain true to your own integrity and still get paid for your work and offer quality services within the current context of managed care.*

Couples and Pregnancy: Welcome, Unwelcome, and In-Between, edited by Barbara Jo Brothers, MSW, BCSW (Vol. 8, No. 2, 1999).* *Gain valuable insight into how pregnancy and birth have a profound psychological effect on the parents' relationship, especially on their experience of intimacy.*

Couples, Trauma, and Catastrophes, edited by Barbara Jo Brothers, MSW, BCSW (Vol. 7, No. 4, 1998).* *Helps therapists and counselors working with couples facing major crises and trauma.*

Couples: A Medley of Models, edited by Barbara Jo Brothers, MSW, BCSW, BCD (Vol. 7, No. 2/3, 1998).* *"A wonderful set of authors who illuminate different corners of relationships. This book belongs on your shelf . . . but only after you've read it and loved it." (Derek Paar, PhD, Associate Professor of Psychology, Springfield College, Massachusetts)*

When One Partner Is Willing and the Other Is Not, edited by Barbara Jo Brothers, MSW, BCSW (Vol. 7, No. 1, 1997).* *"An engaging variety of insightful perspectives on resistance in couples therapy." (Stan Taubman, DSW, Director of Managed Care, Alameda County Behavioral Health Care Service, Berkeley, California; Author,* Ending the Struggle Against Yourself)

Couples and the Tao of Congruence, edited by Barbara Jo Brothers, MSW, BCSW (Vol. 6, No. 3/4, 1996).* *"A library of information linking Virginia Satir's teaching and practice of creative improvement in human relations and the Tao of Congruence. . . . A stimulating read." (Josephine A. Bates, DSW, BD, retired mental health researcher and family counselor, Lake Preston, South Dakota)*

Couples and Change, edited by Barbara Jo Brothers, MSW, BCSW (Vol. 6, No. 1/2, 1996).* *This enlightening book presents readers with Satir's observations–observations that show the difference between thinking with systems in mind and thinking linearly–of process, interrelatedness, and attitudes.*

Couples: Building Bridges, edited by Barbara Jo Brothers, MSW, BCSW (Vol. 5, No. 4, 1996).* *"This work should be included in the library of anyone considering to be a therapist or who is one or who is fascinated by the terminology and conceptualizations which the study of marriage utilizes." (Irv Loev, PhD, MSW-ACP, LPC, LMFT, private practitioner)*

Couples and Countertransference, edited by Barbara Jo Brothers, MSW, BCSW (Vol. 5, No. 3, 1995).* *"I would recommend this book to beginning and advanced couple therapists as well as to social workers and psychologists. . . . This book is a wealth of information." (International Transactional Analysis Association)*

Power and Partnering, edited by Barbara Jo Brothers, MSW, BCSW (Vol. 5, No. 1/2, 1995).* *"Appeals to therapists and lay people who find themselves drawn to the works of Virginia Satir and Carl Jung. Includes stories and research data satisfying the tastes of both left- and right-brained readers." (Virginia O. Felder, ThM, Licensed Marriage and Family Therapist, private practice, Atlanta, Georgia)*

Surpassing Threats and Rewards: Newer Plateaus for Couples and Coupling, edited by Barbara Jo Brothers, MSW, BCSW (Vol. 4, No. 3/4, 1995).* *Explores the dynamics of discord, rejection, and blame in the coupling process and provides practical information to help readers understand marital dissatisfaction and how this dissatisfaction manifests itself in relationships.*

Clinical Issues with Interracial Couples: Theories and Research

Volker Thomas, PhD
Terri A. Karis, PhD
Joseph L. Wetchler, PhD
Editors

Clinical Issues with Interracial Couples: Theories and Research has been co-published simultaneously as *Journal of Couple & Relationship Therapy*, Volume 2, Numbers 2/3 2003.

The Haworth Press, Inc.

New York • London • Victoria (AU)
www.HaworthPress.com

Clinical Issues with Interracial Couples: Theories and Research has been co-published simultaneously as *Journal of Couple & Relationship Therapy*™, Volume 2, Numbers 2/3 2003.

The development, preparation, and publication of this work has been undertaken with great care. However, the publisher, employees, editors, and agents of The Haworth Press and all imprints of The Haworth Press, including The Haworth Medical Press® and Pharmaceutical Products Press®, are not responsible for any errors contained herein or for consequences that may ensue from use of materials or information contained in this work. Opinions expressed by the author(s) are not necessarily those of The Haworth Press, With regard to case studies, identities and circumstances of individuals discussed herein have been changed to protect confidentiality. Any resemblance to actual persons, living or dead, is entirely coincidental.

Cover design by Jennifer M. Gaska

Library of Congress Cataloging-in-Publication Data

Clinical issues with interracial couples: Theories and Research / Volker K. Thomas, Joseph L. Wetchler, Terri A. Karis, editors.
       p. cm.
"Clinical issues with interracial couples: theories and research has been co-published simultaneously as Journal of couple & relationship therapy, Volume 2, Numbers 2/3 2003."
Includes bibliographical references and index.
      ISBN 0-7890-2179-X (hard : alk. paper) – ISBN 0-7890-2180-3 (soft : alk. paper)
      1. Marital psychotherapy. 2. Interracial marriage–Psychological aspects. I. Thomas, Volker.
II. Wetchler, Joseph L. III. Karis, Terri A. IV. Journal of couple & relationship therapy.
RC488.5.C594 2003
616.89'156–dc21
                                            2003007638

Indexing, Abstracting & Website/Internet Coverage

This section provides you with a list of major indexing & abstracting services. That is to say, each service began covering this periodical during the year noted in the right column. Most Websites which are listed below have indicated that they will either post, disseminate, compile, archive, cite or alert their own Website users with research-based content from this work. (This list is as current as the copyright date of this publication.)

Abstracting, Website/Indexing Coverage . . . . Year When Coverage Began

- **CINAHL (Cumulative Index to Nursing & Allied Health Literature), in print, EBSCO, and SilverPlatter, Data-Star, and PaperChase <www.cinahl.com>** **2001**

- **CNPIEC Reference Guide: Chinese National Directory of Foreign Periodicals** **2001**

- **Contemporary Women's Issues** **2001**

- **e-psyche, LLC <www.e-psyche.net>** **2001**

- **Family & Society Studies Worldwide <www.nisc.com>** **2001**

- **Family Index Database <www.familyscholar.com>** **2003**

- **Family Violence & Sexual Assault Bulletin** **2001**

- **Gay & Lesbian Abstracts <www.nisc.com>** **2002**

- **IBZ International Bibliography of Periodical Literature <www.saur.de>** **2001**

- **Index to Periodical Articles Related to Law** **2002**

- **Referativnyi Zhurnal (Abstracts Journal of the All-Russian Institute of Scientific and Technical Information–in Russian)** **2001**

(continued)

- *Social Services Abstracts <www.csa.com>* **2001**
- *Social Work Abstracts <www.silverplatter.com/catalog/swab.htm>* . . . **2001**
- *Sociological Abstracts (SA) <www.csa.com>* **2001**
- *Studies on Women Abstracts <www.tandf.co.uk>* **2001**
- *Violence and Abuse Abstracts: A Review of Current Literature on Interpersonal Violence (VAA)* **2001**
- *Women's Resources International Abstracts* **2001**

Special Bibliographic Notes related to special journal issues (separates) and indexing/abstracting:

- indexing/abstracting services in this list will also cover material in any "separate" that is co-published simultaneously with Haworth's special thematic journal issue or DocuSerial. Indexing/abstracting usually covers material at the article/chapter level.
- monographic co-editions are intended for either non-subscribers or libraries which intend to purchase a second copy for their circulating collections.
- monographic co-editions are reported to all jobbers/wholesalers/approval plans. The source journal is listed as the "series" to assist the prevention of duplicate purchasing in the same manner utilized for books-in-series.
- to facilitate user/access services all indexing/abstracting services are encouraged to utilize the co-indexing entry note indicated at the bottom of the first page of each article/chapter/contribution.
- this is intended to assist a library user of any reference tool (whether print, electronic, online, or CD-ROM) to locate the monographic version if the library has purchased this version but not a subscription to the source journal.
- individual articles/chapters in any Haworth publication are also available through the Haworth Document Delivery Service (HDDS).

Clinical Issues with Interracial Couples: Theories and Research

CONTENTS

Introduction   1
Volker Thomas
Terri A. Karis
Joseph L. Wetchler

CLINICAL ISSUES WITH INTERRACIAL COUPLES:
THEORIES AND RESEARCH

Homogamy Outlaws: Interracial Couples' Strategic Responses
to Racism and to Partner Differences   3
Kyle D. Killian

How Race Matters and Does Not Matter for White Women
in Relationships with Black Men   23
Terri A. Karis

Latino/a and White Marriages: A Pilot Study Investigating
the Experiences of Interethnic Couples in the United States   41
Elizabeth Wieling

Lives Together, Worlds Apart?
The Lives of Multicultural Muslim Couples   57
Manijeh Daneshpour

Interracial Relationships in Hawaii: Issues, Benefits,
and Therapeutic Interventions   73
Paula M. Usita
Shruti Poulsen

INTERRACIAL ISSUES WITH SAME-SEX COUPLES

Interracial and Intercultural Lesbian Couples:
The Incredibly True Adventures of Two Women in Love   85
Janie Long

Latino Cross-Cultural Same Sex Male Relationships:
   Issues of Ethnicity, Race, and Other Domains of Influence   103
      Andres Nazario

INTERVENTIONS WITH INTERRACIAL COUPLES

Assessment and Intervention with Black-White
   Multiracial Couples   115
      Carolyn Y. Tubbs
      Paul C. Rosenblatt

Intercultural Therapy with Latino Immigrants
   and White Partners: Crossing Borders Coupling   131
      Gonzalo Bacigalupe

Asian American Intermarriage: A Socio-Political
   Construction and a Treatment Dilemma   151
      MaryAnna Domokos-Cheng Ham

Therapists' Perspectives on Working
   with Interracial Couples   163
      Shruti S. Poulsen

Index   179

ABOUT THE EDITORS

Volker Thomas, PhD, is Associate Professor of Marriage and Family Therapy and Director of the Marriage and Family Therapy Program in the Department of Child Development and Family Studies at Purdue University. Dr. Thomas has been on the editorial boards of the *Journal of Marital and Family Therapy, The Family Journal, and Counseling and Values.* He served as Editor-in-Chief of the AFTA Newsletter from 1998-2002. His research interests include family assessment, therapy with children of economically disadvantaged families (e.g., Head Start families), parental grief of a loss of a child, and multicultural issues in family therapy. Dr. Thomas is co-editor of a forthcoming book on *Family Assessment: Integrating Multiple Perspectives.* He has served on the Commission on Accreditation for Marriage and Family Therapy Education, and is Chair Elect of the Family Therapy Section of the National Council on Family Relations. Dr. Thomas is a licensed Marriage and Family Therapist in Indiana and has a small private practice.

Terri A. Karis, PhD, is Assistant Professor in the Marriage and Family Therapy Program and Department of Psychology at University of Wisconsin-Stout. She is a co-author (with Paul Rosenblatt and Richard Powell) of *Multiracial Couples: Black and White Voices,* which was named as an outstanding book of the year (1995) on the Subject of Human Rights in North America by the Gustavus Myers Center for the Study of Human Rights. Her research interests include the construction of white racial identities, white mothers of black children, and racial dynamics in therapy. Dr. Karis is a Clinical Member of the American Association for Marriage and Family Therapy, a licensed Marriage and Family Therapist in Wisconsin, and a licensed Psychologist in Minnesota. She maintains an active clinical practice in Minneapolis.

Joseph L. Wetchler, PhD, is Professor of Marriage and Family Therapy, and Director of the Master's Program in the Marriage and Family Therapy Program at Purdue University Calumet. He is a Clinical Member and Approved Supervisor of the American Association for Marriage and Family Therapy. Dr. Wetchler was the recipient of the *1997 IAMFT Award for Outstanding Contribution to Research in Family Life.* He is the Editor of the *Journal of Couple & Relationship Therapy,* and has served on the Editoral Boards of *the American Journal of Family Therapy,* the *Journal of Family Psychotherapy,* the *Journal of Feminist Family Therapy,* the *Journal of Marital and Family Therapy,* and the *Journal of Activities in Psychotherapy Practice.* Dr. Wetchler is a co-editor (with Lorna Hecker) of *An Introduction to Marriage and Family Therapy* and a co-author (with Fred Piercy & Douglas Sprenkle) of the *Family Therapy Sourcebook 2nd ed.* He is also the author of numerous journal articles on family therapy supervision, family therapy for child and adolescent problems, family therapy for substance abuse, couple therapy, and the self of the therapist. Dr. Wetchler has been a co-investigator on a large project funded by the National Institute on Drug Abuse to study couple therapy approaches for substance abusing women. He regularly consults to social service agencies and therapists in private practice, and maintains an active family therapy practice in Northwest Indiana. Dr. Wetchler is a licensed marriage and family therapist in Indiana.

Introduction

Volker Thomas
Terri A. Karis
Joseph L. Wetchler

Interracial couple relationships have been around since humans began to classify each other based on racial categorization. Although interracial couples face challenges that are directly and indirectly related to differences in their racial backgrounds, couple and family theories have had little to say about how to work with these differences. With the paradigm shift from modern to post modern thinking, couple and family therapists have become increasingly interested in the multiple and shifting ways that people view the world, and increasingly aware that not all couples are alike. Not all couples are white, married, and heterosexual, and there is a growing understanding that clinical practices based on these assumptions may not be adequate when working with interracial couples. Recognizing the diversity of our clients, the intent of this publication is to contribute to more respectful and inclusive clinical practices that can address the treatment issues we face in the first decade of the 21st century.

The goal of this volume is to give voice to and provide space for couples whose relationships have all too often been silenced or overlooked. Attempting this, we faced an interesting dilemma. Recognizing that interracial couples have historically been marginalized and pathologized *because* of their racial differences, how could we provide a space to focus

Volker Thomas, PhD, is Associate Professor and Program Director, Marriage and Family Therapy Program, Department of Child Development and Family Studies, Purdue University, 1269 Fowler House, West Lafayette, IN 47907.

Terri A. Karis, PhD, is Assistant Professor, Marriage and Family Therapy Program, University of Wisconsin-Stout, PO Box 790, Menomonie, WI 54751.

Joseph L. Wetchler, PhD, is Professor and Program Director, Marriage and Family Therapy Program, Purdue University Calumet, Hammond, IN 46323.

[Haworth co-indexing entry note]: "Introduction." Thomas, Volker, Terri A. Karis, and Joseph L. Wetchler. Co-published simultaneously in *Journal of Couple & Relationship Therapy* (The Haworth Press, Inc.) Vol. 2, No. 2/3, 2003, pp. 1-2; and: *Clinical Issues with Interracial Couples: Theories and Research* (ed: Volker Thomas, Terri A. Karis, and Joseph L. Wetchler) The Haworth Press, Inc., 2003, pp. 1-2. Single or multiple copies of this article are available for a fee from The Haworth Document Delivery Service [1-800-HAWORTH, 9:00 a.m. - 5:00 p.m. (EST). E-mail address: docdelivery@haworthpress.com].

on these differences without contributing to further stereotyping and marginalization? While racial differences can be thought of as either biological givens or cultural constructions, we might also think of them as created by racism, and not simply reflections of racism. In highlighting the unique race-related struggles that interracial couples confront on a daily basis, we run the risk of oversimplifying the complex realities of their lives, and of overlooking partners' similarities, and couples' strengths and loving connections. In addressing this dilemma we were fortunate to put together a panel of outstanding authors who not only are experts in this area, but many of whom also live in interracial couple relationships themselves. They drew not only upon their rich academic knowledge, but also on their invaluable lived experiences.

We tried to cover clinical issues of interracial couples from theoretical as well as research perspectives. For example, the Killian, Karis, and Wieling articles report on qualitative research conducted with African American and white, and Latina/o and white couples. Other articles, such as those by Tubbs and Rosenblatt, Daneshpour, Bacigalupe, Ham, and Usita and Poulsen discuss theoretical and clinical issues of couples in which one partner is white and the other is non-white. Although a primary focus is on racial difference, in conceptualizing this volume we worked with a definition of diversity that goes beyond race. Thus, the chapters by Long and Nazario explore issues of interracial lesbian and gay couples respectively. All chapters address issues of power as they relate not only to racial differences, but also to gender differences, and to the interactions between the two. Finally, while most articles are written with a main focus on the couples and their presenting issues, the last article by Poulsen explores therapists' perspectives on working with interracial couples, and the potential complexities when the therapist is the same race as one partner, but of a different race than the other partner.

We hope that this collection will provide the reader with an overview of possible issues interracial couples face in this culture. However, the volume is not intended to serve as a definitive guide for how to work with a certain interracial constellation. There is no unitary construct of THE Black/White, Latino/White, Asian/European, or Muslim/Christian couple. This would lead to stereotyping and oversimplification of the heterogeneous realities of the couples to whom the authors tried to give voice in this publication.

CLINICAL ISSUES WITH INTERRACIAL COUPLES: THEORIES AND RESEARCH

Homogamy Outlaws: Interracial Couples' Strategic Responses to Racism and to Partner Differences

Kyle D. Killian

SUMMARY. This study explores how black-white interracial couples experience and respond to racism and how they negotiate racial and ethnic difference in their relationships. Twelve black-white couples were interviewed individually and conjointly, and the descriptive data were analyzed using a grounded theory approach. Results reflect interracial couples' strategic responses to negative public reactions and how they resist and comply with the discourse of homogamy in their relationship. Implications for couple and family therapists working with interracial couples are discussed. *[Article copies available for a fee from The Haworth Document Delivery Service: 1-800-HAWORTH. E-mail address: <docdelivery@ haworthpress.com> Website: <http://www.HaworthPress.com> © 2003 by The Haworth Press, Inc. All rights reserved.]*

Kyle D. Killian, PhD, is Assistant Professor of Family Therapy, University of Houston-Clear Lake, Box 201, 2700 Bay Area Boulevard, Houston, TX 77058-1098.

The author wishes to thank Anna M. Agathangelou, Terri Karis, and the other editors for their very helpful comments and suggestions for improving this article.

[Haworth co-indexing entry note]: "Homogamy Outlaws: Interracial Couples' Strategic Responses to Racism and to Partner Differences." Killian, Kyle D. Co-published simultaneously in *Journal of Couple & Relationship Therapy* (The Haworth Press, Inc.) Vol. 2, No. 2/3, 2003, pp. 3-21; and: *Clinical Issues with Interracial Couples: Theories and Research* (ed: Volker Thomas, Terri A. Karis, and Joseph L. Wetchler) The Haworth Press, Inc., 2003, pp. 3-21. Single or multiple copies of this article are available for a fee from The Haworth Document Delivery Service [1-800-HAWORTH, 9:00 a.m. - 5:00 p.m. (EST). E-mail address: docdelivery @haworthpress.com].

http://www.haworthpress.com/store/product.asp?sku=J398
10.1300/J398v02n02_02

KEYWORDS. Interracial, couples, family therapy, race, ethnicity, difference, homogamy

INTRODUCTION

Heterogamy between partners has become increasingly common in recent years (Kalmijn, 1993; Surra, 1990) with black-white couples quadrupling in number since 1970 (Domokos-Cheng Ham, 1995). However, the dominant discourse of mate selection in the larger society and in the fields of psychology and marriage and the family still remains homogamy. Heterogamous couples, in which partners differ on race, ethnicity,[1] social class, and education, are an exception to this principle of homogamy (Gadberry & Dodder, 1993; Houts, Robins, & Huston, 1997; Kalmijn, 1998; Knox, Zusman, & Nieves, 1998; Surra, 1990). "Birds of a feather flock together" and "stick to your own kind" are familiar phrases representing ethnocentric, prejudicial attitudes and practices of both exclusion and homogamous mate selection. Interracial couples employ various strategic responses to acts of overt and covert racism from families, social networks, and the larger society, social systems that directly or indirectly punish those who cross the border of race. This article explores these survival strategies and their implications for interracial couples and the helping professionals who work with them. Drawing from individual and conjoint interviews with 12 black-white couples, I present couples' experiences with, and their strategic responses to, racism in the larger society and discuss ways partners deal with racial and ethnic differences in self and other. Finally, I discuss implications of these strategies for couple and family therapists working with interracial couples.

THE DOMINANT DISCOURSE OF HOMOGAMY

Dominant discourses are systems of "statements, practices, and institutional structures that share common values" (Hare-Mustin, 1994, p. 19) and sustain a particular worldview (Clifford, 1986). One such discourse, homogamy, holds that people are attracted to one another because of their similarities in background. Shared characteristics, such as race, religion, education, income, age, and other demographic and status variables, have been considered to be major factors in the mate selection process (Surra, 1990) and thought to predict relationship success and satisfaction. Heterogamous mate selection practices run counter to this discourse of homogamy. Various notions or "rationales" of why persons do not, or *should* not, select partners across the border of race continue to be prevalent in our society. Porterfield (1982) stated that "it is not surprising that strong norms against racial intermarriage should be accompanied by beliefs that such marriages are fraught with special hazards and are likely to fail" (p. 25). Embodying this prevailing ideology of the larger society, homogamy is also utilized by white supremacists as a rationale for maintaining social and geographic segregation of persons from different races in an effort to maintain white racial purity (Ferber, 1998; Root, 2001).

Have the norms of intolerance toward interracial relationships changed? Sixty-four percent of Americans approve of interracial marriages today compared to an approval rate of only 20% in 1968 (Gregory, 1993). Thus, while the number of interracial couples has risen remarkably over the past three decades and the level of approval is also on the rise, about one-third of Americans still outright disapprove or are not certain if they approve of interracial marriage. This supports past findings that partners from different racial backgrounds are likely to experience disapproval from society (Belkin & Goodman, 1980; Porterfield, 1982; Rosenblatt, Karis, & Powell, 1995). While laws change, and schools and communities have become desegregated across the U.S., social barriers to interracial relationships persist. In this article, I examine how the discourse of homogamy operates at two systemic levels, that of the larger community and society within which couples move and interact, and the level of the couple relationship in which partners choose strategies to negotiate their differences.

DEFINING RACISM AND DISCRIMINATION

The formation of a couple identity involves a search for mutuality, which, in turn, involves attempts to reach agreement on what is important in the relationship and how the couple will deal with the outside world. Because of the prevalence of racism in the larger social context (Brown, 1987; Paset & Taylor, 1991; Porterfield, 1982), partners in interracial relationships historically have experienced hostility and rejection. Stemming from a set of prejudiced beliefs and attitudes, racism is manifested in both overtly hostile actions and more subtle, "dysconscious" acts directed against persons of color (Rains, 1998). Racist actions range from denial of goods and services, to psychological intimidation, to verbal and/or physical assault, to murder. Racial discrimination may be defined as concrete actions which adversely affect the personal safety, security, or social and economic opportunities of persons whose skin color or ethnic heritage differs from that of the perpetrator. Racism and discrimination are manifested in the attitudes and behaviors of individuals as well as in the actions of larger societal institutions. Persons who discriminate against interracial couples may believe it is "immoral" or "unnatural" for persons of different racial groups to form couple relationships. While individual racism manifests itself in the behavior of one person or small groups of people, institutional racism involves the adverse, discriminatory behavior and policies of larger institutional structures. Institutions such as school boards, banks, and real estate agencies have engaged in discrimination against individual persons of color and interracial couples (Dalmage, 2000). Thus, opposition to interracial couples and persons of color takes concrete, material forms. If choosing a partner from a different racial background made no difference in a person's life, then research participants would have few stories to tell about their experiences of racism. But racism does manifest itself in myriad ways in a racially stratified culture, and since it affects everyone, it necessarily has an impact on black and white couples as well. Racism's impact is different for different people, including white and black partners in interracial relationships.

METHOD

Sample

The sample comprised 12 black-white couples who had been married for a minimum of one year and had at least one child together. Participants ranged from 23 to 49 years of age and were diverse in regard to family of origin background, social class, education, and income. Because approximately 75% of black-white married couples are black male-white female (Domokos-Cheng Ham, 1995; Rosenblatt, Karis, & Powell, 1995), the sample comprised nine black male-white female couples, and three black female-white male couples.

Procedure

Data were collected through semi-structured, in-depth interviews with the individual spouses and couples (36 interviews in total). Each interview was 1.5-2 hrs long. I prepared specific queries in advance and also kept the interview flexible to allow for the inclusion of material deemed important by the participants. First, I interviewed the spouses separately in order to solicit thoughts and feelings that might not have been shared in their partners' presence. Then, immediately prior to conducting the couple interviews, I asked each partner individually to share additional thoughts or perceptions that had occurred to him/her since our first meeting. I audiotaped the interviews with the participants' permission and kept field notes to capture important ideas and observations.

A Grounded Theory Approach to Analysis

Following transcription of the interviews, the data were coded and analyzed using the grounded theory approach (Charmaz, 1983; Glaser & Strauss, 1967; Strauss & Corbin, 1998) aided by HyperRESEARCH, a software program (ResearchWare, 1999). The first stage of inductive analysis method involves the categorization and sorting of data into codes or labels that serve to separate, compile, and organize descriptive data (Charmaz, 1983). HyperRESEARCH permits the researcher to assign multiple codes to the same data, and then store and retrieve coded data. Coding categories can be retrieved and combined over a set of interviews through data reports, which are organized through the use of descriptors and/or the selection of multiple codes. A method of constant comparison was used to capture commonalties (recurring themes, phrases, and discourses) in the experiences of the participants. This method is intended for studies with multiple sources of data and, thus, is appropriate for this study because each participant spouse is considered a separate data source. The individual responses of the participants were analyzed first individually, and then spouses' perspectives were compared for similarities and differences within couples.

INTERRACIAL COUPLES' EXPERIENCES OF HOMOGAMY'S EFFECTS

In my study, most partners made frequent references to the racism and prejudice they had experienced. Here a white female talks about her awareness of a persistent intolerance:

Barbara: There is a lot of prejudice out there. It seems like people are almost accepting that there are black people in the world, and white people and Mexican and all this, but the bottom line for most people is that you don't get married [to them] and you certainly don't have kids [with them].

The interviews were replete with examples of incidents occurring in the public context, from subtle cues of avoidance and exclusion from conversations, to more obvious behaviors, such as people staring in restaurants and turning around on the street to get a second look. Here are examples from three different couples:

Interviewer: Could you two give me examples of public reactions?

Steve: Well, at the mall. We have the stare-down contests.

Tahnee: Restaurants. Once we sit down, people will just watch us. [A local restaurant] has little cubicles so that it is semi-private when you eat. A few years back there was an older couple sitting across from us and they just kept staring and staring.

Katrina: Sometimes, depending on where we are, like at the mall or whatever, there's a group of young black girls and they will be like, "Damn, he shouldn't be with her." Little things–people just have this perception where if you don't look like somebody else you shouldn't *be* with them.

Hillary: These people masquerade and go around and pretend that they are oh-so-cool and everybody's alright, but I see when people are in the office and Ian comes in, they're wondering what relationship he is to me, and if I tell them he's my husband, they don't know how to react.

STRATEGIC RESPONSES TO RACISM AND HOMOGAMY

Couples utilize a host of strategies to cope with negative attention in public situations. Six strategies presented here are "fighting fire with fire," "making a special effort," disassociating from one another, restricting itinerary, not discussing public reactions, and deprioritizing racial and ethnic differences. Here are some excerpts from the interviews that highlight these six strategies.

"Fighting Fire with Fire"

Interviewer: What was your reaction to their reaction?

Barbara: I was mad; I would stare them back down. That's what I would do, because I was a college student (laugh).

Steve: I get a kick out of it, because I like to stare at them, you know, I get right in their face, "Look, you got a problem with this?" As long as I look a little nutty, they will keep their distance and that works. . . .

Anita: The least amount of negative energy I get, I'll do one of two things: I either scowl back at that person or I'll hug Fred tighter. I used to do that a lot; now I just sort of get into Fred and not care too much about what people are thinking because this is the person I love. . . .

"Making a Special Effort"

Debra: I do remember [Larry] saying one time when the kids were little that it was important when we did go out as a family that we were clean, that we presented ourselves well, that we looked nice, not that we needed to dress expensively, but that you didn't want to go out and make a bad impression. Because when we go out, maybe people are going to take a second glance more often, and for those people who might tend to have negative impressions anyway, there's no reason to reinforce those impressions.

Disassociating from One Another

Fred: There are a couple of circumstances that we find ourselves in, like riding public transportation late at night or on the north side–

Anita: Yeah, we have something called "north-mode," and that's where we try to neutralize and don't try to look as provocative.

Fred: We may sit on separate sides and we don't look like we're together.

Anita: Yeah, we'll want to protect each other. If we're going very deep into the north side to visit my sisters and stuff, 'cause we have to pass through there, then we really just *chill*, chill *big*.

Interviewer: Is there any other place where you might go into north-mode?

Anita: Places where there are either a lot of black people or white–

Fred: Usually black men.

Anita: Yeah, 'cause they're like "What are you doing with my sister?" or "What are you doing with him?," and you don't want to excite certain kinds of people.

Restricting Itinerary

Interviewer: Is "comfortable" about being in a place where you are trusted and known, a place where you are more secure?

Tahnee: Definitely, because I feel insecure in a lot of places when I go out with my son. [Negative attention] also limits where I choose to go and shop and stuff because I hate always being like a museum piece.

Katrina: Honestly, I don't think Mel and I would go into the deep south of Georgia and not have any qualms about how we are going to be reacted to. I think we would have to think about it.

Larry: We won't go too far off the interstate. Danger is danger, and I'd feel safer every time at the back of the McDonald's than at a rest area.

Not Discussing Negative Public Reactions

It appears that another strategy for dealing with racism in the larger society is not discussing everyday experiences of prejudice and racism with one's partner. During conjoint interviews, four couples suggested that they had few to no racist incidents to report. Interestingly, during individual interviews and even during conjoint interviews, black partners in these same four couples did refer to negative reactions at the work place and in public situations. Both male and female black partners may adopt a code of silence out of family of origin allegiance or racial community loyalty (i.e., "some things just aren't talked about") or concerns that their partner may not be empathic to their experiences. Here is what a white female spouse said in an individual interview about the phenomenon of negative public reactions:

> Linda: I've tried to ask Robert about this; he doesn't like to talk about that kind of thing. Sometimes I've wanted to drag it out of him–"Have you ever noticed anything?" and he will say, "Nooo." And I'll say, "What do you mean 'nooo'?" and he'll say, "Oh, nothing *really*." So I think he's noticed things, but I don't know whether he's sure something happened and he doesn't want to tell me, or he's not sure if something happened and he's really being too sensitive.

Since Linda had previously stated that negative public reactions were something she "just doesn't notice," the answer to the interviewer's question becomes whether or not Robert has really noticed anything. But he is reluctant to discuss such matters with her. This code of silence adopted in some interracial relationships may serve a protective function. For some couples, discussing race may be actively avoided precisely because it is so significant, so intimidating in its implications for their relationship.

Deprioritizing Racial Differences

Four couples attempted to cope with the negative attention and stereotypes associated with the discourse of homogamy by defining themselves as altogether unremarkable or unexceptional. For example, one couple described themselves as being "like any other couple," "real boring," and "perfectly normal." Interestingly, the black male partner in this same couple stated that when he and other family members had chosen interracial partners, the extended family had deemed their choices as "strange" and "just not normal." It is possible that couples hope to avoid or neutralize these kinds of distinctions by seeming as "boring" as possible. To resist the dubious distinction of being a case of "mixed blood"–a curiosity of popular culture–and to acquire a sense of normalcy often denied them by others, some couples choose to de-emphasize partner differences, and differences between themselves and other same-race couples.

Another means by which interracial couples comply with the discourse of homogamy is by attributing saliency to particular demographic, ethnographic and status variables other than race and ethnicity. For example, an interracial couple who are Jehovah's Witnesses attributed disapproval or hostility from others as being a prejudiced reaction to their shared membership in a religious minority rather than to their racial difference. This couple adopted a strategy of grounding their partnership in shared social locations such as religious affiliation. This strategy serves to protect them against daily challenges by a society which views them as aberrant and problematic. Other ecosystemic variables (e.g., race and ethnicity) and their interconnections with the variable of religious affiliation are relegated to the margins of their consciousness. In effect, the way they make meaning of their compatibility as partners permits their partial compliance with, or conformity to, the principle of homogamy.

During interviews, six couples deprioritized or minimized racial differences, focusing instead on the similarities between themselves and their partner. These couples acknowledged differences in perception and experience along racial lines, but only when repeatedly asked to discuss "differences" between the two partners. Larry, a black male, voiced his dislike of the term "interracial" and a deep conviction that there were no "races": "I think there is only one race–the human race. Other people always make a big deal about race and color and all, but I don't pay them any mind . . . it doesn't matter what color you are." For him, the white woman he loved was necessarily "from his group"–the group of human beings–and he focused on their compatibility in terms of class and religion.

In addition, several couples suggested that little to none of their family of origin ethnicities had been integrated into their new family system. Here is what one couple had to say about including rituals, traditions, and foods from their families of origin in their new relationship:

> Dennis: I think that we just leave everything behind when we're together. We don't establish new beliefs or anything. We're just sort of on our own.

Mira: I think there are things that we both brought, but if there're any differences, we worked through them just to find a way for our relationship to survive. I can't think of any examples or specifics. I don't think of any of the ethnic things we came from as being a part of us.

Interviewer: So there's a sense of leaving some stuff in the past and starting from scratch?

Dennis: That's basically it, yeah. We're dealing with things different 'cause we're on our own.

Mira: Maybe family values or morals have been brought, but not necessarily *ethnic*.

Dennis: For instance, (laugh) I'm not in the kitchen cooking pig's feet or chitlins, 'cause she does most of the cooking. So we didn't actually bring that part with us; I like soul food, I like fish, and I want to set an example, but I can't really do it.

Mira: I guess I don't view it as *ethnic*, I just view it as family things that we brought. . . .

Dennis: I'm not being funny here, but everything that wants to stay, stays, and everything that wants to go goes.

Interviewer: So it's less about what was kept and more about what got pitched. Like for instance, fish. That's something you wanted and you missed. Would you be able to make it?

Dennis: (quietly) No. . . . You can't cook chitlins . . . you can't cook fish in this house.

Mira: I can't stand the smell (laugh).

Dennis: I'd have to go to my mom's.

Mira: My mom's chocolate chip cookie recipe has been kept. I still do that.

Mira states that differences were something that they had to work through in order for their relationship to survive, and she views ethnicity as being something completely separate from who they are as people and as a family system. Other than Mira's mother's cookie recipe and general family values, this couple did not retain traditions, rituals, or favorite foods. Mira's dislike of the smell of fish and chitlins curtails Dennis' opportunities to cook and consume the foods he values as part of his ethnic identity and through which he would like to "set an example" with their daughter. Thus, the strategy of "starting from scratch" and leaving ethnic and racial identity behind is another way of complying with the discourse of homogamy.

DISCUSSION

Survival Strategies

What causal conditions[2] lead to the social phenomenon of disapproving gestures, expressions, and statements directed toward interracial couples? Negative public reactions probably would not occur if the people interracial couples encounter did not hold racist attitudes or a prejudice against mixed race couples. The context of these reactions includes locations such as walking down the street, shopping at the mall, and eating a meal at a restaurant. The duration of incidents is from several seconds to hours, depending on the specific context. The frequency appears to range from once a week to four or five times a week, and is mediated by the source of the data, with black partners noticing it more than white partners. Intensity is also mediated by the data source, with black partners tending to discuss incidents in greater and more personal detail.

Placing couples' strategies for responding to public reactions within the conditions of space, culture, and history, one can see that in a public space, interracial partners have no control over how someone initially reacts to them. People often feel free to be intrusive, obnoxious, and hostile in public. In terms of culture, the principle of homogamy continues to dominate mate selection in the U.S., and many people are covertly or overtly racist and segregationist in their views of persons of color. In terms of history, interracial relationships were illegal in sixteen states until 1967, and changing laws does not change people's beliefs and attitudes. The incidents described in this study suggest that a significant number of people still view interracial relationships with fear and loathing. Therefore, strategic responses by interracial couples take place in a context that contains the real possibility of a violent backlash. It is interesting to note that couples' tactics ranged from open defiance (e.g., "I stared right back at them," "I just glower back"), to voicing desperation ("I'm sick of feeling like we're in a circus all the time"), to preemptive avoidance, as in switching "modes" to a stance of non-association or shopping only at stores where the couple or family is already known. Couples who described themselves as "ordinary" de-emphasized the frequency of public reactions and so saw no need to discuss strategies. This response, in itself, represents a significant strategy for handling this phenomenon.

Some strategies carry consequences. For example, Fred and Anita's shift to "north mode" means that in certain parts of town they will present the appearance of not knowing one another, and this has become a part of the context shaping their relationship dynamics. Another example is Tahnee's avoidance of certain stores when she is in the company of her husband or son. The range of places to which she is comfortable traveling is constrained, and this also becomes an intervening condition. Perhaps the most widespread outcome of the phenomenon of negative public reactions is a theme of personal pain and frustration evident in nearly all the interviews. This hurt represents a real consequence of racism and intolerance in our society and a genuine, daily consideration for couples.

Living Inside and Outside of Homogamy: Dyadic Double Consciousness

In an attempt to survive within a social context in which interracial couples are viewed as aberrations, couples may subvert such beliefs and work to consistently bring to the fore their similarities and homogeneity in their relationship. Over the course of the interviews, the idea of *duality* emerged: Couples see themselves one way, and they see the society perceiving them in another. This theme of self-consciousness and a sense of duality was reflected by four couples in this study, and has also been noted in other studies (Reddy, 1994; Rosenblatt, Karis & Powell, 1995, pp. 31-34). One way to understand this phenomenon is through Du Bois' notion of *double consciousness*.[3] According to Du Bois, black persons view and speak about themselves one way within their families and communities, and adopt a different consciousness or sense of self, which corresponds to whites' perceptions of them when they are around persons from the dominant group.

Some interracial couples also seem to experience a form of double consciousness. They have their own sense of who they are and what their life is really about, and at the same time, through encountering negative cultural stereotypes of interracial couples, and through interactions with others, are aware of the ways in which the larger society views them. Consistent with the discourse of homogamy, depictions of interracial couples are frequently fraught with conflict, controversy, and innuendo, and, probably in the interest of higher ratings and sales, television programs and tabloids rarely feature exogamous couples whose relationships are stable and satisfactory to both partners. Such depictions serve the interests of white supremacists wishing to protect the purity of their race. The dominant society's view of interracial couples, communicated through the various media, is presented for the consumption and/or indoctrination of the mass public and impacts interracial couples as well. The way interracial couples present themselves to the public may be organized by their resistance to media portrayals (e.g., news magazines, tabloids, talk shows, the internet). Thus, this *dyadic* double consciousness in interracial partners has implications for the ways in which some couples present themselves to interviewers, co-workers, and to helping professionals. Couples' repeated references to being "boring" and "like any other couple" might stem from a dyadic form of double consciousness, and represent acts of resistance to a larger society that refuses to leave them and "the issue" of interracial couples alone. This coping strategy of countering what they perceive as an agitated, obsessive preoccupation with racial difference also represents a particular, more indirect means of negotiating difference within the relationship. This way of negotiating, or *navigating around* difference, is yet another strategy of which therapists must be aware in their clinical work with interracial couples.

IMPLICATIONS FOR THERAPY
WITH INTERRACIAL COUPLES

Interventions are more likely to be therapeutic if therapists (1) are aware of and sensitive to their own racial and ethnic identity(ies) and to their beliefs about interracial relationships, (2) recognize the reasons behind the emergence of couple strategies for dealing with racism, and (3) work with couples to explore the implications of such strategies and make explicit their vision for their relationship. First, therapists are most likely to acknowledge the significance of race, ethnicity, and culture in daily life, and in therapy, if they possess a clear, and positive, ethnic identity and an awareness of their own racial identity. Ethnicity embodies a sense of commonality that satisfies a basic need for historical continuity and identity (McGoldrick, Pearce, & Giordano, 1996;

Pinderhughes, 1989). Therapists who wish to aid couples in examining issues related to race, ethnicity, and identity first must do this type of work themselves. Helping professionals who experience discomfort when faced with racial and ethnic differences often possess an ethnic identity that is conflicted or negative (Pinderhughes, 1989) and frequently deny the importance of difference as a way of distancing from their own negative reactions. A common white assumption is that it is impolite to talk about race, and a colorblind approach demonstrates their "goodness" or "niceness" (Killian, 2001). Therapists must also explore their own attitudes and beliefs about persons of color and interracial couples and families. Unexamined assumptions, myths and stereotypes about interracial unions and persons of color must be addressed if clinical interventions are to be therapeutic (Davidson, 1992). Therapists organized by their bias can go to extremes of denying that race carries any significance or continuously emphasizing a client's racial or ethnic background to the extent that the client's unique personal history is undercut (McRoy & Freeman, 1986; Sue & Sue, 1990). In addition, therapists must be able to assist interracial couples and families in differentiating relationship issues from racial and ethnic issues (Okun, 1996). Therapists can also help couples be aware of their shifting interpretations about presenting issues, where a problem may simply be about "personalities" in one situation, and then about gender or race in another. Self-monitoring, supervision, and continuing education can work to ameliorate negative iatrogenic effects in one's clinical work with this population.

Second, it is helpful for therapists to understand that couples' strategies are necessary for survival in a racist society. Even the strategies of not discussing racist incidents or partner differences on race and ethnicity may be functional for couples who have implicit agreements to avoid conflict. Gottman (1994) concluded that "conflict-minimizing" couples represent a type of stable couple system. Some partners in interracial couples have learned from their families of origin and in other intimate relationships to maintain a code of silence around issues of race, identity, and family history. Reticence to discuss racist incidents or partner differences in a relationship may not constitute a clinical issue.

At the same time, couples' pervasive patterns or processes are worthy of exploration. Issues might include avoiding conversations about a co-worker's prejudice at work, poor service at a restaurant, and disapproving looks in other public places, suspending all discussions of ethnic and racial differences, and/or completely suppressing the ethnic traditions of either partner. Censoring one's experiences of being both conspicuous and invisible in a racist society, or burying one's ethnic or racial identity can exact a terrible toll on the physical and psychological health of individual partners and disrupt intergenerational continuity for the family system. Therapists can help couples explore the costs and benefits of strategies of silence, and subvert the discourse of homogamy by coaching conversations that are inclusive of categories of difference, not as markers of division and tension, but as sources of wholeness, strength, identity, and continuity. Described in detail elsewhere (Killian, 2001a; Killian, 2001b), clinical interventions with interracial couples include the use of cultural genograms, internalized other interviewing, and the re-authoring of couple and family identities through narrative therapy techniques.

CONCLUSION

Marrying interracially carries personal and systemic consequences. Manifestations of opposition to interracial couples take the form of stares, people turning around and taking a second look, disapproving expressions, and harassment at work and in public places. Participants described strategic responses to such phenomena, including staring back, explicitly questioning/challenging others' behaviors, restricting itinerary, and not discussing racist incidents with one another. Such responses sometimes carry consequences, including constraints on freedom to travel to certain locales and to explicitly associate with one another in public. While some social scientists (Gordon, 1964; Washington, 1993) have promulgated the notion that social equality would be symbolized by an increase in the rate of interracial marriage (St. Jean, 1998), we should not assume that an increase in *social tolerance and acceptance* of interracial relationships is concomitant to the increase in frequency in intermarriage witnessed in the past 30 years. All 12 couples in this study disclosed painful experiences that indicate prejudice and resistance against their union from the larger society.

Interracial couples respond to partner differences in different ways. The decentralization of race serves a function for some couples and such a stance should be acknowledged as a strategy of survival in a larger social context that is still overtly and covertly hostile to both persons of color and white persons who choose a black partner. Therapists who wish to be effective with interracial couples and families must do the work of attaining a clear sense of their own racial and ethnic identity(ies) and values and becoming conscious of any beliefs and attitudes that adhere to the discourse of homogamy. Culturally competent therapists can carefully explore with couples the costs and benefits associated with strategies of silence and invite partners to imagine alternatives that allow for greater intimacy, mutuality, and intergenerational continuity.

NOTES

1. Social scientists and lay people frequently conflate race and ethnicity (Callinicos, 1993). Traditionally, ethnicity refers to a sense of common heritage made up of similarities in religion, nationality, and culture. In contrast, race is a term closely linked to physiognomy, focusing on morphological characteristics and common *genetic* descent. Complicating differentiation of race and ethnicity is the fact that both are socially mediated and understood, and ethnicity can also be seen as a "sanitized" version of race for those professing a "colorblind" stance (Agathangelou, 1997). Thus, ethnic and racial identities are social constructions imbued with positive and negative meanings and statuses from inside and outside particular communities. For analysis on how race and ethnicity represent sociopolitically motivated categories, see Milton Kleg (1993), *Hate, Prejudice and Racism.*

2. I am indebted to Strauss and Corbin (1998) for their paradigm model, which helped organize the analysis and discussion of the phenomenon of negative public reactions in the interview data.

3. W. E. B. Du Bois was one of the first scholars to discuss the social and psychological experience of persons of color in the U.S. He suggested that blacks were simultaneously "inside and outside the West," and introduced the concept of double consciousness, in which minorities develop two senses of self, one derived from their own daily perceptions and experiences within their respective communities and another *internalized* sense of self derived from the perceptions, dominant expectations, and the Euro-intellectual tradition of the dominant society (see Gilroy, 1993).

REFERENCES

Agathangleou, A. M. (1997). The Cypriot "ethnic" conflict in the production of global power. Ann Arbor, MI: UMI Dissertation Services.

Belkin, G. S., & Goodman, N. (1980). *Marriage, family and intimate relationships.* Chicago: Rand McNally.

Charmaz, K. (1983). The grounded theory method: An explication and interpretation. In R. M. Emerson (Ed.), *Contemporary field research* (pp. 109-126). Prospect Heights, IL: Waveland.

Clifford, J. (1986). Introduction: Partial truths. In J. Clifford & G. E. Marcus (Eds.), *Writing culture: The poetics and politics of ethnography.* Berkeley: University of California Press.

Dalmage, H. M. (2000). *Tripping on the color line: Black-white multiracial families in a racially divided world.* New Brunswick, NJ: Rutgers University Press.

Davidson, J. R. (1992). Theories about black-white interracial marriage: A clinical perspective. *Journal of Multicultural Counseling and Development, 20,* 150-157.

Domokos-Cheng Ham, M. (1995). *Conversation: Biracial couples creating multiracial families.* Workshop at the annual conference of the American Association for Marriage and Family Therapy, Baltimore, MD, November 3.

Ferber, A. (1998). *White man falling: Race, gender and white supremacy.*

Gadberry, J. H., & Dodder, R. A. (1993). Educational homogamy in interracial marriages: An update. *Journal of Social Behavior and Personality, 8,* 155-163.

Gilroy, P. (1993). *The Black Atlantic: Modernity and double consciousness.* Cambridge, MA: Harvard University Press.

Glaser, B., & Strauss, A. L. (1967). *The discovery of grounded theory.* Chicago: Aldine.

Gordon, M. (1964). *Assimilation in American life: The role of race, religion, and national origins.* Oxford University Press.

Gottman, J. M. (1994). *What predicts divorce? The relationship between marital processes and marital outcomes.* Hillsdale, NJ: Lawrence Erlbaum Associates.

Gregory, D. (April 26, 1993). What color is love? *First,* 50-53.

Hare-Mustin, R. T. (1994). Discourses in the mirrored room: A postmodern analysis of therapy. *Family Process, 33,* 19-35.

Houts, R. M., Robins, E., & Huston, T. L. (1997). Compatibility and the development of premarital relationships. *Journal of Marriage and the Family, 58,* 7-20.

Kalmijn, M. (1993). Trends in black/white intermarriage. *Social Forces, 72,* 119-146.

Kalmijn, M. (1998). Intermarriage and homogamy: Causes, patterns, trends. *Annual Review of Sociology, 24,* 395-421.

Killian, K. D. (2001a). Reconstituting racial histories and identities: The narratives of interracial couples. *Journal of Marital and Family Therapy, 27,* 23-37.

Killian, K. D. (2001b). Crossing borders: Race, gender, and their intersections in interracial couples. *Journal of Feminist Family Therapy, 13,* 1-31.

Knox, D., Zusman, M., & Nieves, W. (1998). College students' homogamous preferences for a date and mate. *College Student Journal, 31,* 445-448.

McGoldrick, M., Giordano, J., & Pearce, J. K. (Eds.). (1996). *Ethnicity and family therapy. 2nd ed.* New York: Guilford.

McRoy, R. G., & Freeman, E. (1986). Racial-identity issues among mixed-race children. *Social Work in Education, 8,* 164-174.

Pinderhughes, E. (1989). *Understanding race, ethnicity, and power.* New York: Free Press.

Porterfield, E. (1982). Black-American intermarriage in the United States. *Marriage & Family Review, 5,* 17-34.

Rains, F. V. (1998). Is the benign really harmless? Deconstructing some "benign" manifestations of operationalized white privilege. In J. L. Kincheloe, S. R. Steinberg, N. M. Rodrguez, & R. E. Chennault (Eds.), *White reign: Deploying whiteness in America* (pp. 77-102). New York: St. Martin's Griffin.

Reddy, M. (1994). *Crossing the color line: Race, parenting, and culture.* New Brunswick, NJ: Rutgers University Press.

ResearchWare, Inc. (1995). *HyperRESEARCH: A content analysis tool for the qualitative researcher.* PO Box 1258, Randolph, MA 02368-1258.

Root, M. P. P. (2001). *Loves' revolution: Interracial marriage.* Philadelphia: Temple University Press.

Rosenblatt, P. C., Karis, T. A., & Powell, R. D. (1995). *Multiracial couples: Black and white voices.* Thousand Oaks, CA: Sage.

St. Jean, Y. (1998). Let the people speak for themselves: Interracial unions and the General Social Survey. *Journal of Black Studies, 28,* 398-414.

Strauss, A., & Corbin, J. (1998). *Basics of qualitative research, 2nd ed.* Newbury Park, CA: Sage.

Sue, D. W., & Sue, D. (1990). *Counseling the culturally different: Theory and practice* (2nd ed.). New York: Wiley.

Surra, C. A. (1990). Research and theory on mate selection and premarital relationships in the 1980s. *Journal of Marriage and the Family, 52,* 844-865.

Washington, J. R., Jr. (1993). *Marriage in black and white.* Lanham, MD: University Press of America.

How Race Matters and Does Not Matter
for White Women
in Relationships with Black Men

Terri A. Karis

SUMMARY. Drawing on a qualitative research study, this article provides a beginning exploration for how race both matters and does not matter in white women's relationships with black men. As a means of protecting themselves and their families from pathologizing stereotypes about interracial couples, women make claims that race does not matter. At the same time, they describe ways that stereotypes impact their self identities and their couple interactions. Different situations and relationships create shifts in racial interpretations, and contact with extended family members can change racial meanings. The article offers suggestions for how to create a therapeutic space for discussing race without over-determining its significance. *[Article copies available for a fee from The Haworth Document Delivery Service: 1-800-HAWORTH. E-mail address: <docdelivery@haworthpress.com> Website: <http://www.HaworthPress.com> © 2003 by The Haworth Press, Inc. All rights reserved.]*

KEYWORDS. Interracial couples, white women, multiracial families, racial interpretation

Terri A. Karis, PhD, is Assistant Professor of Psychology in the Marriage and Family Therapy Program, University of Wisconsin-Stout, P.O. Box 790, Menomonie, WI 54751 (E-mail: karist@uwstout.edu).

The author is grateful to Paul Rosenblatt, Bruce Kuehl, and Volker Thomas for comments on earlier drafts of this paper.

[Haworth co-indexing entry note]: "How Race Matters and Does Not Matter for White Women in Relationships with Black Men." Karis, Terri A. Co-published simultaneously in *Journal of Couple & Relationship Therapy* (The Haworth Press, Inc.) Vol. 2, No. 2/3, 2003, pp. 23-40; and: *Clinical Issues with Interracial Couples: Theories and Research* (ed: Volker Thomas, Terri A. Karis, and Joseph L. Wetchler) The Haworth Press, Inc., 2003, pp. 23-40. Single or multiple copies of this article are available for a fee from The Haworth Document Delivery Service [1-800-HAWORTH, 9:00 a.m. - 5:00 p.m. (EST). E-mail address: docdelivery@haworthpress.com].

http://www.haworthpress.com/store/product.asp?sku=J398
10.1300/J398v02n02_03

In recent years the family therapy field has begun to consider the larger social context, and it has become axiomatic that the racial backgrounds of individuals have a significant impact on a couple's relationship. Crohn (1998), for example, assumes that there is tremendous potential for value conflicts in an interracial relationship, based on the understanding that "[e]thnicity, religion, race, gender, and class . . . influence every aspect of how people view the world and what they consider 'normal'" (p. 295). As the most stigmatized and controversial type of interracial relationship, partnerships involving white women and black men are viewed by many as "dangerous and doomed to tragedy" (Root, 2001). Despite their societal high profile, and the assumption that there would be relationship problems *because* of racial differences (Beigel, 1966; Black, 1973), these couples have been clinically invisible, expected to respond to interventions and services designed for racially homogamous couples and their families (Faulkner & Kich, 1983; Saba, Karrer, & Hardy, 1990).

When black-white interracial couples talk about their lives they routinely claim that race makes no difference in their relationships. They often emphasize that they are "ordinary" couples who, just like same-race couples, struggle to make ends meet, get the laundry done, and care for their children (Rosenblatt, Karis & Powell, 1995). A recurrent theme is that race does not matter within the privacy of couples' homes, but only becomes relevant when they are reminded of it in public (Karis, 2000).

How can we make sense of the apparent discrepancy between the stance taken by at least some interracial couples, and the widespread clinical assumption that racial differences matter? My explanation rests on an exploration of how the social location of being interracially partnered invites couples, and particularly white women, to claim that race does not matter, and on an understanding of race as a relational concept whose significance fluctuates depending on situations and relationships. My thinking is informed by my previous relationship experience as a white woman married to a black man, by clinical practice, and by a qualitative research study focused on how white woman articulate, challenge, and reproduce white racial identities within committed heterosexual relationships with black men, and as mothers of biracial children (Karis, 2000).

Following brief summaries of the research study, and of the unique positioning of white women in multiracial families, I hope to illustrate how race can matter, and also not matter. Simultaneously holding both of these perspectives provides a foundation for therapeutic understanding of white women who are in relationships with black men.

RESEARCH METHODOLOGY

Participants

Seventeen women participated in this study; 12 were partnered with black men at the time of their interviews, and 5 had previously been married to black men. With one exception, all women were mothers of biracial children. For those who were still partnered, relationship length ranged from 4 years to 35 years. Three of the couples had been together 8 to 10 years, and 8 of the couples had been together 15 to 35 years. For women who were no longer interracially married, relationship length ranged from 7 years to 21 years; and the time since their divorces ranged from 1 year to 34 years.

At the time of the interviews, women were 28 to 65 years old, and had a total of 33 biracial children, ranging in age from just less than a year old to 40 years old. All of the women currently lived middle class life-styles and were college graduates; 10 had advanced degrees.

Data Collection and Analysis

Participants were recruited through my own social network and through snowball sampling, with the process being informed by theoretical sampling goals (Miles & Huberman, 1994). Each woman participated in an in-depth semi-structured individual interview that lasted from one-and-a-half to two-and-a-half hours. All interviews were tape recorded and completely transcribed. Using an active interviewing approach (Holstein & Gubrium, 1995), interviews focused on women's racial identities, their understanding of racial differences, and their multiracial family lives. As a form of interpretive practice, active interviewing involves the researcher and the research participant constructing new meanings and perspectives, rooted in "the interpretive resources at hand" (Holstein & Gubrium, 1995, p. 16), including the life experiences of both, the researcher's orientation to the topic, and localized orientations to the topic.

Data included tape recordings of individual interviews, interview notes and transcripts, theoretical and personal process notes, and my own experiential data based on personal experiences and previous research experience. Far from being viewed as biased, the researcher's interpretations are seen as plausible, useful, and essential to doing sensitive theorizing (Strauss, 1987).

Research methodology was shaped by social constructionist and feminist paradigms. Data analysis drew on hermeneutical interpretation, Frankenberg's (1993) racial difference paradigms, the Stone Center's Relational/Cultural (R/C) Theory (Walker, 1999), and Lakoff and Johnson's (1980) theory of metaphor.

WHITE WOMEN IN MULTIRACIAL FAMILIES

Carmen Luke (1994) conceptualizes women in interracial relationships as "outsiders within" (p. 51): While they still have white skin and its accompanying privileges, being in intimate family relationships with people of color potentially subjects them to discrimination, prejudice and racism that "rebound" (Frankenberg, 1993, p. 112) onto them, something not experienced by white women in monoracial white families. As an "insider" within dominant white culture, the same system that privileges a white woman excludes her nonwhite partner and children as outsiders. Because whiteness is transparent as the universal norm (Mahoney, 1995), white people generally take their racial identities for granted, and do not consider issues of race relevant to their daily lives. Being in a racially mixed family means that white women face situations in which ignoring race is no longer an option, and whiteness loses some of its taken-for-granted status. For example, when in public a woman may be treated differently depending on whether she is alone, or with her family (Luke, 1994). Such experiences heighten women's awareness of previously unnoticed white racial privilege. At the same time, because racial identities are produced and consolidated, in part, by cultural proscriptions against interracial sexual relationships (Ferber, 1995), white women's relationships with black men are a threat to whiteness, and women may be viewed by other whites as "less than white."

Many women in multiracial families have specific language for naming the significant shifts in public and private identities that result from their dual positioning as racial insiders and outsiders within. Women name racial identity shifts using metaphors such as white with a black soul, a spy, masquerading as a typical white person, a white woman in an interracial family, and being a not totally white person incognito among white people (Karis, 2000). These terms reflect women's experience of the discrepancy between their white physical characteristics and their daily racial interactions, and emphasize increases in racial awareness, connections to their non-white family members and to black communities, feeling different from other white people, and the lack of visible cues to mark these experiences.

THE CLAIM THAT RACE DOES NOT MATTER WITHIN INTERRACIAL COUPLE RELATIONSHIPS

There are a number of ways to understand the claim, made by many white women, that race does not matter within their interracial couple relationships. While this assertion could reflect the innocence of normative whiteness (Edgington, 1999) or a liberal colorblind view of racial difference (Mahoney, 1995), I want to highlight the influence of the social location of being an interracial couple in a racially stratified culture. This location seems to invite white women to draw a dichotomous distinction between their private family lives and the larger public sphere. Saying that race does not matter might be viewed as a form of "backtalk" (Stewart, 1990), an assertion that white women's relationships with black men are not defined by sexualized racial stereotypes.

Stereotypes About Black-White Interracial Couples

I'm always aware of wondering how we as a couple are perceived. So that shifts my identity of myself I guess . . . I assume that we don't really blend into the crowd, anywhere. I've a little pocket of wondering if I'm categorized as one of those "white women who goes with black men," whatever that means. I assume there is . . . a set of perceptions that go with that. (Peggy)[1]

One way to understand the assertion that race does not matter within interracial couples relationships is to view it as a protective response to negative cultural stereotypes which make loving across racial lines unimaginable. Black-white couple relationships exist within a social/historical context that pathologizes them as deviant. Frankenberg (1993) details the elements of this cultural "discourse against interracial relationships" (p. 77). Its foundation is a paired construction of racialized black masculinity and white femininity; black men are viewed as a constant threat to the myth of white racial purity and superiority. Reductionist stereotypes pair supersexual, aggressive, and exotic black men with loose, misguided white women, who are in the "relationship solely for sex or rebellion" (Dalmage, 2000, p. 47). Implicit in the discourse is the assumption that each partner in an interracial relationship comes from a racially and culturally homogenous family and social background, with no acknowledgment of potential similarities between partners, such as class and educational backgrounds. Both partners are viewed as having crossed racial and cultural boundaries that are considered fixed and absolute, rooted in essential biological differences (Frankenberg, 1993). Interracial couples express concern that helping professionals will see them through the lens of this dichotomous conceptualization of racial difference, and conclude that they should not be together (Killian, 2001).

Drawing a Line Between the Private Family Sphere and the Public Sphere

> You are not thinking of everybody's color when you're looking for your socks . . . race disappears in the house. (Cindy)

Those who are interracially partnered often claim that race does not matter in their relationships, within the privacy of their homes, but only becomes significant in public when others remind them of it (Rosenblatt et al., 1995). For white women with black men, this dichotomous splitting into separate public and private spheres might be an unconscious means of shielding themselves and those they love from negative racial stereotyping. White women frequently emphasize that they did not marry "a black man," but simply the person they love. A recent study of interracial relationships supports this view, concluding that "[l]ove alone motivated . . . women and men to cross the color line" (Root, 2001, p. 6). At the same time, the fact that so many who are interracially partnered call attention to this taken-for-granted relationship norm, might itself be viewed as a form of backtalk, an oppositional response to the discourse against interracial relationships.

Because race is socially constructed and not an essential difference, couples are able to connect across racial lines and create loving relationships. While it is understandable that white women frequently draw a line between the racist public sphere and their private family lives, this dichotomous distinction also has drawbacks. Recognizing the interconnections between individuals, families, and the larger systemic context of a racially stratified culture makes it impossible to maintain the conventional distinction between private and public, with family relations being viewed as fundamentally different than those in the rest of society (Ferree, 1990). This does not mean that couple or family dynamics precisely replicate those at larger systemic levels, but couples are not immune to the impact of the discourse against interracial couples simply because they emphasize that they are "with the person I love."

Despite the claim that race does not matter within the privacy of their homes, when women discuss their relationships, they make racial interpretations about couple and family dynamics (Karis, 2000). Their stories reveal ways in which race matters for white women in interracial couple relationships, and illustrate the shifting significance of race, and the fluidity of racial interpretations. What is interpreted as a racial matter at one moment may not be interpreted as a racial matter at another point in time, or in another setting, even by the same woman.

Race as Situationally and Relationally Constructed

The limitations of current racial discourse make it difficult for members of multiracial families to communicate about the complicated racial realities of their lives (Dalmage, 2001). The assertion that race does not matter within the privacy of interracial couples' homes might mean that race does not matter in the stereotypical ways that society assumes.

Race is a complex, multidimensional concept that "mutates and adapts across social-historical contexts, and different life-spheres" (powell, 1997a, p. 100). Although it is widely recognized that race has no scientific biological reality, the racial essentialist paradigm continues to co-exist with racial paradigms that emphasize the social, political and experiential realities of race. Race, like gender, "is 'real' in the sense that it has real, though changing, effects in the world and real, tangible, and complex impact on individuals' sense of self, experiences, and life chances" (Frankenberg, 1993, p. 11).

Social constructionist views of race recognize racial categories as being created day by day "through our thoughts and actions as we assign and attach meaning to various physical features" (Dalmage, 2000, p. 12). As those who are interracially partnered attempt to make sense of the differences and similarities that matter in their lives, they make interpretations. There is an interpretive continuum along which concerns are prioritized, and because race is just one among a range of concerns and values, it is not always in the forefront of a person's consciousness (Hartigan, 1999). In one moment a person may consider the racial aspect of a situation to be significant, whereas at another time, or in relation to a different event, a person may interpret a situation as being about personality or gender differences, about work stress, about a tired child, about being on the verge of getting sick, or about a multitude of other daily concerns. As the quote about looking for socks illustrates, in multiracial family homes it is an everyday experience that racial meanings are suspended or are just not salient. Racial identities, while always present, shift between being actively or passively articulated (Hartigan, 1997).

It is important to emphasize that racial interpretations are modified by situations and relationships. In the following section I will offer examples of instances when race mattered within white women's interracial couple relationships. There is heterogeneity within the category of white-women-partnered-with-black-men, and these illustrations might best be thought of as clues for how race *could* matter for white women in interracial relationships, rather than as set themes or patterns that characterize the majority of such relationships.

Some of these "racial moments" have a direct connection to the negative cultural discourse against interracial couples. They illustrate the interrelationship between race and gender, show how a shift in focus from couple to extended family dynamics can bring racial interpretations to the forefront, and demonstrate the ability to hold a dual awareness of how race can both matter and not matter.

HOW RACE MATTERS
WITHIN INTERRACIAL COUPLE RELATIONSHIPS

Although many of the women in my study denied that stereotypes about interracial couples directly impacted them, they also gave numerous examples of how these stereotypes influenced their sense of self and/or their behavior with partners. Postmodernist perspectives on identity offer a means of making sense of this contradiction. Identities are viewed as multiple, shifting, and "internally fractured," leading to an understanding of "identity as process, as performance, and as provisional" (Bondi, 1993, p. 97).

Additionally, when it comes to racial matters, white women may not see *themselves* clearly. Because whiteness is the dominant norm, it is generally transparent to white people (Flagg, 1993). Despite increased racial awareness about their non-white family members, the characteristics of whiteness, combined with efforts to disconnect from the discourse against interracial relationships, may preclude self-transparency.

Stereotypes Impact Couple Relationships and Women's Self Identities

One way that the discourse against interracial relationships shaped relational dynamics was that some white women deliberately avoided behaviors that might appear to confirm the stereotypes. In the first scenario Jenise does not want others to assume that she, as a white woman, is being used for her financial resources. In the second Rose wants to avoid giving the impression that she, as a white woman, will put up with disrespectful behavior from a black partner.

> Anytime we would go out for dinner, even if I were paying, I would never want to be the one to give the money, especially if we had a black server. Because I wouldn't want them to say, "Oh, look. She's taking him out to dinner." Even now, we're married. Obviously our money is the same, but I never want to be the one to hand out a credit card. . . . I didn't change my behavior. Maybe sometimes it made me demand different behavior out of him. When we were at college parties I wanted him to make sure to really show I was his girlfriend, show respect, whereas maybe I wouldn't have otherwise, if I hadn't known the beliefs or the ideas. (Jenise)

> I am embarrassed to admit, but [I was influenced by] the stereotype of the black guy who has all these girlfriends, and the white girlfriend will put up with it kind of thing. I remember clearly telling Oliver I did not want to hear from co-workers that he even talked to an ex-girlfriend. That would be perceived as he was playing me, and because he was black that would really be talked [about] . . . I trust Oliver . . . it wasn't out of fear that he would cheat on me. It was out of fear that people would play it up and gossip about it. . . . And I was already being talked about, and I didn't want to deal with it. That probably wasn't fair to do, but I did it. (Rose)

In both of these narratives women's behaviors were shaped by their awareness of how they, as white women and as interracial couples, might be viewed. In talking about their behaviors, women emphasized that they wanted to publicly demonstrate that there were no grounds on which people could substantiate negative stereotypes. While these situations were described as "for show" out in public, these interactions were not totally separate from each couple's private, at-home relationship.

Each woman explicitly made a point of saying that *she* did not think of her partner as disloyal or disrespectful, yet as a means of protecting them both from others' stereotyping, she tried to manage the impressions that he made. While Jenise had talked with her partner about her public strategy, Rose and Oliver had not discussed her behavioral requests of him. This silence may serve a protective function in a couple relationship (Killian, 2001), but it raises questions such as, "How did Oliver make sense of Rose's requests? Did he think that she actually considered him disloyal?" One drawback of the strategy of relegating race to the public sphere is that couples will not have an avenue for talking about those moments when racial stereotypes impact their relationship.

A second way that the discourse against interracial relationships impacted some white women was in how they experienced their own identities. The following example illustrates one way that negative stereotypes about interracial couples can affect a woman's sense of self. Debbie's experience of being in an interracial relationship led her to her feel less visible as an individual, less self-confident, and socially isolated. She felt visible *because* she was partnered with a black man, but only as an extension of him, an objectification that resulted in feeling socially ostracized.

> One really significant thing that I felt changed for me being involved with a black man was that the way I was perceived by a lot of people was they thought of me as being lower class and as being loose or being . . . promiscuous . . . it kind of made me feel a little paranoid, whenever we would go out in public together. Whereas before I was always very confident and kind of out-there . . . I was really popular. And I felt kind of squelched after a while. . . . Plus I just think that in public they don't remember you, they remember the black man that you were with, in a way. I just feel like all strikes were sort of against you because white men thought you were sort of slutty, and black women resented the fact that you were with a black man. Older people thought, "Oh my gosh, that's awful that they're together." So I sort of withdrew a little bit. And it just changed my whole demeanor about how I felt about myself. I think I felt less of myself at times. (Debbie)

While some women feel constrained or diminished as a result of having violated family or cultural rules about crossing the color line, other women, in breaking those rules, find a sense of freedom. As the following account illustrates, this freedom may be connected to having moved away from a number of interrelated aspects of one's family background, including having crossed racial boundaries.

I hadn't thought this thought for a long time, but I did think it when I was first married. There is a freedom in marrying a black man. And I think that freedom is the freedom to be yourself. I felt that in the first five years that there was something: I did not have to live the way my folks lived. Now whether that was white or poor or German or Catholic, I don't know what it was that they were living. But I was choosing something new. And because of that there was a freedom about what I brought to it, that couldn't be categorized. So this was a whole new thing where I could do something special. (Annie)

These contrasting stories demonstrate that individuals respond differently to the discourse against interracial couples. Even though both women were subjected to negative stereotypes, their particular ways of making meaning about being interracially partnered resulted in vastly dissimilar experiences. Although these quotes focus on women's experiences of themselves, it seems clear that there would be relational implications to the identity shifts that are described. Despite efforts to relegate race to the public sphere, white women bring racialized selves to the private sphere.

Because my study drew only on the stories of white women, we are left to speculate about how their shifting self-perceptions were experienced by their partners, and how this played out in relationship dynamics. Did Debbie talk with her partner about feeling squelched and invisible? If so, did she talk in racial terms, or use gender or personality interpretations to make sense of her experience? If she did not talk directly with her partner, did he notice that her demeanor had changed? How might he have made sense of this change? Did he take it personally? Exploring the possible impact of the discourse against interracial couples on relationship dynamics may offer couples a way of making sense of their experiences that moves beyond individualized, perhaps blaming, interpretations.

Contact with Extended Family Members Changes Racial Meanings

Contact with extended family members can shift interpretations about whether race matters. The following example illustrates such a shift, and shows the benefit, in one couple's relationship, of explicitly acknowledging racial meanings. Lynette describes a situation in which she draws on a racialized gender interpretation to make sense of a couple issue. While she and her husband Joseph have a domestic arrangement in which she takes the lead with home repairs, this division of labor does not work in the same way when Lynette's white family members enter the picture.

> We need to replace the shower in our basement. I called my father and said, "You're coming up next month, do you think you could help me replace this?" My dad and I do this stuff a lot; I do most of the home repairs. My husband, I know, feels a little inadequate, like his maleness is being threatened because I do this stuff. But in our politically correct language, my husband is a big picture person. I am a detail person. He'll put it in, but there will be all of these details that are off. And I'm going to see those details forever. So I want it done right. And I'm more mechanically inclined than he is. I think he would even admit to that, with a little chagrin. At the same time, the men in my family are the ones who do this stuff. So I think sometimes he feels like he's being looked down on as a man, as a *black man*, when my dad helps do something with me.
>
> I told him we were going to do this–he's the one that wants the shower. But now he doesn't want my dad and I to do it. He says, "Well, I don't want your dad to be working on this. I want to manage the project." It's like, "Well, what the hell does that mean? Are you going to do it? You don't know how to do it. What does it mean to manage it? We don't have the money to pay anybody, so what are you going to manage?" So he's like, "Well, I can get [my friend]. He knows how to do this stuff and he and I can do this."
>
> At the same time this is a together time for my dad and I. This is the time that we have to spend to communicate. So it's important to me to do this, but we've done other projects together and there will surely be something else around the house. So long as he's got somebody else who knows what they're doing, I'll let it go. Because I know that this is deeper than an issue of, "I don't want your dad working on his vacation." That while all of those reasons are there, that it's cutting in deeper to his masculinity, and his identity, and how my family perceives him as being a capable man. (Lynette)

Lynette's account reflects her intuitive understanding that, although private home repair conversations with her partner might generally be framed in terms of gender, and her partner's sense of inadequacy in the face of her competence, there is a racialized gender dynamic that moves to the foreground when her white male family members enter the picture. During home repair conversations it is unlikely that Lynette is thinking about Joseph as "my *black* husband." At the same time, she has learned that her husband Joseph's experience is that Lynette's family will potentially look down on him, not just as a generic (white) man, but as a *black* man. Racialized gender constructions that characterize white men as strong, capable, and in charge necessarily implicate black men as passive and incompetent (Frankenberg, 1993), and insinuate that Joseph may not be in charge in his family, or be capable of handling manly tasks.

This account highlights how racial meanings are fluid and shifting. When the couple is alone they tend to interpret the issue of household chores as being about gender, and racial interpretations are not in the foreground. The presence, or imagined presence, of white family members makes racial interpretations more salient. While the literature on interracial couples often cites lack of acceptance by extended families as one of the challenges faced by couples (Frankenberg, 1993), this example shows that relational dynamics with extended families can play out in subtle ways. Lynette's family likes Joseph, accepts their relationship, and offers both material and emotional support. Yet these factors do not preclude them from making racial interpretations, or prevent Joseph and Lynette from interpreting family member's behaviors through a racial lens.

This situation illustrates that race matters within an interracial couple relationship, and not just when they are in public. Lynette's ability to take her husband's perspective into account is based on her understanding that although he is an individual–Joseph, the person she loves–he is not simply an individual (powell, 1997b), but also is a member of a racial group. This dual awareness is one example of how race simultaneously matters and does not matter.

HOLDING A DUAL AWARENESS: HOW RACE MATTERS AND DOES NOT MATTER

Lynette's narrative, like those of most of the women in my study, demonstrates the co-existence of increasing consciousness about previously taken-for-granted racial privilege, movement away from an "epistemology of ignorance" (Mills, 1997) regarding the racial realities experienced by nonwhite family members, and unconscious normative white racial practices. While Lynette displays an understanding of how racial oppression impacts her husband, awareness about how membership in a racial group structures her own ways of knowing and being in the world is less developed.

In the following quote Lynette elaborates on her understanding of her husband as a black man. On a day-to-day basis, she acknowledges that, like many white women, she does not think about her husband as black. At the same time, she holds a dual awareness, and does not forget that he is black. Notice, though, that she focuses on what is important to *him* because of *his* race, and does not comment directly on how *her* race is relevant.

> I don't forget that he's black either, because that's part of who he is. And if I were to just do that, literally white-washing, I'd deny a part of who he is and what his experiences in the world are . . . the way I've long thought about it is that race is a pressure from the outside in, not from the inside between the two of us. There are issues, there are times when, just like in any marriage, in that give-and-take, there will be some things that are important to my husband because of his race. That I have to know that this is such an important thing to him, that regardless of how I'm feeling, I need to back off. You have to have sensitivity for what the other person is experiencing in the world. And there have been times when, and this is part of [our] learning and growing experiences as white people, when our black family members come home and say, "I've had a really bad day. This asshole at work did this such-and-such."
>
> Now when I came home from school and had something bad happen, my mother would often say, "Well maybe it wasn't quite the way you were looking at it. Maybe they didn't really mean that. Maybe they meant this instead," which is a less painful interpretation of what it is. As human beings, we have a hard time dealing with other people's pain. As white people, we have a hard time dealing with racism. And so I think many of us make the mistake of when our children or spouses come home and say, "This person was doing this to me just because I was black," then doing what my mother did, and saying, "Oh well that surely isn't what they meant. Maybe they meant this. You are being too sensitive." Which denies their whole experience of the world. And if you continue in that you're going to drift apart. Because your spouse does not feel that you empathize with what they go through every day. (Lynette)

Lynette's well-developed dual awareness about her partner helps her understand him as an individual, *and* as a member of a racial group. She demonstrates awareness that "whitewashing" race-related comments, in order to distance from the pain they carry, will not contribute to maintaining an empathetic connection with her partner. At the same time, Lynette does not directly acknowledge how her whiteness might shape who she is and what is important to her. She does, however, move beyond the individualism of normative whiteness when she identifies herself with other white people ("this is part of [our] learning and growing experiences as white people"; "As white people, we have a hard time dealing with racism.").

Lynette's narrative shows that she has moved away from her mother's "good (white) girl" (Moon, 1998) teaching that promoted a conflict avoidant minimization of difference as a means of re-establishing harmony. While the intent of this approach is to be helpful, it is based on the normative white assumption that experiences in the world are solely an individual matter that require a willingness to simply change oneself or one's outlook. This perspective does not take into account racial and gender stratification that differentially impact groups, and makes individual efforts insufficient.

Although Lynette's dual awareness of herself is less developed than her dual awareness of her partner, her ability to see him both as an individual and as a member of a racial group is significant, and is a perspective that may not be shared by white extended family members. If they have not developed this dual awareness, white extended family members may accept a black partner by viewing him as an individual exception to his racial group (Rosenblatt et al., 1995). Holding tightly to the stance that race does not matter obscures full understanding of the complex ways in which race both matters and does not matter in the relationships of white women and black men.

CONCLUSION AND THERAPEUTIC IMPLICATIONS

1. Because interracial couples live in a culture that pathologizes their relationships, they have good reason to insist that race does not matter within their couple relationships. When asked directly, they may draw a public/private dichotomy, saying that race matters in public but not at home. When they talk in detail about their lives, they are likely to say things that contradict this position.

Create a therapeutic space that is big enough to hold the shifting ways in which race both matters and does not matter in their lives.

2. Keep in mind that racial meanings are shifting and fluid. Events and behaviors can be interpreted as being about race, about gender, about family of origin differences, about personality, or about lots of other things. These interpretations shift, even within one person's account of an incident. Pay particular attention to how and when interpretations shift. A shift from a gender interpretation to a racial interpretation can be revealing, and provides an opening for exploring previously unexamined racial assumptions and their possible connection to couple dynamics.

3. Remember that both partners are members of racial groups, with racial identities that are either actively or passively articulated, and they are also unique individuals who generally do not think of their partner as "a black man" or a "white woman." Pay attention to those moments when there is a shift from a racial identity being passively articulated to it being actively expressed. These moments may offer a clue that there are underlying feelings or issues.

4. White partners might need help in moving beyond colorblind individualistic views to hold a dual awareness of their partners and themselves as both individuals *and* members of racial groups. Even when they have a finely developed dual awareness of their partners, white women may not be cognizant of how whiteness structures their own ways of being in the world.

5. Pay attention to the ways that race and gender are intertwined. Silence about the racial aspects of couple dynamics might stem, for example, from a gendered position of setting aside one's authority, in deference to a male partner, or from a colorblind racial perspective that reflects normative whiteness.

6. Even if racial content is not explicitly presented, it is beneficial to show that you have some understanding of the social location of interracial couples, yet do not make assumptions about this particular couple's experience. Demonstrating that you can talk about race without over-determining its significance creates a therapeutic space for couples to discuss those moments when race does matter.

Because interracial couples experience "border patrolling" (Dalmage, 2000, p. 42) from both blacks and whites, they may be cautious about discussing race with black or white therapists. Given the racial identity shifts experienced by white women in multiracial families, white therapists should not assume shared common ground with these clients, based on whiteness. Because white people generally have been socialized to take their racial identities for granted (Thompson & Neville, 1999), white therapists especially may need to actively demonstrate a nuanced racial understanding that might just be assumed for therapists who appear to be non-white.

NOTE

1. In order to protect the confidentiality of participants, all names have been changed.

REFERENCES

Beigel, H. G. (1966). Problems and motives in interracial relationships. *Journal of Sex Research, 2*, 185-205.

Black, A. (1973). Expectations and realities of interracial marriage. In I. Stuart and L. Abt (Eds.), *Interracial marriage*. New York: Grossman Publishers.

Bondi, L. (1993). Locating identity politics. In M. Keith & S. Pile (Eds.), *Place and the politics of identity* (pp. 84-101). New York: Routledge.

Crohn, J. (1998). Intercultural couples. In M. McGoldrick (Ed.). *Re-visioning family therapy: Race, culture, and gender in clinical practice* (pp. 295-308). New York: Guilford Press.

Dalmage, H. M. (2000). *Tripping on the color line: Black-white multiracial families in a racially divided world*. New Brunswick, NJ: Rutgers University Press.

Edgington, A. (1999). Growing up in Little Rock. In C. Cuomo & K. Hall (Eds.), *Whiteness: Feminist philosophical reflections* (pp. 37-44). Lanham, MD: Rowman & Littlefield.

Faulkner, J., & Kich, G. K. (1983). Assessment and engagement stages in therapy with the interracial family. In C. Falicov (Ed.), *Cultural perspectives in family therapy* (pp. 78-90). Rockville, MD: Aspen Systems.

Ferber, A. L. (1995). Exploring the social construction of race. In N. Zack (Ed.), *American mixed race: The culture of microdiversity* (pp. 155-167). Lanham, MD: Rowman & Littlefield.

Ferree, M. M. (1990). Beyond separate spheres: Feminism and family research. *Journal of Marriage and the Family, 52*, 866-884.

Flagg, B. J. (1998). *Was blind but now I see: White race consciousness & the law*. New York: New York University Press.

Frankenberg, R. (1993). *White women, race matters: The social construction of whiteness*. Minneapolis: University of Minnesota Press.

Hartigan, J. (1997). Locating white Detroit. In R. Frankenberg (Ed.), *Displacing whiteness: Essays in social and cultural criticism* (pp. 180-213). Durham: Duke University Press.

Hartigan, J. (1999). *Racial situations: Class predicaments of whiteness in Detroit*. Princeton, NJ: Princeton University Press.

Holstein, J. A. & Gubrium, J. F. (1995). *The active interview.* Thousand Oaks, CA: Sage.

Karis, T. A. (2000). *Racial identity constructions of white women in heterosexual black-white interracial relationships.* Unpublished doctoral dissertation: University of Minnesota.

Killian, K. D. (2001). Reconstituting racial histories and identities: The narratives of interracial couples. *Journal of Marital and Family Therapy, 1,* 27-42.

Lakoff, G. & Johnson, M. (1980). *Metaphors we live by.* Chicago: University of Chicago Press.

Luke, C. (1994). White women in interracial families: Reflections on hybridization, feminine identities, and racialized othering. *Feminist Issues,* 49-72.

Mahoney, M. (1995). Segregation, whiteness and transformation. *University of Pennsylvania Law Review, 143,* 1659-1684.

Miles, M. B., & Huberman, M. A. (1994). *Qualitative data analysis.* Thousand Oaks, CA: Sage.

Mills, C. (1997). *The Racial Contract.* Ithaca: Cornell University Press.

Moon, D. (1998). White enculturation and bourgeois ideology: The discursive production of "good (white) girls." In T. Nakayama & J. Martin (Eds.), *Whiteness: The communication of social identity* (pp. 177-197). Thousand Oaks, CA: Sage.

powell, j. a. (1997a). The "racing" of American society: Race functioning as a verb before signifying as a noun. *Law and Inequality, 99,* 99-125.

powell, j. a. (1997b). The colorblind multiracial dilemma: Racial categories reconsidered. *University of San Francisco Law Review, 31,* 789-806.

Root, M. P. P. (2001). *Love's revolution: Interracial marriage.* Philadelphia: Temple University Press.

Rosenblatt, P. C., Karis, T. A., & Powell, R. D. (1995). *Multiracial couples: Black and white voices.* Thousand Oaks, CA: Sage.

Saba, G. W., Karrer, B. M., & Hardy, K. V. (1990). Introduction. In G. Saba, B. Karrer, & K. V. Hardy (Eds.), *Minorities and family therapy* (pp. 1-15). New York: The Haworth Press, Inc.

Stewart, K. (1990). Backtalking the wilderness: 'Appalachian' en-genderings. In F. Ginsburg & A. Tsing (Eds.), *Uncertain terms: Negotiating gender in American culture* (pp. 43-56). Boston: Beacon Press.

Strauss, A. (1987). *Qualitative analysis for social scientists.* New York: Cambridge University Press.

Thompson, C. E. & Neville, H. A. (1999). Racism, mental health, and mental health practice. *The Counseling Psychologist, 27,* 155-223.

Walker, M. (1999). *Race, self, and society: Relational challenges in a culture of disconnection.* (Work in Progress No. 85). Wellesley, MA: Stone Center.

Latino/a and White Marriages:
A Pilot Study Investigating the Experiences
of Interethnic Couples in the United States

Elizabeth Wieling

SUMMARY. The purpose of this study was to explore the experiences of six heterosexual couples who identified as being in a mixed ethnic and/or racial marriage where one partner is of Latino/a descent and the other is of non-Latino/a White descent. There are virtually no studies that investigate this type of cross-cultural marriage. Therefore, this exploratory pilot study provides some in-depth descriptions of how these couples experience their interethnic relationships. A set of open-ended questions was sent to couples living throughout the United States and a follow-up phone call was conducted with each person for member checking purposes and to give participants an opportunity to elaborate on their responses. The primary categories that emerged from the data are: (1) the experiences and perceptions of being in a marriage with someone from a Latino/a or Euro-American ethnic group, (2) the perceived reactions from family, friends and social institutions, and (3) the perceived levels of acculturation and multiculturalism. *[Article copies available for a fee from The Haworth Document Delivery Service: 1-800-HAWORTH. E-mail address: <docdelivery@haworthpress.com> Website: <http://www.HaworthPress.com> © 2003 by The Haworth Press, Inc. All rights reserved.]*

Elizabeth Wieling, PhD, is Assistant Professor, Family Social Science, 290 McNeal Hall, 1985 Buford Circle, St. Paul, MN 55108 (E-mail: lwieling@che.umn.edu).

[Haworth co-indexing entry note]: "Latino/a and White Marriages: A Pilot Study Investigating the Experiences of Interethnic Couples in the United States." Wieling, Elizabeth. Co-published simultaneously in *Journal of Couple & Relationship Therapy* (The Haworth Press, Inc.) Vol. 2, No. 2/3, 2003, pp. 41-55; and: *Clinical Issues with Interracial Couples: Theories and Research* (ed: Volker Thomas, Terri A. Karis, and Joseph L. Wetchler) The Haworth Press, Inc., 2003, pp. 41-55. Single or multiple copies of this article are available for a fee from The Haworth Document Delivery Service [1-800-HAWORTH, 9:00 a.m. - 5:00 p.m. (EST). E-mail address: docdelivery@haworthpress.com].

KEYWORDS. Interethnic, interracial, marriage, Latino/a, White

Although interracial and interethnic[1] marriages were illegal in many states until 1967 when the Supreme Court, in *Loving v. Commonwealth of Virginia*, overthrew anti-miscegenation laws, there is historical evidence that such unions were occurring before 1967 (Rosenblatt, Karis, & Powell, 1995). The numbers of interracial marriages have consistently increased over the past decades across ethnic and racial groups. The total number of interracial marriages grew from 310,000 in 1970 (0.4% of all marriages) to approximately 1.3 million in 1994 (2.2% of all marriages). The census does not specifically report on the number of Latino/a[2] and non-Latino/a Whites.[3] This figure may be difficult to obtain given that persons of "Hispanic" origin may be of any race. However, the 2000 census reports that the numbers of "Hispanics" married to someone from an "other" origin (not Hispanic) increased from 891,000 in 1980 to 1,647,000 in 1999. Likewise, the number of "Whites" married to someone of "other" race has increased from 450,000 to nearly 1 million. Although both groups have almost doubled their rate of marriages to persons of "other" race, "Whites'" rate of intermarriage is much lower than those of "Hispanics." This may be due to Whites' privileged position and continued prejudice towards "others." It is important to note that a large percentage of Latinos/as have white skin color, thus potentially making them more likely candidates for an interethnic marriage to an Anglo-American White person. Berg (1995) reports that currently the majority of interethnic marriages occur between persons who are "non-Hispanic Whites" and persons of "Hispanic" descent. Given that Latinos/as comprise the fastest growing population in the United States, it is not surprising that this group might show greater numbers of interethnic marriages.

Most interracial and/or interethnic studies have focused on Black-White relationships but there is virtually no literature investigating the marital relationships of Latino/a and White couples. Some notable exceptions are Salgado de Snyder and Padilla's (1982) study on intermarriages of Mexican Americans. This study reports that Latina women are more likely than Latino men to intermarry and that these marriages will likely be to someone from a higher socioeconomic class. They conclude by stating that intermarriage itself is not necessarily a good index of acculturation and that "Mexican Americans, in spite of marrying outside their ethnic group, maintain cultural ties and an ethnic identity" (p. 362). Further, these marriages show flexibility in allowing each partner to transmit both cultural orientations. Kearl and Murgia's (1985) study considered the costs of minority members entering into exogamous union with someone from the majority culture. They found that minority females use marriage as a vehicle for assimilation into majority culture. The cost is that a woman is typically much younger than her spouse. More recently, Negy and Snyder's (2000) study compared Mexican American and non-Hispanic White American interracial couples to Mexican-American couples and non-Hispanic White couples. They looked at issues of marital satisfaction, acculturation, parental-role orientation, and implications for clinical intervention. This study reported that overall, the interethnic couples were more similar to non-Hispanic White couples than they were to Mexican American couples across domains such as marital distress, and distress regarding their children. In addition, this study reported that the interethnic couples did not experience greater relationship distress than monoethnic couples, despite previous literature suggesting that racially and/or ethnically mixed marriages are inherently more stressful due to cultural differences (Negy & Snyder, 2000).

The purpose of this study was to explore the experiences of six heterosexual couples who identified as being in a mixed ethnic and/or racial marriage where one partner is of Latino/a descent and the other is of European-American descent. Given the dearth of studies investigating this type of cross-cultural marriage, this exploratory pilot study provides some in-depth descriptions of how these couples experience their relationships.

METHODS

A phenomenological qualitative tradition guided the conceptualization of this study. The primary purpose was to gain a better understanding of the experiences of Latino/a and White couples. The researcher constructed an open-ended questionnaire and mailed it to a convenience sample of heterosexual couples who self-identified as being racially and/or ethnically mixed. A telephone interview was conducted with each person to provide an opportunity for participants to elaborate on their answers and as a means for the researcher to check for accuracy of data interpretation. The data were collected over a period of three months.

Researcher

I am a multiracial and multiethnic woman with dual citizenship in the United States and in Brazil. I was born in the United States but grew up in Brazil as the daughter of a German-American father and a Spanish,

Afro-Brazilian, Portuguese, and Native Brazilian Indian mother. I came to the United Stated in 1985 to pursue my college education. I earned a doctoral degree in marriage and family therapy and have been working as assistant professor in a marriage and family therapy program for the past four years. I am passionate about the study of cross-cultural relationships and family dynamics and have made this my primary area of research. I have also been married to an Irish and German American for 12 years, which further propelled my interest in investigating the experiences of Latino/a and White couples. My personal experience as a daughter of a multiethnic and multiracial couple were quite positive. However, I believe that growing up in an upper-middle class family in Brazil makes my experience significantly different from what it might have been in the United States as many of the issues surrounding discrimination and negative stigma due to intermarriages are different in Brazil. My marriage has also been positive and was particularly accepted by my family and friends. My own interethnic experiences were reflected in many of the comments reported by the participants in my study.

Participants

Six heterosexual couples volunteered to participate in the study. I knew four of the couples and was referred by one of the respondents to the other two as potential participants. The couples live in different parts of the United States and have a range of family characteristics. In terms of the ethnic and/or racial composition of this sample, three couples represent Latina women married to White men and the other three couples represent the reverse. Below is a brief summary of each couple. Fictitious names were created to protect participant anonymity.

Anna and Richard. Anna (age 42, bilingual) grew up in Puerto Rico and came to the United States to pursue her college education as an architect. Richard (age 43, bilingual) is a German American who grew up in Boston and is a graphic designer. Anna and Richard have been married 20 years and have two children.

Paula and Stephen. Paula (age 26, bilingual) is also from Puerto Rico and was raised in a Latin neighborhood in New York City. She received a master's degree in psychology and is now a stay-home mother of her two-year-old daughter. Paula intends to pursue a doctoral degree in Higher Education. Stephen (age 30) is an Irish and Italian American who grew up in New Jersey and works as a certified public accountant. Paula and Richard have been married three years.

Silvia and Ed. Silvia (age 30) is Mexican American and was raised in Texas. She received a bachelor's degree in elementary teaching and describes not knowing much about her culture. She intends to pursue a master's degree in Chicano studies and to learn Spanish. Ed (age 39) does not know much about his ethnic identity because he was adopted. His adoptive family is Irish American, and he grew up in Iowa. Silvia and Ed have been married four years and do not have children.

Shirley and Carlos. Shirley (age 45, bilingual) is a French and Norwegian American who grew up in Chicago. Shirley has a doctoral degree in English and is a college professor. Carlos (age 49, bilingual) is originally from Mexico but was raised in California. He has a master's degree in Engineering and works for an electric company. This is a second marriage for Shirley and Carlos, and they have been together six years. From their previous marriages they have children who are no longer living with them.

Dana and Osmar. Dana (age 21) is an Italian and German American from Florida. She is currently a third-year history major in college. Osmar (age 22, bilingual) has Cuban heritage and is also from Florida. He is a third-year college student majoring in engineering. Dana and Osmar have been married 1 1/2 years and have no children. They both intend to pursue graduate degrees.

Trish and Antonio. Trish (age 33) is a Polish American from Minnesota. She is currently pursuing a master's in business administration. Antonio (age 35, bilingual) is Mexican American and grew up in Nebraska. He is finishing his bachelor's degree in computer engineering. They have been married for one year and have a two-year-old son. They both work full-time in addition to going to school.

Interview Protocol

The questionnaire was composed of several demographic questions, one grand tour question, and seven follow-up questions. The grand tour question asked participants to describe their experiences of being married to someone from another race and/or ethnic group. Follow-up questions focused on participants'

a. thoughts on interracial relationships,
b. previous experience dating outside of race,
c. expectations,
d. perceived level of acculturation,
e. reactions from family, friends, and society,

f. experience with multiethnic and/or multiracial children, and
g. experience with discrimination based on their interethnic and/or interracial marital status.

Couples were instructed to complete the questionnaire jointly and to make note of any areas of difference regarding their experience. During the telephone interview, both the wife and husband were consulted simultaneously (each spouse was on a separate phone) with four of the couples and only the wife was interviewed with the other two couples. All telephone interviews were recorded and transcribed for data analysis. Participants reported an average of 1 1/2 hours to complete the questionnaire and the telephone interviews lasted approximately 45 minutes.

Data Analysis

Once I received the completed questionnaire from each couple, a preliminary analysis of data was conducted for each spouse and then compared to their partner's response. The follow-up telephone interview focused on member checking to ascertain whether I had accurately understood their answers, and provided participants with an opportunity to elaborate on their previous responses. Data analysis followed Spradley's (1979, 1980) Developmental Research Sequence that includes coding transcripts and written records for significant words and phrases, clustering this initial information into domains of meaning, clustering emergent themes and sub-themes, and identifying essential invariant structures. Lastly, categories were identified encompassing particular themes. The process of gathering written data from each spouse and conducting telephone interviews helped increase the trustworthiness of the data by triangulating data sources and checking for accuracy of interpretation with participants. Peer checks were also conducted during data analyses.

FINDINGS

Three core categories emerged from the data; each category includes dominant themes, and some have sub-themes. It should be noted that there is a close relationship between the dominant categories and the nature of questions that were asked of participants. Utilizing a questionnaire as the primary means of data collection heavily influences the type of information gathered, and it often increases the likelihood of categories being established a priori. Every effort was made to include the direct quotes from the participants to highlight how they expressed and perceived their experiences.

Category I. Experiences and Perceptions of Being in a Marriage with Someone from a Different Racial and/or Ethnic Group

Theme I: Idealized Perception of the "Other"

Nearly all participants reported having had a previous romantic relationship with someone from a different racial or ethnic group before they married. Ten participants stated that they were "very interested in other cultures" and "always imagined that they might marry someone from a different race." Anna and Richard stated,

> We were fascinated with each other's culture . . . so when we met and we had so much in common . . . we just knew we were meant for each other. We felt that the cultural background of the other person provided us with something that we had a hard time getting from people in our own group.

Paula and Stephen echoed these experiences by reporting, "we kind of had an idealized vision of what the other person was like because of their culture . . . even though a lot of it you get from society and the media . . . we found that a lot of it was true and it's worked for us." They went on to explain that "it is important to be careful though because there are also many negative stereotypes that really don't fit." Trish and Antonio talked about how they were "curious and intrigued with the other culture." They added, "I guess we just had an idealized perception of what someone from this other culture would be like." Two participants stated that they had "never really thought much" about whether or not they would marry in or out of their racial or ethnic background but that they "must have been open to it" or they would not have chosen to date someone from a different ethnic background.

Latinos'/as' Reasons for Idealizing Whites. When I followed up with participants regarding how they believed they acquired this "idealized" view of their spouses' culture, all the Latinos/as responded in a similar fashion. They said that some of the intrigue was due to the United States society's bias of "White" being equated with a "better than" status. This seemed to raise both feelings of curiosity and sadness for Latino/a participants. Carlos stated:

> It is so complex because we learn that White women are beautiful and maybe even superior . . . at some point those ideas become ingrained. On the other hand, we know that there is something wrong with that and we don't want to sell out our culture and our people. The bottom line is that my wife and I have similar values and outlook in life . . . I never really found that with someone from my own group.

Other Latinos/as reported that because they saw themselves as being somewhat acculturated to White values, they thought it was easier to believe that a White partner might be more desirable and a better fit than a Latino/a partner. Antonio added, "I now realize that much of my attitude was racist against my own people." Therefore, previously he may "not have considered someone from [his] own ethnic group as a suitable partner." Osmar, Antonio, and Silvia reported only recently becoming aware of the many negative stereotypes they held regarding people from their own ethnic background and "felt saddened by [their] ignorance."

Whites' Reasons for Idealizing Latinos/as. Four White participants stated that they had been exposed to Latinos growing up and that they had become "fascinated" with the Latino/a culture. Shirley had traveled extensively in Central and South America and became fluent in Spanish. She reported, "I loved their [Latinos/as] warmth and kindness . . . I liked the way families interacted with each other and I always knew that I would like a similar type of family." Ed said, "I know this may sound bad but part of me was attracted to the idea of a wife that would not be submissive, but that would be more attentive to my needs . . . I guess I had that idealized stereotype of a Latina woman." Stephen reported a similar view, "I always thought Hispanic women were beautiful and I thought they would value children more because it's a cultural thing."

Theme II: Similar Outlook on Life

All participants reported that their primary reason for being attracted to each other and getting married had more to do with their "similar outlooks on life," and "sharing mutual values and attitudes" than with the fact that they belonged to different ethnic groups. Three couples specifically addressed how they saw "many more areas of similarities than difference in how [they] approached life." Dana and Osmar said:

> We were amazed at how two people that grew up with such different values could end up wanting such similar things in a spouse and

out of life. I (Osmar) know people try to say that sometimes we intermarry because we want to get back at our family for something or we don't want someone from our own group because we don't think they are good enough . . . but that is not the case with us.

Influence of Time and Children. Several couples stated that once they had been together for a longer period of time and /or when they had had children, there was a shift in their values that reflected more of the cultural values they had been raised with. Shirley and Richard captured this sentiment when they stated, "it wasn't until we had kids that we were forced to really think hard about some of our values and how we wanted to raise our children . . . but we worked it out and I (Shirley) think all couples go through that regardless of race."

Again, couples suggested that, for the most part, they perceived themselves as "normal" and that it was society that often made their relationship an anomaly. These couples experienced a cultural bias that pathologized their interracial relationship. Ed said, "if anything, it's the unrealistic standards that some family members and friends put on us that can make the situation [marriage] more complex."

Theme III: Additional Societal Pressures

All couples with the exception of Trish and Antonio believed that there were "additional external pressures to making the relationship work." They made statements like, "if the slightest thing goes wrong in the relationship, people are quick to blame it on our cultural differences." "I don't get how some people can be so ignorant and want to blame our problems on our different races," and "sometimes I get fed up with the looks and whispering . . . I mean what year is this?" These participants believed that because they were more highly educated and because they tended to live in more liberal parts of the United States, some of the negative stereotyping was minimized. They talked about the importance of living in such environments, particularly for the sake of their children. Lastly, three participants stated how it was crucial not to ignore the "real racism, bias, and prejudice that is still prevalent in society" despite the increased numbers of interracial and interethnic marriages.

Theme IV: The Influence of Children

Three of the six couples have children together and one other couple said they would like to have children in the future. They reported that having children increased awareness regarding their "true values," but also influenced the part of the country they wanted to live in and desire for proximity to extended family. All couples with children stated they wanted to continue living in communities that were "more progressive." Anna and Richard said, "it's important to live in a place where they can see other children and parents that are mixed . . . we don't want them to grow up thinking this is a problem or that there is something wrong with it." Dana and Osmar added, "the important thing is for our son to grow up in an environment where they are respected and valued for who they are."

These parents talked about having a grandparent (typically the Latina grandmother) come live with them for a while during the time their child was an infant. Additional areas of concern revolved around making a specific point to transmit both White and Latino/a values to their children. Osmar stated, "I want my children to be proud of all of who they are . . . not just one cultural group." Dana added, "I see mixed children who are forced to make a choice about what ethnic group they want to be, this is not good for children." When asked what factors they believed influenced whether children grow up with both cultural identities, parents reported that the "strength of the parent relationship," "positive attitude from friends and family," "community," and "level of education and awareness of parents" were key factors.

Category II. Perceived Reactions from Family, Friends and Social Institutions

Theme I: Mixed Reactions on the Basis of Ethnic Background and Gender

All couples reported that they perceived their family and friends' reactions to their interethnic relationship as being "different" to how these persons responded to their siblings or friends' monoethnic relationships. These reactions were remarkably similar on the basis of the Latino/a or White status of each spouse. The three Latinos/as reported that their families were quite open and supportive of their choice to intermarry and only raised concerns regarding how the children would be raised. Friends were supportive, even though some had hesitations because of what they perceived as an "additional stress on the relationship." Paula stated, "my family loved Richard right away . . . and they just didn't have an issue with it [the marriage]." Anna commented, "the only thing my family said was that they wanted children and they wanted to be involved." All Latina women reported "no concern" with fear of rejection when introducing their future spouse to friends and family. Five of the White participants stated that some family members, friends, and persons at church and at work had serious reservations about their interethnic relationship. Concerns included the children, whether the "Latino/a families would be over-involved" in their lives, and wondering *why* they would choose someone that was "so different from them." Dana said, "my parents freaked out at first . . . but then they did calm down and gave Osmar a chance . . . now they think he is wonderful." Stephen described his family's reactions as "totally inappropriate at first . . . my family and some of my friends actually said that they thought I was marrying 'down.' " Richard reported that his "family could not come to grips with their stereotypes of Hispanic women and the fact that Anna was highly educated and not submissive." All Whites reported that although there was hesitation at first, their families and friends were open minded enough to "give their spouse a chance." However, three White and two Latino/a participants stated that if their partner "had been Black, that would have been a whole other story." The implication was that it would have been more difficult for their families to accept that type of interracial relationship. Lastly, 11 participants stated that the fact that their partner was educated made a significant difference in how the Latino/a person was received. Antonio said, "my father-in-law had the nerve to tell me that he knew he could trust me to take care of his daughter because I was like one of them . . . responsible and educated and all." Interestingly, the White participants did not indicate a similar shift in their families after the birth of their children.

An additional difference in terms of the reactions that these couples received from friends and family was based on gender. The three White women stated that some of their family members questioned the interethnic relationship because they worried about them getting into a marriage with a "machista" who would dominate and abuse them. These three women stated that they were "deeply offended" by this negative stereotype of Latino men that did not fit their husbands. Shirley stated, "there is just so much ignorance out there about what machismo represents . . . yes, there are Latino men who mistreat their wives but we are fools to believe that it happens any less with Whites or Asians or . . . ." Anna and Paula stated that their families saw this interethnic marriage as a "move up" for them, meaning that they would obtain upward social and economic mobility. The White men said that their friends made jokes about how marrying a Latina would mean "getting easy access to sex, good cooking, and a well kept home." Stephen stated, "I was often appalled by some of the things my friends would say. . . . I didn't want to believe that people could be so ignorant."

Category III. Perceived Levels of Acculturation and Multiculturalism

Theme I: Acculturation and Multiculturalism–From Latino/a Minority Group to White Majority Group

All Latinos/as in this study self-identified as being "highly acculturated." However, most of them stated that they had not abandoned their culture of origin, but had become "multicultural." Carlos stated, "I have been educated in this country . . . it is hard to be successful in the school system, at work, etc., without learning White people's rules . . . of course I have acculturated but I have not lost my culture." Anna reported, "I consider myself to be a multicultural person. Yes, that means I have acculturated to dominant values but I have not given up my Hispanic culture."

Theme II: Acculturation from White Majority Group to Latino/a Minority Group

Seven of the White participants stated that they believed acculturation for them was much different than the process of acculturation for their spouses. Shirley stated:

> There is no doubt that White privilege makes the issue of acculturation different for my husband and I. I have the flexibility to pick and choose the areas that I want to "adapt" to. Whereas he must acculturate in order to survive in many of our institutional and social systems.

Trish echoed this sentiment and added, "this acculturation issue is much different for the two of us because I belong to the dominant culture . . . I can choose to acculturate in areas that are convenient for me . . . he does not have the same privilege." Stephen said, "my hope is that with the increased numbers of the Latino community, that this will eventually bring more of a balance into what we consider the 'cultural norms' of our society." But it remains to be seen whether an increase in numbers will translate into an increase in power.

DISCUSSION

Open-ended survey and telephone interviews were conducted with six heterosexual couples of Latino/a and White descent regarding how they experienced their interracial and/or interethnic marriages. The major themes reflected were:

a. both Latinos/as and Whites in this sample had an idealized vision of the "other,"
b. Latinos/as and Whites had different reactions from family, friends, and social institutions based on their own ethnic background and gender,
c. these couples believed they had similar views of the world, and
d. Latinos/as believed they had to become multiracial and thus acculturate to dominant values while Whites reported that they had the privilege of choosing what they wanted to acculturate to.

Because relatively few studies have looked at Latino/a-White couple relationships, these findings provide at least a superficial understanding regarding some of the experiences, attitudes, and family and social dynamics present in these marriages. Many of the experiences reported in this study are found in the research conducted by Rosenblatt et al. (1995) and reported in their book *Multiracial Couples: Black & White Voices*. For example, White women in their sample also had a more difficult time gaining family acceptance for their interracial relationship. Also, it was couple' similarities and shared views of the world that attracted them to each other. Likewise, Johnson and Warren's (1994) book *Inside the Mixed Marriage* incorporates the experiences of couples in many different ethnic groups and explores the topic of mixed marriages in general. Many of the ideas reported in the book were reflected in the experiences of these six couples.

Clinical Implications

Given that the couples that participated in this study did not comprise a clinical sample, caution must be taken in drawing conclusions to a clinical population. However, the themes that emerged indicate that there may be particular couple and family dynamics and life cycle transitions that increase the possibility of stress for interracial and/or interethnic couples. It might be beneficial for therapists to assess couples' level of acculturation and to investigate the attraction or motivation that drew them to one another. In addition, it might be helpful to explore perceptions of support from family and friends and how the couple relationship might have shifted as a result of having children. It has been argued that one of the reasons for the higher rates of divorce among interethnic couples may not be the result of higher rates of distress in these relationships but rather the higher independence of these individuals that may make them more likely to dissolve a marriage (Negy & Snyder, 2000). This independence could be framed as valuable resource for these couples. Therapists may want to encourage couples to build on the skills they developed in dealing with family, friends, and society in going against the traditional norms of intra-group marriages. These skills may also be helpful to pass on to their children who will need to be prepared to interact with the world as interracial persons.

Limitations

This study has several limitations with respect to small sample size and lack of categorical saturation. In addition, as was reported by participants, the high level of participants' education might have played a significant role in how these couples experienced each other. Again, despite the limitations, I hope the study makes a small contribution to this body of literature. I would like to conclude by adding that my personal experience of being married to a White person is quite similar to the experiences reported by the Latina women in this sample.

NOTES

1. Interethnic in this paper refers to a marriage between persons from an ethnic majority and ethnic minority group in the United States.

2. Although the U.S. Census Bureau uses the term "Hispanic" to refer to populations that have Spanish ancestry, I will refer to these groups as "Latinos/as" in this paper because it is a more inclusive term that may include persons from Brazil and some of the Caribbean Islands.

3. Please note that when the term White is used, it refers to persons who are not of Latino/a descent. Some Latinos/as are also Whites and therefore this type of relationship would not necessarily constitute a mixed marriage. Also, the U.S. Census classifies "Hispanics" as Caucasians.

REFERENCES

Berg, R. R. (1995). Low fertility among intermarried Mexican Americans: An assessment of three hypotheses. Unpublished doctoral dissertation. *The University of Texas at Austin.*

Johnson, W. K., & Warren, D. M. *Inside the mixed marriage.* Lanham, MD: University Press of America.

Kearl, M. C., & Murgia, E. (1985). Age difference in spouses in Mexican American intermarriage: Exploring the cost of minority assimilation. *Social Science Quarterly, 66,* p. 453-460.

Negy, C., & Snyder, D. K. (2000). Relationship satisfaction of Mexican American and non-Hispanic White American interethnic couples: Issues of acculturation and clinical intervention. *Journal of Marital and Family Therapy, 26*(3), 293-304.

Rosenblatt, P. C, Karis, T. A., & Powell, R. D. (1995). *Multiracial couples: Black & white voices.* Thousand Oaks, CA: Sage Publications.

Salgado de Snyder, N., & Padilla, A. M. (1982). Cultural and ethnic maintenance of interethnically married Mexican Americans. *Human Organizations, 41,* 359-362.

Solsberry, P. W. (1994). Interracial couples in the United States of America: Implications for mental health counseling. *Journal of Mental Health Counseling, 16,* 304-317.

Spradley, J. (1980). *Participant observation.* New York: Holt, Rinehart & Winston.

Spradley, J. (1979). *The ethnographic interview.* New York: Holt, Rinehart & Winston.

U.S. Census Bureau. (1994). Subject Report on Marital Characteristics.

U.S. Census Bureau. (2000). Statistical Abstract of the United States.

Lives Together, Worlds Apart?
The Lives of Multicultural Muslim Couples

Manijeh Daneshpour

SUMMARY. The lives of multicultural Muslim couples is the focus of this paper. It is based on interviews with couples in which the husband is a Muslim of Middle Eastern descent with a wife of European-American or Asian-American descent. These women converted to Islam before or after marriage, or have remained Christian. The opportunities, strengths and challenges in such relationships are discussed, including issues that emerge connected to family, community, and society. In addition, current multicultural therapy competencies are reviewed and approaches, interventions, and strategies that may be useful in the treatment of multicultural Muslim couples are presented. *[Article copies available for a fee from The Haworth Document Delivery Service: 1-800-HAWORTH. E-mail address: <docdelivery@haworthpress.com> Website: <http://www.HaworthPress.com> © 2003 by The Haworth Press, Inc. All rights reserved.]*

KEYWORDS. Multicultural Muslim couples, multicultural therapy, treatment issues with Muslim couples, Muslim-Christian couples relationships

---

Manijeh Daneshpour, PhD, LMFT, AAMFT Approved Supervisor, is Director of the Marriage and Family Therapy Program, St. Cloud State University.

[Haworth co-indexing entry note]: "Lives Together, Worlds Apart? The Lives of Multicultural Muslim Couples." Daneshpour, Manijeh. Co-published simultaneously in *Journal of Couple & Relationship Therapy* (The Haworth Press, Inc.) Vol. 2, No. 2/3, 2003, pp. 57-71; and: *Clinical Issues with Interracial Couples: Theories and Research* (ed: Volker Thomas, Terri A. Karis, and Joseph L. Wetchler) The Haworth Press, Inc., 2003, pp. 57-71. Single or multiple copies of this article are available for a fee from The Haworth Document Delivery Service [1-800-HAWORTH, 9:00 a.m. - 5:00 p.m. (EST). E-mail address: docdelivery@haworthpress.com].

And among His Signs is that He created for you mates from among yourselves that you may live in tranquility with them and He has put love and mercy between your (hearts); verily in that are signs for those who reflect. (Qur'an 30:21)

Reasonable estimates of the Muslim presence in the U.S. now go as high as seven million (Khan Shamim, 2000). While a large percentage of this number represents immigrants to America from the Middle East, Africa and Europe, the number of converts also appears to be growing. This chapter is focused on multicultural Muslim couples. It is based on interviews with couples in which the husband is a Muslim of Middle Eastern descent with a wife of European-American or Asian-American descent. These women converted to Islam before or after marriage, or have remained Christian. Although there are no data available about how many American converts marry people of Middle Eastern descent, there is a growing number of such relationships, which creates numerous opportunities as well as challenges for these couples.

In this article, the opportunities, strengths and challenges in such relationships will be discussed, including issues that emerge connected to family, community, and society. In addition, current multicultural therapy competencies will be reviewed and approaches, interventions, and strategies that may be useful in the treatment of multicultural Muslim couples will be presented.

METHODOLOGY

This was a comprehensive qualitative investigation of the lives of ten multicultural Muslim couples between the ages of thirty-two and fifty-six who had been married from ten to twenty-two years. The participants were asked if they would participate in this study and were offered a brief, one-page description of the purpose of the study. They were informed of what they would get out of participating in the study, who would see the results, where they could obtain more information about the study, and how long it would take to complete the interview. Eight couples live in Minnesota; one couple lives in Oregon and the other lives in California. The eight couples that live in Minnesota were interviewed at their homes. The interviews were audio taped and all participants signed a consent form. The two couples that were not in Minnesota were interviewed over the phone using speakerphone and with their written consent; the interviews were audio taped as well.

In this sample the husbands were from Middle Eastern countries including Iran, Iraq, Jordan, and Palestine, which are racially considered to be what is referred to as "White," but is technically of Arian decent. Eight of the wives interviewed were European American, and two were Asian American. The interview questions explored aspects of the couples' lives, including their nuclear family background, dating history, courtship experiences, wedding, social life, public life, living and community environment, parenting and child-rearing experiences, education and employment experiences, values, religious differences, and areas of stress and disagreement. The final section of the interview explored issues regarding marital adjustment, communication, and decision-making. Couples also responded to questions regarding experiences with therapists and their expectations of the therapy profession. All tapes were transcribed after each interview to compare and contrast couples' responses to different questions in order to develop some general themes and patterns.

The sample consisted largely of couples that were highly educated, and professionally employed, with middle class backgrounds. Hence, although the findings are not easily generalizable to all interracial couples, they suggest some patterns and themes that have appeared significant.

It is important to keep in mind that indeed I am from Iran, teach multicultural therapy courses, and have done extensive research with the Iranian population and thus can be considered to be familiar with Middle Eastern culture. Therefore, the conclusion can be drawn that my background might have created some biases in understanding the challenges and opportunities these couples have faced. Nevertheless, as a postmodernist, I do not believe in an objective reality, and furthermore, this article is simply based on my interpretation and understanding of the lives of these couples.

MULTICULTURAL MUSLIM COUPLES' SIMILARITIES WITH OTHER COUPLES

The lives of all these couples are very similar to the lives of same-race/culture/ethnicity couples, as depicted in popular and contemporary media and literature. These couples describe their attractions to each other in ways parallel to partners of the same religion/race/ethnic background. They indicate mutual interests, values and beliefs, ease in being in each other's company, and physical attractiveness toward each other.

One of the couples interviewed consisted of an Iranian husband and a wife from the Asian country of the Philippines. She has never converted to Islam and to this day is a practicing Catholic. They reported sharing many common values and beliefs. The most common shared values for this couple were respect, honesty, trust, faithfulness, appreciation of diversity, family (including family of origin), and religion or spirituality. Expanding on this concept, the couple discussed the fact that their mutual values seemed to attract them to each other and at times it even seemed they had grown up in the same family, been taught the same things and had been raised in an almost identical manner. They attributed their marital success to the shared values they held between each other.

Two European-American women discussed how their tendency to share the same values and beliefs with their husbands of Middle Eastern descent reduced the level of potential conflict between them. The couples mutually felt that their shared values were particularly helpful when it came to maintaining consistency in their roles as partners and parents.

The areas of greatest stress or tension for all the couples, regardless of ethnic or racial background, tend to be very similar. Such examples of stress and tension usually consist of finances, juggling roles and responsibilities, parenting, communication related to dynamics of the relationship, and decision-making issues (Wehrly et al., 1999). The couples in this study tended to report similar stressors and tensions. In their response to questions concerning the impact of their racial, religion or ethnic differences, they tended to point out the existence of greater hurdles to overcome than their lack of racial or ethnic similarities.

MULTICULTURAL MUSLIM COUPLES' CHALLENGES

Even though multicultural Muslim couples tend to have many relationship strengths and stressors that are similar to couples that do not have such racial or ethnic differences, they nevertheless do face other unique challenges due to these minor but important differences. Depending on the length of time spent in this country, as well as the level of acculturation and assimilation, the cultural values and worldviews of Middle Easterners and Americans may present dramatic differences, and as a result may have an impact on the dynamics of the marriage. For immigrants and first-generation Middle Easterners, conflicts and differences related to communication patterns, language, gender roles, religious practices, parenting styles, customs, and foods were manifestations of profound cultural values and worldview differences. For the couples in this study, many of these issues related to cultural differences and conflicts were more prevalent in the early years of the couple's relationship, which will be discussed in the following sections.

Religious Compatibility

All couples talked about the importance of the religious aspects of their lives. Men whose wives converted to Islam agreed that indeed it was better to introduce their wives to Islam and encourage them to become Muslim prior to the marriage, but it seemed that women had some difficulty understanding this idea. Middle Eastern men struggled to point out their reasoning and simply explained that in enlightening their soon-to-be-wives of the views, practices and strong beliefs of Islam prior to being married, it would simply make it easier for the wives to have a better understanding of the religious background they hold and would in the future like for their wives to hold as well. European-American women struggled with their lack of understanding of the religion, and their partners' insistence got them even more confused. However, the same individuals admitted that Islam was very easy for them to accept within the passing of time in the actual marriage, whereas prior to the event such a conversion seemed near to impossible. Two others felt that their relationships were stable and lasting even without the conversion to Islam.

However, regardless of the timing of the conversion, whether before or after the marriage or not at all, all couples acknowledged that they had many conflicts and misunderstandings regarding their individual religious values at the beginning of their marriage even though flexibility, understanding, and tolerance for different perspectives played an important if not crucial role in the stability of their current relationship.

Community and Social Issues

Several couples struggled with differences regarding cultural and religious customs, particularly at social gatherings. At the beginning of their relationships, partners had problems understanding exactly what was to be expected of them and deciding how it was they were to deal with such a dilemma.

Given the fact that a non-Muslim is not bounded by Islamic values regarding dress code, mixed gender parties, consuming alcohol and eating non-halaal foods,[1] some non-Muslim women voluntarily chose to follow these customs in an effort to sustain a pleasant family life or simply as a goodwill gesture to walk the extra mile for their Muslim partners. For others, these issues became the major source of struggle.

Several Middle Eastern husbands in this study pointed out that by getting married to a non-Muslim woman, they knew that expecting their non-Muslim wives to behave in an Islamic fashion was not a sound expectation. They also knew that as a couple they would be invited to certain parties and dinners where it would not be unlikely for all non-halaal items to be served and even though he may not wish to consume such items, his wife could very well have wishes different to his. Therefore, both the husband and wife expressed the difficulty in the early years of their marriage in dealing with such problems due to the lack of understanding of what is expected of the other party.

Non-Muslim Celebrations

Some couples discussed the struggle in celebrating holidays, births and other such occasions with family and friends. In the occasion of births, problems were commonly raised among the Christian grandparents regarding the baptizing of the child, a very important aspect in the Christian religion yet not at all acknowledged in the Islamic faith. Similar differences arose on such Christian holidays as Easter and Christmas in which great feasts are held and presents are distributed, which are again not an acknowledged aspect in the Islamic faith. In this study, all eight couples whose wives converted to Islam struggled with these issues. Women described that unless they made sure that their side of family understands their husband's reservations about such celebrations, the situation got very tense at such a joyful occasion and left bitter memories.

Along the same line, family of origin problems can also arise for women who have converted to Islam. A European-American woman with an Arab husband talked about how she–now a Muslim–had problems and conflict related to cultural values and worldview differences concerning celebrating Christian holidays both with her husband and her own family. This couple's cultural and religious differences resulted in both lack of support and acceptance from her family, which made the initial phases of their relationship difficult, if not a real challenge. When the family began to see their daughter's continual conflict between her commitment to the relationship and her commitment to them, and her American family of origin culture, her family began to relax and understood the situation from what can be referred to as a different perspective. However, numerous concessions were made by all and involved the wife's willingness to respect, learn more about, and adapt to Arab and Islamic culture, making it possible for the couple to come to a level of understanding and compromise. And in return the husband participated in more gatherings when alcoholic beverages were not served and went to visit the wife's family on days that were not a Christian holiday, which resulted in the absence of the extended family.

Hugging and kissing cheeks of male and female friends across gender is another practice which is not permissible in Islam. Several couples talked about the confusion and anger at the beginning of their relationship regarding these issues. One European-American woman talked about how all of the sudden everything she was doing was considered wrong and it took her several years before understanding the religious reasoning behind it.

These differences that exist between Middle Easterners, Asians and European-American cultures are legitimate and may be of valid concern, but these couples appeared willing and able to rise above the differences even though they struggled a great deal during the first few years of their marriage. The willingness of one or both partners to respect and learn about the others' cultural backgrounds, including rituals, customs, and traditions, seemed to have far-reaching implications in the relationship between the partners and in the relationship both have with the families of origin, in-laws, friends, and associates.

Friendship Circles

Converting to Islam for these European-American and Asian-American women also had an impact on their friendships. Several couples, especially European-American women, discussed the difficulty they had with support of their non-Muslim friends at the beginning of their relationship. Some talked about friends wanting to go out and due to the possibility of drinking involved, they could not participate. Some talked about feeling different and not having much in common with friends anymore. Many talked about breaking ties with good friends due to ideology differences and began becoming friends with couples like themselves who were isolated from their own family and friends after converting to Islam.

Acceptable Dress

Islam prescribes dress codes for both men and women. Today, not many Muslim men and women, living in secular Muslim countries or the West, follow the dress code perfectly. However, most Muslim women still do not normally wear sleeveless shirts, shorts, bikinis or other such revealing articles of clothing. A practicing Muslim man who is faithful to the ideology of the Islamic faith will inevitably prefer his wife and children to be dressed in a proper, that is, a non-revealing manner. If the wife is non-Muslim she is under no obligation to follow a strict Islamic dress code, or in that case a dress code at all. Nevertheless, she may choose to dress in a proper manner to please her husband, to avoid offending him, and to furthermore prevent the attraction of other men to her feminine beauty.

The European-American women in this study talked about the difficulty they initially had understanding the reasoning behind the dress code. After having decided to become a Muslim, however, they accepted the dress code. Almost every European-American woman discussed their family's resistance and furthermore misunderstanding about the Islamic dress code. Families tended to mistakenly view the struggle for modesty of the women to be rather a sign of their oppression. Some women admitted that they had given up trying to explain their views to their families while others claimed that their families had come around and furthermore defended the Islamic dress code in front of other non-Muslims, when spoken ill of.

Issues of Parenting and Child Rearing

Multiracial couples usually insist that their children have an identity based on the collective background of both parents (Brandell, 1988; McRoy & Freeman, 1986; Wardle, 1987). In this sample the two multifaith couples indicated that they believed in raising their children to embrace and celebrate the Middle Eastern and American cultures collectively and equally, thus exposing their children to the values, roles, norms, attitudes, behaviors, and even the languages of both cultures.

However, child rearing and parenting are the most important and complicated issues multicultural Muslim couples face, with the major concern being how to help their children practice their Islamic faith in this society, that for the most part, tends to stereotype and furthermore misunderstand the Islamic faith. In Islamic cultures, even those with secular governments such as Pakistan, Egypt, Bangladesh, Turkey, and Indonesia, the entire social environment supports learning and understanding Islam. Although cultural practices might deviate from the true meaning of Islam, nevertheless, children learn Islam in bits and pieces at home, school, through radio, TV and through their participation in Islamic groups. Grandparents and other relatives also play a role to help parents teach Islamic values to their children. In the West, parents are faced with a totally different environment. In most cases, they have to be the only "bridge" between Islam and their children. Several couples discussed their frustration with teaching Islamic principles. Due to the fact that the husbands' families live in the Middle East and the wives are not very familiar with the Islamic values and principles, husbands felt overwhelmed serving as the only connection to the Islamic faith for their whole family, which created even more frustration for the non-Muslim wife. Several European-American women said that after discussing different issues with other Muslim couples, they realized that their husbands' interpretations of what is Islamic and what is not is a mixture of family of origins' values and also cultures and traditions which might be very different for other Middle Eastern cultures.

The majority of the couples I interviewed spoke of wanting their children to have a sense of and appreciation for their Middle Eastern cultural backgrounds and heritages, since they are already exposed heavily to U.S. culture. Several couples gave examples of how, beginning very early in their children's lives, they attempted to introduce them to the various aspects of their Middle Eastern cultural backgrounds, based on their Islamic faith. Couples stated that it is very challenging to raise children with Islamic values (i.e., no dating, no drinking, no dancing or listening to music, etc.) while they are exposed to U.S. cultures, which for the most part contradict almost all of these values. Parents emphasized the importance of talking with their children about issues of identity: providing identity-bolstering seminars, books, and films, and providing instructions for their children about what to say and how to respond in situations in which they are faced with making difficult choices. In addition, parents spoke of the significance of strong adult role models for their children, and of support from extended family, friends, and good connections to a strong Muslim community. They cited the necessity of their children's learning to speak Arabic or Persian and enjoying customary foods. According to these couples, Middle Eastern "culture" has special importance for them and their children, due to its connection to their Islamic faith. However, they indicated that the decision to introduce their children to Middle Eastern culture came later, after wives had converted to Islam, and even then most couples indicated that raising children was the most challenging part of their relationship.

Several European-American women remembered that in the early years of child-rearing it had been frustrating not knowing what was "Islamic" and what was "cultural" when they had to implement rules for their children. One European-American woman believed that her husband demanding to be the absolute authority figure in the family was an Islamic rule, and she needed to teach her children absolute obedience. However, later on, she realized that her husband's father was a powerful man, and therefore her husband continued that pattern, and his behavior had nothing to do with the Islamic faith. Therefore, there was a significant struggle in understanding that religion, culture, and upbringing are each separate categories and can easily become blended, and therefore dement the true beliefs of what they know as their "Islamic faith."

Gender and Power

This was a very controversial and difficult topic to discuss with the couples in which the wife had converted to Islam. All wives in this study indicated that prior to meeting their husbands their perception of the Middle Eastern cultures in general were very different. They believed that these cultures are patriarchal and not very inclusive to women in public life. However, many years later, they realized that when dealing with the Islamic perspective of any topic, there should be a clear distinction between the normative teachings of Islam and the diverse cultural practices among Muslims, which may or may not be consistent with the Islamic principles.

For example, three women that were married to Iranians discussed the issues of power and gender differently as opposed to European-American women who were married to Arabs even though the teachings of the Islamic faith are supposed to be the same. Nevertheless, all couples interviewed emphasized that if they would have married someone from their own cultures the issues of gender and power would have been very different. Specifically, Arab men discussed their cultural expectation to be the provider and the protector of the family and seeing their wives working and making significant contributions to their married lives were challenging for them. On the other hand, they expected their wives to take more power in family decision-making, but their wives preferred their involvement in family affairs and joint decision-making.

It was also evident that they used or misused their Islamic faith to gain more power, which was challenged by their wives once they became more knowledgeable about the true teaching of the religion. One European-American woman talked about how at the beginning, she perceived her husband to be a very good Muslim and therefore superior in many different aspects of morality and later on, once she read books and attended religious gatherings, she realized that she herself had actually become a better Muslim!

Nevertheless, in this sample, male power existed more so at the beginning of their relationship than later, but women often eventually understood that the power role of their husbands has not been Islamicly validated, but rather an adaptation of their father's or forefather's demented belief of male roles in Islam, and the interpretation varies from one culture to another.

APPROACHES, INTERVENTIONS, AND STRATEGIES FOR THERAPY WITH MULTICULTURAL MUSLIM COUPLES

The mental health field has only recently begun to address the issues and concerns of the multicultural population (Wehrly et al., 1999). Mental health professionals have had limited experience working with multicultural couples and have often relied on dated literature that depicts interracial/interfaith relationships as being fraught with pathology and doomed to failure. Some multicultural couples in this study reported working with professionals who made judgments about their relationship problems based on the partners' cultural and religion differences. These judgments were based on the assumption that racial, religion, or cultural background differences always result in relational difficulties. McGoldrock, Giordano, and Pearce (1996) suggest that the greater the cultural differences between spouses, the more problems they have adjusting to marriage. This was true for two couples in this study, but we need to urge mental health professionals to be careful about making this assumption without a thorough assessment of each couple.

It is also absolutely essential that therapists who work with multicultural Muslim couples examine and explore their own attitudes and beliefs about these relationships. Myths and stereotypes continue to cloud societal images of individuals who marry persons of another culture/religion. The therapist's awareness of his or her own attitudes and beliefs is a foundation for doing competent and effective therapy with multicultural couples (Solsberry, 1994). It is crucial that therapists are not only aware of their personal biases, but that they also recognize the negative effects that such biases can have on the therapy process (McRoy & Freeman, 1986). One couple talked about how they felt judged when the therapist assumed their marital problems are solely related to their religion and did not validate their other more important relationship concerns.

Myths and stereotypes about multicultural marriage also have the potential to have a negative impact on the multicultural couple's relationship. These myths and stereotypes are often at the root of the opposition that these couples experience as rejection and alienation from family and friends. One couple talked about their frustration with the therapist because she was not able to validate their sense of alienation, and it seemed to them that she was siding with people who reject and alienate them. Davidson (1992) suggests that therapists be critically aware of these theories and myths, recognizing their inherent racial/cultural biases and guarding against their influence in the therapy process. Couples may enter therapy in an attempt to discuss and understand the objections to their relationship (Wehrly, 1996). The therapist must be able to empathize with the couple and validate feelings that the partners may be experiencing. It may also be necessary to refocus the couple's attention on to the strengths of the relationship. A major strength that is often overlooked or minimized is the ability of couples to transcend or appreciate their vast differences. Further, the therapist should assist the couple in recognizing and drawing on the strength of the relationship to empower the couple to resist stereotypes and grapple with family issues.

Several couples talked about their families' opposition that this marriage is for ulterior motives (i.e., staying in the U.S., obtaining legal status or residency). It is certainly possible that a person has married a European-American for ulterior motives and in doing so is fulfilling stereotypes and myths. If, in the context of the therapy process, this is revealed, it should be explored, and the therapist should assist the couple in identifying and clarifying the partners' reasons for being together. Attempts should be made to help the couple determine if, because of love or other positive factors, the relationship has a viable chance of survival (Davidson, 1992; Okun, 1996).

Davidson (1992) suggests that in some cases a clinical professional may work with the couple and family members (if they are still around) to discuss different issues related to multicultural marriage. Family members may be invited to examine whether their accusations about ulterior motives expose their prejudice rather than indicating weakness in the couples' decision to marry. In general, all couples in this study believed that multicultural couples' marriages still present concern for members of this society, especially multicultural Muslim marriages. In working with couples and their families, it is important for therapists to help them become aware that in accepting the relationship, they may be making different and also very difficult choices. This may carry some high demands (Davidson, 1992), including that of role modeling what it means to live harmoniously in a multicultural society.

According to Solsberry (1994), a therapist who works with a client of the same race, who is interracially married, may assume that there are no racial or cultural differences between the therapist and the client. The multicultural marriage, however, generally places the client in a position that is currently different from that of the therapist. As indicated by Sue, Arrendondo, and McDavis (1992), the culturally skilled therapist has knowledge and understanding of the life expectancies, cultural heritages, and historical backgrounds of culturally different clients. However, the influences of being married to a person of a different race, religion, and culture positions a client who is of the same background as the therapist to potentially have a very different cultural experience and worldview than the therapist. For multicultural Muslim couples the therapist might feel more connected to the European-American partner and assumes that she understands her issues better without recognizing the differences between them. One European-American woman talked about her frustration with the therapist trying very hard to emancipate her from supposedly an oppressive relationship without understanding the vast ideological and value differences between them.

It is important, when multicultural couples present concerns regarding the relationship, that therapist explores the basis for and possible origins of these concerns. Ibrahim and Schroeder (1990) also suggest that an assessment be conducted to help the therapist understand each partner's worldview and cultural identity, as well as to help each partner understand the other's worldview and cultural identity. According to Okun (1996), differences in expression of emotion, expression of physical affection, beliefs of partners regarding roles, power distribution, cultural influences on family structure, views about parenting, and the meaning of love should be considered in any multicultural marriage. According to Ibrahim and Schroeder (1990), in addition to examining worldview and other cultural matters, the following may also be explored: the couple's satisfaction with the relationship, the effectiveness of communication between the partners, the commitment and level of solidarity in the relationship, the developmental differences that each partner has experienced or expects to experience, the occupational status of both partners, and the family role expectations of both partners. In examining concerns that may be a function of the cultural differences that exist between the partners, it is important to help couples explore the following: how each partner defines his or her cultural identity, the meaning that cultural identity has for each of them, and how the meaning given to each one's cultural identity influences and affects the relationship and the dynamics within the relationship (Okun, 1996). The exploration of each partner's worldview and cultural basis can assist the couple in understanding some of the reasons for the partners' conflicts (Ibrahim & Schroeder, 1990). The same dynamic exists for multicultural Muslim couples. It is important to note that even when individuals marry someone from the same culture and ethnic background, they still have to deal with different family values and role expectations. Thus, it is necessary to normalize many of these issues and not blame it on cultural difference.

CONCLUSION

Based on a research study of ten couples, this study provided an overview of the unique experiences of multicultural Muslim couples in the United States. Growing opportunities for interactions between people of differing cultural backgrounds makes it likely that the number of multicultural relationships will continue to increase. In addition, there is going to be continued growth in the segment of the U.S. population that accepts Islam as their religion; therefore, the expansion of the meanings of multicultural couples should include Christian-Muslim couples when discussing couples and families. Therapists will need to assess their own views on this population and be able to assess these couples' needs, strengths, and differences. It is paramount for mental health professionals to increase their knowledge and broaden their understanding of multicultural couples and their Islamic faith if they want to help these couples thrive in their relationships.

NOTE

1. Non-halaal can simply be defined as foods that are not permitted in Islam to be consumed by a Muslim such as pork and meats which have not been processed in an Islamic way; in technical terms this word is referred to as "lawful" in the Quran.

REFERENCES

Brandell, J. R. (1988). Treatment of the biracial child: Theoretical and clinical issues. *Journal of Multicultural Counseling and Development, 16,* 176-187.
Davidson, J. R. (1992). Theories about Black-White interracial marriage: A clinical perspective. *Journal of Multicultural Counseling and Development, 30,* 150-157.

Ibrahim, F.A. & Shroeder, D. G. (1990). Cross-cultural couples counseling: A developmental psychoeducational intervention. *Journal of Comparative Family Studies, 21*, 193-205.

McGoldrick, M., Giordano, J., & Pearce, J. K. (1996). *Ethnicity and family therapy* (2nd edition). New York: Guilford.

McRoy, R. G., & Freeman, E. (1986). Racial-identity issues among mixed race children. *Social Work in Education, 8*, 164-175.

Okun, B. F. (1996). *Understanding diverse families: What practitioners need to know.* New York: Guilford.

Shamim Khan, A. (2000). Marriages between Muslims and Non-Muslims. *Islamic Horizon*, July/August.

Solsberry, P. W. (1994). Interracial couples in the United States of America: Implications for mental health counseling. *Journal of Mental Health Counseling, 4*, 304-377.

Sue, D. W., Arredono, P., & McDavis, R. J. (1992). Multicultural counseling competencies and standards: A call to the profession. *Journal of Multicultural Counseling and Development, 20*, 64-88.

Wardle, F. (1987). Are you sensitive to interracial children's special identity needs? *Young Children, 42* (2), 53-59.

Wehrly, B., Kenney, K. R. & Kenney, M. E. (1999). *Counseling Multiracial Families.* Thousands Oaks, CA: Sage.

Wehrly, B. (1996). *Counseling interracial individuals and families.* Alexandria, VA: American Counseling Association.

Interracial Relationships in Hawaii: Issues, Benefits, and Therapeutic Interventions

Paula M. Usita
Shruti Poulsen

SUMMARY. Given the increase in rates of intermarriages, it is vital that we understand the issues and benefits of interracial relationships and the ways in which therapists might assist interracial couples. Our focus in this article is on interracial relationships in Hawaii. Because of its history of promoting interracial ties and its plural character, Hawaii is, in many ways, a unique setting for interracial relationships. At the same time, there are relational issues, benefits, and needs faced by both mainstream U.S. interracial couples and interracial couples in Hawaii. There are a variety of therapeutic interventions that could be used to help interracial couples. This chapter examines the factors in Hawaii's past and present that contribute to its particular history of interracial relationships, the common challenges that face interracial couples, personal and relational benefits of interracial relationships, and the therapeutic interventions from which interracial couples may benefit. *[Article copies available for a fee from The Haworth Document Delivery Service: 1-800-HAWORTH. E-mail address: <docdelivery@haworthpress.com> Website: <http://www.HaworthPress.com>* © 2003 by The Haworth Press, Inc. All rights reserved.]

Paula M. Usita is affiliated with San Diego University.
Shruti Poulsen is affiliated with Purdue University.
Address correspondence to: Paula M. Usita, PhD, University Center on Aging, San Diego State University, 5500 Campanile Drive, San Diego, CA 92182-1872 (E-mail: usita@mail.sdsu.edu).

[Haworth co-indexing entry note]: "Interracial Relationships in Hawaii: Issues, Benefits, and Therapeutic Interventions." Usita, Paula M., and Shruti Poulsen. Co-published simultaneously in *Journal of Couple & Relationship Therapy* (The Haworth Press, Inc.) Vol. 2, No. 2/3, 2003, pp. 73-83; and: *Clinical Issues with Interracial Couples: Theories and Research* (ed: Volker Thomas, Terri A. Karis, and Joseph L. Wetchler) The Haworth Press, Inc., 2003, pp. 73-83. Single or multiple copies of this article are available for a fee from The Haworth Document Delivery Service [1-800-HAWORTH, 9:00 a.m. - 5:00 p.m. (EST). E-mail address: docdelivery@haworthpress.com].

KEYWORDS. Interracial relationships and Hawaii, mixed-race marriages, therapy and interracial marriages

The state of Hawaii has a long history of interracial relationships, dating back to the early 1800s (Labov & Jacob, 1998). Because of Hawaii's tradition of intermarriages, interracial couples' experiences in Hawaii may be qualitatively different from interracial couples' experiences living on the mainland U.S. However, interracial couples, no matter where they reside, confront potential challenges from their families, racial communities, and dissimilar upbringings. At the same time, interracial couples in Hawaii and elsewhere in the U.S. have the potential to experience personal and social benefits from their relationships. Our goal in this paper is to describe the reasons that interracial couples in Hawaii may enjoy a different experience from their counterparts living in the mainland U.S. while emphasizing that all interracial couples–no matter where they live–have the potential to confront similar challenges and gain similar benefits from their cross-race intimate relationship. We conclude the paper with a discussion of select therapeutic interventions from which interracial couples in Hawaii and elsewhere in the U.S. may benefit.

HAWAII:
A UNIQUE SETTING
FOR INTERRACIAL RELATIONSHIPS

Hawaii is a unique setting for interracial relationships. There are a myriad of factors that contribute to the historical acceptance of interracial ties in Hawaii. We will focus on four factors: social geography, Hawaii's history of promoting interracial relationships, Hawaii's immigration history, and local identity among Hawaii residents.

Social geography. Social geography refers to how a physical geography is peopled, and with how the social composition of a physical region influences social contact and economic opportunities (Frankenberg, 1993; Katz & Monk, 1993). In Hawaii, the social geography is quite different than the rest of the U.S. Hawaii is a racially heterogeneous society compared to the mainland U.S. Whereas non-Hispanic Whites are the majority racial group in states on the mainland U.S., Asians or Pacific Islanders are the largest racial group in Hawaii, followed by non-Hispanic Whites; Hispanics; Blacks; and American Indians, Eskimos, or Aleuts (U.S. Census Bureau, 2001). Further, racial and ethnic groups live in proximity on the islands, which appears to contribute to cross-race relationships among young adults (Root, 2001). During the 1990s, intermarriage rates were around 46% in Hawaii (Fu & Heaton, 1997).

Hawaii's history of promoting interracial relationships. Hawaii is a unique setting for interracial relationships also because of its history of promoting cross-race ties. While statehood in 1959 brought with it a certain degree of conformity to Anglo culture (Labov & Jacobs, 1998), public sanctioning of marriages between Hawaiians and foreigners existed in the 1820s (Adams, 1937; McDermott, Tseng, & Maretzki, 1980). Yet, other influences that still exist in Hawaii appear to promote the acceptance of interracial relationships.

Hawaii's immigration history. Hawaii is a state with a strong immigrant tradition. Immigrants were sought from different nations to assist with Hawaii's sugar cane and pineapple industries. Immigrants from Portugal, Japan, China, Korea, and the Philippines, for instance, have had a hand in Hawaii's agriculture (McDermott, Tseng, & Maretzki, 1980). The immigrants laid roots in Hawaii and eventually became involved in other work sectors of the island economy. As immigrants experienced educational, professional, financial, and political success, intermarriages became more acceptable (McDermott, Tseng, & Maretzki, 1980). Anti-miscegenation laws, which existed in some mainland states until as recently as 1967, have never existed in Hawaii (Kitano, Yeung, Chai, & Hatanaka, 1984).

Local identity: Unification of Hawaii residents. Some scholars on intermarriage believe that Hawaii has been able to maintain a unique view of intermarriage, in part, because of its "local culture" (Labov & Jacob, 1998). Hawaii residents of various ethnic and racial backgrounds share a strong local identity and speak a command language known as pidgin (Hormann, 1972). Presumably, the local identity unifies residents, separates them from their co-ethnics and non co-ethnics from the mainland, and preserves Hawaii's unique cultural landscape (Okamura, 1994). Because locals share a collective identity, interracial relationships among locals may be viewed as further promotion of the local identity.

ISSUES FOR INTERRACIAL COUPLES IN HAWAII AND ELSEWHERE

Hawaii may be a more accepting location in which to experience cross-racial relationships than the mainland because of the greater potential for cross-ethnic and racial contact. However, interracial couples in Hawaii confront many similar challenges to their counterparts in the mainland U.S. because in a basic sense all couples intermarry, bringing to the marriage differences such as gender, socio-economic background, and religion (Falicov, 1995). The differences may widen for interracial couples, whether or not they live in Hawaii, if the following exist: family opposition, social intolerance, language and communication difficulties, different views on sexuality, and different beliefs surrounding child-rearing.

Family opposition to interracial relationships. Sociologists generally believe that any ethnic group interested in building a cohesive political and social structure will discourage interracial relationships (Pope, 1986). One of the most difficult issues that an interracial couple often faces is strong opposition to their relationship from their families. Parental approval generally will have great psychological importance to a couple's marital relationship, and it can impact a couple's relationship at every phase of their lifecycle (Falicov, 1995; Ratcliff, Moon, & Bonacci, 1978). Parental and family response can impact lifecycle rituals and events such as the wedding ceremony or the birth of a child in ways that can be negative or positive (Falicov, 1995). For example, some interracial couples may forgo a wedding ceremony in light of their family's disapproval and lack of support for the relationship. Additionally, marital difficulties can be compounded by each spouse's sense of divided loyalties or unresolved family issues. The availability of racial communities may also influence family views on mixed cultural relationships. According to Kitano, Yeung, Chai, and Hatanaka (1984), when there are no large, cohesive racial communities, and limited marital choices, there is a lesser degree of control over marital choice and a greater acceptance of interracial marriage among these groups due to limited marital choices. It is important to note that resistance to the interracial relationship may exist at the early stages of the relationship or when family come to understand the couples' seriousness, but that acceptance of the interracial union does occur in many instances (Root, 2001).

Societal intolerance of interracial relationships. Societal intolerance of interracial relationships can contribute to stressors for the partners. Some segments of society still view such unions as something of an anomaly that does not readily fit into the racial stratification system. Such ambivalence in society creates a similar ambivalence for the interracial couple themselves, because those beliefs could be internalized (Motoyoshi, 1990). According to Pope (1986), interracial couples, and especially black-white couples, cannot ignore the impact of racial tensions and divisions in U.S. society. Cultural and racial differences often become magnified during a crisis situation, and the lack of support and isolation from the society at large poses a threat to the stability of interracial relationships (Falicov, 1995; Solsberry, 1995). Certain racial combinations may be more accepted and tolerated than others. For instance, African American and Caucasian American couples historically have tended to experience the most hostility and opposition from society whether in Hawaii or in mainland states (Chan & Wethington, 1998; Qian, 1999). Interracial couples will sometimes intentionally isolate themselves from their own communities in an attempt to establish independence from their group's prejudices and disapproval. However, this mechanism can result in total isolation from support including those that the natural extended family system might afford (Falicov, 1995; Ratliff, Moon, & Bonacci, 1978). Therefore interracial couples may face ostracism and opposition not only from society at large, but also from their earliest attachment figures (Gaines et al., 1999). Whereas it is important to bring up the difficulties that interracial couples may face from individuals within and outside of their racial communities, including their families, because those difficulties could create tension within the relationship, it is also important to recognize that most interracial couples are aware of the biases against interracial marriages that exist in society and have given considerable thought to how they will approach the matter within and outside of their communities. Root's (2001) research with over two hundred men and women in interracial relationships illustrates the mindfulness with which interracial couples approach potentially tense situations.

Language barrier and communication issues in interracial couples. A common language functions to strengthen the marital bond and facilitates communication in any relationship. Language is a very important component in the experience of ethnicity and culture, and also in the sharing of this experience with others. Interracial couples facing a language barrier are especially prone to communication challenges (Ho, 1990; Kitano et al., 1984; Ratliff, Moon, & Bonacci, 1978). Research illustrates that interracial couples in the U.S. that consist of an immigrant who is not fluent in English and a partner who is fluent in English only, experience communication breakdown and frustration (Glenn, 1986). Further, for the partner whose first language may not be that of the majority culture, acculturation and adjustment to the new environment may be more complex and difficult (Ratliff, Moon, & Bonacci, 1978), and the interracial couple may undergo difficulties because of that partner's adjustment issues. Whereas language differences pose communication challenges to interracial couples, it must also be recognized that interracial couples and families work together at strengthening communication (Usita & Blieszner, in press).

Sexuality and interracial relationships. In the area of sexual adjustment, interracial couples may have to deal with different cultural codes regarding sexuality, "rules" that each individual will bring to the relationship, and possibly language differences that might complicate communication in this area (Ho, 1990). According to Ho (1990), religious and cultural beliefs inform attitudes toward sex and its role in marriage. Cultural codes and beliefs regulate various aspects of sexuality such as when and how sexual intercourse may take place. How the interracial couple negotiates these differences will influence the degree of satisfaction in their sexual and marital relationship.

Child-rearing in interracial couples. Raising their biracial children in a manner that is congruent with both partners' childrearing views is another consideration for interracial couples. Researchers agree that childrearing practices are deeply rooted in cultural and racial contexts and finding some middle ground on this issue can be difficult for some interracial couples (Falicov, 1995; Gibbs, 1987; McRoy & Freeman, 1986; Xie & Goyette, 1997). Conflict with a spouse may be avoided by adopting a policy where one parent is totally in charge of childrearing practices and rituals. Another approach is the "hands off" approach where neither parent wants to impose their personal parenting style on the children (Ho, 1990). According to Ho, neither approach is particularly effective in raising culturally balanced children and may lead not only to parenting problems but also to tension in the marital relationship.

BENEFITS OF INTERRACIAL RELATIONSHIPS FOR COUPLES

Although many of the issues interracial couples face may be construed as negative, interracial couples also experience personal and relational benefits from their cross-race intimate relationships. Indeed, the "blessings" of being involved in an interracial relationship are numerous, and include feeling that one has been personally enriched by being with an interracial partner, being thankful of the opportunities to bridge cultures, and weathering institutionalized racism (Rosenblatt, Karis, & Powell, 1995). Scholars focusing on intermarriage from a perspective that is resilience-based rather than stress-based (Chan & Wethington, 1998) report that among the psychological benefits to interracial relationships are the increased opportunity for development of social competence, personal growth, and social network expansion. Chan and Wethington (1998) point out that couples who intermarry tend to be older, more educated, and have a higher income, and that all these factors also lead to marital stability over time. Not all couples in interracial relationships experience marital stability, yet, they still benefit from their cross-racial relationships. Immigrant Japanese women in mid- and late-life, who intermarried with Caucasian American and African American men during their young adulthood years, demonstrate resilient personal qualities throughout their life course–they utilize their knowledge and understanding of two languages to build successful personal relationships and professional careers (Usita, 2001).

THERAPEUTIC INTERVENTIONS FOR INTERRACIAL COUPLES

The aforementioned issues suggest that interracial couples deal with important and complex matters in their relationships. Some of those issues may require therapeutic intervention. Therapeutic interventions with interracial couples tend to focus primarily on education and awareness both for clients and therapists (Okun, 1996; Solsberry, 1995; Watts & Henriksen, Jr., 1998). According to Solsberry (1995) therapists must gain awareness and insight of their own attitudes towards intermarriage and engage in an ongoing process of monitoring their own biases during therapy with interracial couples. Therapists are also encouraged to provide an environment in which the clients can also become aware of their own endemic racism and stereotyping. Therapists can be particularly helpful in encouraging couples to identify, acknowledge, and discuss their feelings about interracial marriage and raising biracial children. Additionally, providing therapeutic intervention with as many extended family members as possible can be very useful in addressing issues around parental and family support and acceptance (Solsberry, 1995). Other therapeutic interventions with interracial couples include clinicians being aware and educated about the cultural views of their clients and of client views towards mental health and its treatment (Okun, 1996). Okun also recommends a team consultation approach where a co-therapist or consultant of the client's racial group may be utilized in the process of providing therapy to an interracial couple (p. 282).

Interracial couples planning on marriage may also benefit greatly from premarital counseling or therapy that encourages each partner to assess his or her own assumptions and expectations around cultural and racial differences and issues (Okun, 1996). Clinicians can also share literature and research about interracial couples and can identify community resources for additional support for the couple. Premarital counseling could also include the use of such tools as the Interracial Couple Questionnaire (Watts & Henriksen, Jr., 1998). This questionnaire is designed to facilitate dialogue and understanding of the "couples' perceptions about interracial relationships from each spouse's culture of origin, how interracial relationships affect extended family relationships, how interracial relationships impact children born to the couple, and what interracial couples can do to empower themselves to face the challenges they have experienced and/or will experience" (Watts & Henriksen, Jr., 1998, p. 369). Not only does this questionnaire provide the format for dialogue between the couple on sensitive and difficult issues, but it also works to highlight the couple's strengths and areas for growth in the relationship.

Couples group therapy and genogram therapy are particularly effective therapeutic interventions with interracial couples (McGoldrick, 1998; Solsberry, 1995). A support group consisting of other interracial couples may be useful for interracial couples because it can provide them with role models of successful relationships and can provide additional support around a variety of issues particularly when family support may be limited. The diagramming of the interracial couple's family in a genogram can be a way of eliciting a wealth of information on family-of-origin issues, cultural norms and traditions, support networks, and immigration history, while at the same time facilitating dialogue and understanding between the partners and the therapist (McGoldrick, 1998).

CONCLUSION

Interracial relationships have existed for over a century in Hawaii and will continue into the future. Hawaii is a unique setting for interracial couples because of its population characteristics, tradition of promoting cross-race ties, local identity, and immigration history. Though interracial relationships in Hawaii is more common in Hawaii than in the mainland states, and issues around racial and cultural identity appear to be more fluid and flexible in Hawaii, it can be assumed that interracial couples may experience similar issues and concerns in their relationship as couples in mixed race relationships residing on the mainland. Interracial couples may experience difficulties with certain matters, and, yet, they may also experience benefits, such as psychological growth, from their cross-racial ties. The therapeutic interventions that were described in this paper suggest recognition of the need to support interracial couples. As described, awareness of the larger social world in which interracial relationships exist is important for both therapists and clients to recognize, involvement of couples in therapy prior to legal formalization of their tie, and recognition of family history through genogram therapy and the use of role models in group therapy are interventions that may be particularly effective for interracial couples.

Two areas of study that deserve more attention are the benefits of interracial relationships and interracial relationships among older adults. Much of the research on interracial relationships has focused on the difficulties encountered by couples in mixed-race ties. A growing body of literature is surfacing on the positive dimensions of interracial relationships, such as the fact that relationships involving racially different partners are formed on the basis of love and commitment (Dalmage, 2000; Root, 2001). It is important to continue research on the upsides of interracial relationships because of the long tradition of racial bordered thinking in society (Dalmage, 2000; Root, 2001). Increased knowledge of the positive aspects of interracial relationships would create a more accurate and balanced perspective of interracial ties.

Research on interracial couples in late adulthood is also advisable. Studies of interracial couples in late life have the potential to illuminate how cross-race ties are experienced over the course of time and how particular life issues are addressed, such as eldercare. Over the course of their relationship, older interracial couples may have found themselves dealing with differing views on eldercare for their parents, stemming from their different cultural upbringing, for instance. Research on topics such as eldercare among interracial couples is important for an aging society such as the U.S. Hawaii, because of its plural character and history of interracial relationships, may be an ideal location in which to conduct future studies of the benefits of interracial relationships and interracial relationships among older adults.

REFERENCES

Adams, R. (1937). *Interracial marriage in Hawaii.* New York: Macmillan.

Brown, J.A. (1987). Casework contacts with black-white couples. *The Journal of Contemporary Social Work, 68,* 24-29.

Chan, A.Y. & Wethington, E. (1998). Factors promoting marital resilience among interracial couples. In H.I. McCubbin, E.A. Thompson, A.I.Thompson, & J.E.

Fromer (Eds.), *Resiliency in Native American and Immigrant Families* (pp. 71-87). Thousand Oaks, CA: Sage Publications.

Dalmage, H. M. (2000). *Tripping on the color line*. New Brunswick, NJ: Rutgers University Press.

Falicov, C.J. (1995). Cross-cultural marriages. In N.S. Jacobson & A.S. Gurman (Eds.), *Clinical handbook of couple therapy* (pp. 231-246). New York: The Guilford Press.

Frankenberg, R. (1993). *White women, race matters: The social construction of whiteness*. London: Routledge.

Fu, X. (2000). An interracial study of marital disruption in Hawaii: 1983 to 1996. *Journal of Divorce & Remarriage, 32(3/4)*, 73-92.

Fu, X., & Heaton, T.B. (1997). *Interracial marriage in Hawaii: 1983-1994*. Lewiston, NY: Edwin Mellon Press.

Gaines, S.O., Granrose, C.S., Rios, D.I., Garcia, B.F., Youn, M.S., Farris, K.R., & Bledsoe, K.L. (1999). Patterns of attachment and responses to accommodative dilemmas among interethnic/interracial couples. *Journal of Social and Personal Relationships, 16(2)*, 275-285.

Gibbs, J.T. (1987). Identity and marginality: Issues in the treatment of biracial adolescents. *American Journal of Orthopsychiatry, 57*, 265-278.

Glenn, E.N. (1986). *Issei, nisei, war bride*. Philadelphia: Temple University Press.

Ho, M.K. (1990). *Intermarried couples in therapy*. Springfield, IL: Charles C. Thomas.

Hormann, B.L. (1972). Hawaii's mixing people. In N.P. Gist & A.G. Dworking (Eds.), *The blending of races*. New York: Wiley and Sons.

Katz, C. & Monk, J. (1993). *Full Circles: Geographies of Women over the Life Course*. NY: Routledge.

Kitano, H.H., Yeung, W.T., Chai, L., & Hatanaka, H. (1984). Asian-American interracial marriage. *Journal of Marriage and the Family, 46*, 179-190.

Labov, T. & Jacobs, J.A. (1998). Preserving multiple ancestry: Intermarriage and mixed births in Hawaii. *Journal of Comparative Family Studies, 29(3)*, 481-502.

Labov, T. & Jacobs, J.A. (1986). Intermarriage in Hawaii, 1950-1983. *Journal of Marriage and the Family, 48*, 79-88.

Lee, S.M. & Fernandez, M. (1998). Trends in Asian-American racial/ethnic intermarriage: A comparison of 1980 and 1990 Census data. *Sociological Perspectives, 41(2)*, 323-342.

McDermott, J.F. Jr., Tseng, W., & Maretzki, T.W. (1980). People and cultures of Hawaii: A psychocultural profile. Hawaii: University of Hawaii Press.

McGoldrick, M. (Ed.). (1998). *Re-visioning family therapy*. New York: The Guilford Press.

Motoyoshi, M.M. (1990). The experience of mixed-race people: Some thoughts and theories. *The Journal of Ethnic Studies, 18*, 77-89.

Okamura, J.Y. (1994). Why there are no Asian Americans in Hawaii: The continuing significance of local identity. *Social Processes in Hawaii, 35*, 161-178.

Okun, B.F. (1996). *Understanding diverse families: What practitioners need to know*. New York: The Guilford Press.

Pope, B.R. (1986). Black in interracial relationships: Psychological and therapeutic issues. *Journal of Multicultural Counseling and Development, 14*, 10-16.

Qian, Z. (1999). Who intermarries? Education, nativity, region, and interracial marriage, 1980-1990. *Journal of Comparative Family Studies, 30(4)*, 579-597.

Ratliff, B.W., Moon, H.F., & Bonacci, G.A. (1978). Intercultural marriage: The Korean-American experience. *Social Casework, 59(4)*, 221-226.

Root, M.P.P. (2001). *Love's revolution: Interracial marriage*. Philadelphia: Temple University.

Rosenblatt, P.C., Karis, T.A., & Powell, R.D. (1995). *Multiracial couples: Black and white voices*. Thousand Oaks, CA: Sage.

Solsberry, P.W. (1995). Interracial couples in the United States of America: Implications for mental health counseling. *Journal of Mental Health Counseling, 16(3)*, 304-317.

U.S. Census Bureau (2001). *State and county quick facts*. [On-line]. Available: <http://quickfacts.census.gov/qfd/states/15000html>.

Usita, P.M. (2001). *Strengths, multiplicity, and plasticity of intermarried immigrant women in mid- and late-life*. Unpublished manuscript.

Usita, P. M., & Blieszner, R. (in press). Immigrant family strengths: Meeting communication challenges. *Journal of Family Issues*.

Watts, R.E. & Henriksen, Jr., R.C. (1998). The Interracial Couple Questionnaire. *The Journal of Individual Psychology, 54(3)*, 368-372.

Xie, Y. & Goyette, K. (1997). The racial identification of biracial children with one Asian parent: Evidence from the 1990 Census. *Social Forces, 76(2)*, 547-570.

INTERRACIAL ISSUES
WITH SAME-SEX COUPLES

Interracial and Intercultural Lesbian Couples: The Incredibly True Adventures of Two Women in Love

Janie Long

SUMMARY. Evidence indicates that lesbians, like everyone else, are meeting and entering into relationships with women from increasingly varied cultural backgrounds including race, culture, and class. This article seeks to provide clinicians with both the challenges of these relationships as well as the strengths of these relationships. The historical context in which interracial and intercultural lesbian relationships have evolved is presented in the first section of the paper in order to situate these couples in a historical context. Next the available literature is reviewed focused on challenges these couples may experience as they navigate their world and their relationship. The following section of the paper relies on the literature to review potential relationship strengths in

Janie Long, PhD, is affiliated with the Department of Child Development and Family Studies, Purdue University, West Lafayette, IN 47907-1267.

[Haworth co-indexing entry note]: "Interracial and Intercultural Lesbian Couples: The Incredibly True Adventures of Two Women in Love." Long, Janie. Co-published simultaneously in *Journal of Couple & Relationship Therapy* (The Haworth Press, Inc.) Vol. 2, No. 2/3, 2003, pp. 85-101; and: *Clinical Issues with Interracial Couples: Theories and Research* (ed: Volker Thomas, Terri A. Karis, and Joseph L. Wetchler) The Haworth Press, Inc., 2003, pp. 85-101. Single or multiple copies of this article are available for a fee from The Haworth Document Delivery Service [1-800-HAWORTH, 9:00 a.m. - 5:00 p.m. (EST). E-mail address: docdelivery@haworthpress.com].

http://www.haworthpress.com/store/product.asp?sku=J398
10.1300/J398v02n02_07

intercultural and interracial relationships. It should be noted that much more has been written about challenges than about strengths. Finally, clinical considerations are highlighted for working with interracial and intercultural couples. *[Article copies available for a fee from The Haworth Document Delivery Service: 1-800-HAWORTH. E-mail address: <docdelivery@haworth press.com> Website: <http://www.HaworthPress.com> © 2003 by The Haworth Press, Inc. All rights reserved.]*

KEYWORDS. Lesbian couples, interracial, intercultural

A STORY

In 1995 a movie was released entitled, "The Incredibly True Adventures of Two Girls in Love." I remember hearing about the movie from several lesbian friends and wondering if it would ever be shown in Georgia where I was living at the time. It was not only a movie about two teenage girls in love with each other but it was also about an interracial relationship in which there were definite class differences. Of course, there was the possibility it might come to Atlanta, considered by most people to be a very progressive and liberal city. Surely it would come to one of the "alternative" theatres there. Imagine my shock when it came to one of the major mall theatres in Atlanta. It seemed surreal to me to be going to a major theatre to see this movie, and I admit I was a little scared. My fears included being physically harmed or verbally harassed when entering or leaving the theatre, concern that the theatre would be full of men who wanted to see two females being physical, dread that the theatre would be full of homophobic teenagers who would make unseemly comments (which I had encountered before), and trepidation that the media would be covering the preview and I would be shown on television.

None of these fears came to pass. I remember my huge sense of relief when I discovered that the opening seemed to be very uneventful on the surface . . . no protestors or television crews. What was immediately noticeable, however, was the large number of women waiting in line to purchase a ticket. They were women of all colors, hairstyles, and fashion statements. There wore khakis and button down polo shirts, jeans and birkies, had piercings and tattoos, multi-colored hair, Princess Di cuts, close-cropped Afros, neon Swatches, and Gucci watches. Standing in line a few couples were holding hands but the great majority of women were chatting with women who stood in line near them or engaging other friends who happened by. There was a festive and celebratory mood in the air. Once inside the theatre women sat in couples, dyads, or groups, and when the lights lowered many of the dyads clearly became couples. At the end of the movie the audience clapped thunderously and everyone became very animated when the lights went up. After the movie was over many of the moviegoers ended up at the favorite lesbian coffeehouse and everyone was talking about the movie. Perhaps the most spirited group was a group of black lesbians who were arguing vehemently about the pairing of the white teen and the black teen.

Being by myself I was able to listen to the comments floating around in the vicinity of my table. Being the researcher and teacher that I am, I began to write down some of the things that were being said on napkins just in case I could ever use them. I tucked the napkins away along with my movie ticket stub as mementoes of the evening. When I was asked to write this article I remembered the napkins and retrieved them from my antique trunk and reviewed them along with the professional literature. I quickly noticed that the comments on the napkins were highly correlated with what the literature conveyed so I used the comments as headers throughout the paper. Utilizing these sources, my own experience as a therapist, my own personal experience, and my relationships with lesbian friends who either have been or are currently in interracial or intercultural relationships, I formed the ideas for this article.

SETTING A HISTORICAL CONTEXT

To understand the dynamics of interracial and intercultural lesbian relationships it is important to situate them in historical context. Therefore, I will briefly highlight the history of interracial relationships including the influence of slavery, review immigration patterns that have diversified couples in general, and provide a brief history of lesbian couple relationships within this country. Even though I do not outline the history of the status of women in this society and others, it is important to always be mindful of the influence of the subordination of all women within the culture (Hare-Mustin, 1987). The reader should also keep in mind, " . . . that for women of Color, race class and gender subordination are experienced simultaneously and that their oppression is not only experienced by males in their own groups but also by white females and males" (Hurtado, 1989, p. 839).

A History of Interracial Relationships

African families brought to this country were often torn apart by slavery with many couples deliberately split by white slave owners. It is well documented that white slave owners frequently forced African American women into cohabitation and pregnancy (Franklin, 1966). The cohabitor was often the master himself or his white overseer. Elaine Pinderhughes (1998) writes of the omission of names of fathers on birth records during slavery and comes to the conclusion that it is likely that the omissions often occurred in order to hide the white paternity. Thus many African Americans became entrapped in paradoxical positions like being ashamed of their white paternity and at the same time enjoying the benefits of a lighter skin color. It is not difficult to understand that responses to this treatment during slavery would foster negative feelings on the part of African Americans to interracial relationships. These feelings still live today in many African Americans, especially African American women who are angered by the involvement of African American men with white women. These feelings are related to many factors including the perceived idealization of white women by all men including African American men and the lower numbers of African American males who are available as potential partners. (This discussion is infinitely more complicated than space allows me to address.)

During the period following slavery laws sprang up around the country prohibiting the marriage of whites and blacks that existed for many years. During the Civil Rights movement many of these laws were abolished. In 1967 the U.S. Supreme Court overturned existing laws against interracial marriages, which were still illegal in sixteen states (Association of MultiEthnic Americans, Inc., 2002, ¶ 1). However, as recently as November 2000 the voters of the state of Alabama removed a law from their constitution that stated, "The legislature shall never pass any law to authorize or legalize any marriage between any white person and a negro, or descendant of a negro" (State of Alabama, 1901 Constitution, Section 102). Clearly the laws have changed but slowly.

Evidence of an Increase in the Number of Interracial Lesbian Couples

Census data offer us one view of the numbers of interracial couples in this country. The 2000 U.S. census revealed that most partners (married and unmarried) are of the same race but that unmarried partners are about twice as likely to be of different races than married partners (Fields & Casper, 2001). In the 2000 census 4% of unmarried partners were of different races as compared to 2% of married couples (U.S. Census Bureau, 2001, p. 14). It is impossible to obtain accurate readings of the numbers of same-sex couples including lesbian couples with the current format of the census (Fields & Clark, 1999). However, one could make the case that because the numbers of inter-racial couples are increasing that the number of interracial lesbian couples is also increasing.

Evidence of an Increase in the Number of Intercultural Lesbian Couples

Most early immigrants to the United States came from Europe. In 1890, for example, 86 percent were from Europe. In 1960, Europe still accounted for 75 percent of the immigrants to the U.S. with only 9 percent from Latin America and 5 percent from Asia. By 1999, there had been a dramatic shift in the countries of origin of immigrants living in the United States. In 1999 more than half–51 percent–came from Latin America and 27 percent from Asia, while only 16 percent came from Europe (http://www.prb.org). This shift has brought more racial and ethnic diversity among immigrants. Persons of color are becoming the numerical majority in the United States (Yutrzenka, 1995). This rise has brought about increased complexity in the multiple layers of multiculturalism. Pearlman (1996) suggests that lesbians, like everyone else, are meeting and entering into relationships with women from varied cultural backgrounds including race, ethnicity, and class.

A Brief History of Lesbian Couples

The other history that should be considered as a part of the historical context within this country is that of lesbian couples. In the late nineteenth and early twentieth centuries many women in this country entered into what were known as Boston marriages (Rothblum & Brehony, 1993). These relationships, also known as romantic friendships, were generally committed asexual relationships between two women who, having gone to college and then found jobs, set up household. There were other women, including Eleanor Roosevelt, who engaged in long term intense relationships with women while at the same time being involved in heterosexual marriages (Streitmatter, 1998). Faderman (1999) points out that most of the women involved in these relationships would not have considered themselves "sexual inverts" or "homosexuals," terms that were popular in that day, because whether their relationships were sexual or not they were so much more than sexual. Sexologists like Havelock Ellis characterized women of the women's rights movement as sexual inverts who established leadership in the movement and made other women "spuriously homosexual" (Faderman, 1999, p. 5).

It seems that partially as a backlash to the success of the women rights movement female same-sex love was widely maligned in America between 1920 and 1970 (Faderman, 1999). During the 1970s lesbian feminists were a visible and vocal part of the leadership of the second wave of feminism. For the first time in history women were openly identifying as lesbians. While the tides of acceptance have vacillated since the 1970s it has only been within the past thirty years that lesbian couples have become more open and visible. Lesbian couples are now in fact experiencing a "baby boom" (Johnson & Keren, 1998). Many lesbian couples remain closeted, however, out of fear of losing their jobs, their children, their families-of-origin and even their lives.

SO . . . WHAT'S THE PROBLEM?

As I thought about and worked on this project I constantly asked myself what I thought about racial and cultural differences. As someone who has worked against racism ever since I was a child (which was not a popular stance in my family) the last thing I wanted to do was promote further racist attitudes. As I reviewed the literature I found much that seemed to suggest that interracial and intercultural relationships were bound to be more problematic than not. I then asked myself if this was true or were the authors simply more prone to try to point out challenges that might lie ahead than to focus on what is healthy and good in these relationships. As someone who has worked against heterosexism and homophobia both personally and professionally I also did not want to perpetuate ideas that could be considered in those camps either. Too often race and same-sex relationships are examined in a problematic fashion in social scientific research. Would my writing only add to those impressions? I finally decided to include the literature on challenges as best I could but to also include a focus on relationship strengths.

Ruth Frankenberg (1993) studied the social construction of whiteness. Her work brought forth an analysis of race as a social construction rather than an inherently meaningful category. Frankenberg suggests that there is more variability within one traditionally biologically defined racial category than there is between two categories. In other words there is more variability between whites than between whites and blacks. Frankenberg and others present the view that the salience of racial difference still holds true in our society because of the social and political contexts in which racial difference is constructed. As a socially constructed category race is then linked to relations of power (Austin, 2001). Austin points out that this worldview does not minimalize the social and political reality of race but posits that the reality is social, political and therefore subject to change rather than inherent. It is important that the reader be mindful of these concepts when reading this paper. Whether the reader believes in modernist or postmodernist constructions of reality will influence how they read this article. While I tend to be postmodern in my thinking much of the literature is not. I have attempted to bring some balance to these two perspectives in my discussion. As a reader you will then determine whether or not I have been successful.

CHALLENGES FOR THE INTERRACIAL OR INTERCULTURAL LESBIAN COUPLE

Managing Multiple Differences: "But she's not like you, and she never will be. . . ."

Managing multiple differences can be a challenge facing interracial or intercultural lesbian couples. Differences may include race, ethnicity, class of origin, current socio-economic status, and religion. These differences are often experienced in conjunction with one another further complicating the issues. The differences may conjure up one's own prejudices, but they also heavily influence one's value and belief systems. Some of the cultural differences include: obligations to immediate and extended families, money, time, styles of mothering and child-rearing (Pearlman, 1996).

Interracial lesbian couples both of which hold minority status share the experiences of oppression as women of color and as lesbians. For these reasons they may assume more similarity between them than is the case (Greene & Boyd-Franklin, 1996). They are both still members of different cultures and of different families with potentially different values.

Interracial Relationship Prejudice: "People stare at us everywhere we go. . . . everywhere. And often they make very rude remarks."

Both partners in an interracial relationship experience interracial relationship prejudice. Prejudice and racism may come from family members, friends, co-workers, and the society at large. A partner from the dominant culture may experience racial prejudice for the first time. The couple may no longer be welcome in certain neighborhoods and they may not be safe in others. If both partners are from different minority cultures the prejudice may be compounded by the fact that neither one has dominant culture privilege.

Some lesbians who are in interracial relationships believe that they are more easily identifiable as a couple due to their racial differences (Greene & Boyd-Franklin, 1996; Pearlman, 1996). When this is the case they may become easier targets of discrimination and hate.

Interracial and intercultural lesbian couples must deal with the effects of this discrimination upon their relationships. Greene and Boyd-Franklin (1996) address the devalued position of African American lesbians within the social hierarchy as "triple jeopardy." They often face racial, gender, and heterosexist institutional oppression all of which have influence on their optimal development and the development of their relationships (Greene, 1994a,1994b). Greene and Boyd-Franklin note that some dominant culture partners may then underreact (feel that a partner's anger over racism is inappropriate or exaggerated) or overreact (become critical of a partner for not more actively resisting oppression, or attempt to become the rescuer). The African American partner may then " . . . find the assumption of this protective role presumptuous, unwanted, unneeded, and even patronizing" (Greene & Boyd-Franklin, 1996, p. 56).

After being in a relationship for some time, white partners may fall into the mistaken notion that they somehow know what the experience of racism is like for their partners, ignoring the fact that the minority partner has lived her entire life in a position of oppression. As the white partner becomes more aware of privilege and gains in her knowledge and understanding of the experience, her minority partner may feel somewhat displaced or even threatened about who in the relationship has more authority about race, prejudice, and discrimination. As I once heard a black lesbian express to her white partner, "Oh, so now that you are enlightened, you know more about being black than I do!" Out of feelings of guilt white partners may also try to right the injustices of years of oppression, which may leave her feeling frustrated and angry perhaps due to the lack of psychological armor and defensive coping strategies that minority partners have developed.

Due to their attraction to a member of the dominant culture, partners from minority cultures may struggle with questions of internalized racism. Partners from the minority may also sometimes struggle with anger toward the majority partner as an artifact of the prejudice and discrimination they experience on a daily basis from members of the majority culture. Jealousy and resentment over the lover's privileged status in the dominant culture and within the lesbian community may arise (Greene & Boyd-Franklin, 1996).

Antagonism by the Family of Origin: "Isn't it enough that you are a lesbian but now you're with a white woman ... are you trying to kill me ... ?"

Many interracial lesbian couples like many interracial heterosexual couples face antagonism from their families of origin. Greene and Boyd-Franklin report, however, that while heterosexual interracial couples often lack family support, lesbian interracial relationships face an even greater challenge. A white partner's race may become the focus of the black partner's family's anger. "Her position as an outsider to the family and to the ethnic group make her an overdetermined target to blame or scapegoat for 'turning' the family member into a lesbian" (Greene & Boyd-Franklin, 1996, p. 54).

Both partners may be perceived as lacking loyalty to their own families and/or ethnic or racial groups and may begin to feel ashamed of their involvement in the relationship (Falco, 1991). Partners may feel pulled between their loyalty to their partner versus loyalty to their family and their community. These feelings further complicate the resolution of issues within the relationship.

Adjustment to a New Culture: "I feel like you want me to be too Americanized. No wonder my family wants to send me back ... "

For immigrants, adjustments to a new culture are also sometimes still being negotiated. How much does one want to hold onto one's own traditions and how much does one adopt the traditions of the dominant culture? Sometimes these adjustments are not chosen but are imposed by the dominant culture. Due to bias, women coming from other cultures who were raised in higher classes may find themselves struggling with maintaining a sense of privilege within American culture. For example, some women from India may be treated in the U.S. as though they are from a lower class, when in fact, they were from a very high caste in India. This drop in social standing may be very difficult for the Indian partner to accept thus placing an added strain on the relationship. If the white partner is from a high social class, the Indian partner may resent the perceived differences that society places upon them or may struggle with a diminished sense of self-esteem.

Limited Connection to the Lesbian Community

Lesbians of color do not necessarily share the same priorities as white, Anglo lesbians who often dominate lesbian communities (Laird,

2000). For example, lesbians of color have challenged white lesbian feminists regarding gender assumptions. These differences have created tensions within many lesbian communities and left some lesbians of color feeling unwelcome. Greene and Boyd-Franklin (1996) acknowledge that African American lesbians are marginalized within the lesbian community. Even though there is no literature to support the assumption that other racial minority groups also experience marginalization within the lesbian community, this seems likely, not only due to philosophical differences, but also because of the existence of racism. The lesbian community does not exist in a vacuum but is reflective of the society. Just because lesbians are themselves objects of prejudice and discrimination does not mean that they are somehow immune to racism. Interracial and intercultural couples may distance themselves from lesbian communities in order to protect themselves from further negation and discrimination.

RELATIONSHIP STRENGTHS

Heightened Awareness of the Destructiveness of Racism

Lesbians from the dominant culture may gain a heightened awareness of the amount of racial privilege they have and encounter first-hand the destructiveness and pervasiveness of racism. The more aware one becomes the more one can become an advocate against racism. This new awareness can also assist dominant culture partners in being more empathetic to the experiences of their minority partners. Heightened awareness can bring about increased communication between the couple so that they can talk openly about race, racism, and adjustments that might be necessary in order to maintain their relationship (Pearlman, 1996). For example, a white partner who has tended to operate from a mode of being "color blind" (Frankenberg, 1993) maintains that they do not notice racial differences. While the partner may be wishing to minimize differences between she and her black partner she ends up supporting racism because she is not addressing inequitable relationships in power. Through her own heightened awareness of race and the differences between how she and the partner are treated she may be able to engage in dialogue with the partner that moves her toward more race-cognizance that includes an awareness of structural and institutional inequity. Without this level of understanding the white partner may be perpetuating a level of racism within the relationship that destroys it.

Minority culture partners may be able to express fears related to holding onto their identities with their communities of origin while maintaining a relationship with a white woman. As one of the reviewers of this paper pointed out, a racial minority partner may also be able to work through racial misunderstandings with a white partner with whom they trust enough to be vulnerable.

Cultural Expansion

Lesbian partners in intercultural and interracial relationships often gain a deeper understanding of and appreciation for their partner's culture. Many enjoy the opportunity to experience different social customs, philosophies, and in some cases to learn a new language. Liu and Chan (1996) recognize that having multiple roles and commitments can be sources of strength and resilience. Having multiple identities may offer expanded perspectives on their families and on life experiences in general, thus increasing their flexibility and adaptability. The experience of multiple cultures may allow partners to have an increased potential for shifting or broadening the cultural lens which, given the current demographics, is a very helpful skill to possess.

THERAPEUTIC CONSIDERATIONS

Avoiding Alpha and Beta Bias

Several authors have written about the importance of the need for balance in looking at differences between heterosexual couples and lesbian couples, neither viewing them as having no differences or viewing them as being completely different (Hare-Mustin, 1987; Bernstein, 2000; Basham, 2000). Hare-Mustin warns against "alpha bias" (the exaggeration of differences between groups of people) and "beta bias" (ignoring differences that do exist). This type of binary thinking minimalizes the complexity of relationships. In the context of an interracial or intercultural lesbian couple alpha bias would mean focusing only on racial or cultural differences between partners as an explanation for relationship difficulties. Beta bias would then totally ignore the influence of racial or cultural differences on the couple's relationship. Therefore, in working with these lesbian couples, clinicians would be mindful of different norms and values that have previously been mentioned in this article such as obligations to immediate and extended families, money and time, styles of mothering and child-rearing, sources of self-esteem and sense of self, and differing levels of access to privilege and power (Pearlman, 1996). It is important at this juncture for the clinician to pay close attention to the individual constructions of the partners rather than operating out of cultural stereotypes. However, a balance between putting too much emphasis on the differences and not attending enough to differences is important.

In assessing similarities between heterosexual and lesbian couples clinicians can also examine areas of typical stressors between all couples including family-of-origin issues, gender issues, and difficulties related to money, children, and sex. An example of beta bias in this situation would be to treat sexual difficulties in a lesbian relationship from a heteronormative posture. The couple's sexual relationship would then be considered abnormal if they were not focused on penetration and orgasm. An example of alpha bias would then be to only focus on the differences in each partner's cultural norms regarding sexuality.

Avoiding Stereotypes and Biases

Clinicians may be influenced by stereotypes and biases related to interracial relationships including:

1. the selection of a white partner indicates internalized racism;
2. the selection of a minority partner indicates a need for superiority; or
3. selection of a minority partner is related to the "erotization" of the "other" (Pearlman, 1996, p. 28).

While some therapists believe that unconscious factors play a role in partner selection in any relationship, care should be taken not to project the therapists' own biases onto the clients. Other factors of mate selection that should be examined and acknowledged include the possibilities of "genuine liking, respect, and enjoyment in addition to sexual attraction, which constitute the strengths of many interracial relationships" (Pearlman, 1996). Thus monitoring one's own level of counter transference related to one's own racism, classism, and heterosexism are crucial especially given the fact that both interracial and same-sex relationships are often pathologized.

Class Sensitivity

Therapists who work with lesbians who are in interracial or intercultural relationships must also be class sensitive in addition to being knowledgeable about diverse cultures including lesbian culture. "Thus, the race/class sensitive clinician can articulate perspectives which reframe power struggles and the personalizing of difference and disclose other meanings. Moreover, she has the opportunity and the privilege to offer validation of attraction to difference and serve to affirm both cultural enrichment and expansion when intimacy is joined to cultural difference" (Pearlman, 1996, p. 35).

Gender

Laird (2000) points out that gender meanings and relations vary widely among cultural groups, influenced by such factors as " . . . migration experience, degree of acculturation, social class, geographical location, and a myriad of other factors" (p. 458). She also notes that pressure for sexual and gender conformity is often more extreme for lesbians of color than for white women. Therapists working with interracial couples will want to pay attention to how each partner constructs gender from their own cultural and family backgrounds. Weston's work, in fact, taught her that to focus strictly on gender exclusively " . . . obscures the very aspects of race, class, and nation that give gender shape" (1996, p. 1).

Laird (1999, 2000) has recently called for therapists in their work with lesbian couples to help them resist dominant patriarchical cultural imperatives related to gender. She encourages clinicians to instead help them replace social narratives " . . . that do not offer affirmation of the relationship or open up opportunity with narratives that appreciate and celebrate what may be unique, strong, and adaptive about their lives" (p. 464). In order to allow for this to happen with interracial and intercultural lesbian couples, therapists must be sensitive to and respectful of the many layers of culture with which they are working.

Parenting

"Gay and lesbian families come in different sizes, shapes, ethnicities, races, religions, resources, creeds and quirks, and even engage in diverse sexual practices" (Stacey, 1996, p. 107). Intercultural and interracial couples are certainly a part of this mix. They may have children from previous heterosexual relationships, or they may adopt, or artificially inseminate. They will face the same types of decisions and obstacles that same race couples face but will also be faced with extra considerations. For example, if they choose artificial insemination, what race should the sperm donor be? Other issues may include how families would accept or not accept the child as a grandchild, how they will teach their child about race related matters, and what religious upbringing the child should have. Some couples who not have experienced racial tensions before may have them surface in the context of such complex decision-making. Due to space limitations it is impossible to cover the myriad of decisions that lesbian couples encounter related to parenting. Clinicians are encouraged to read the literature in this area including recent works by Ariel and McPherson (2000), Lott-Whitehead and Tully (1999), Morningstar (1999), Muzio (1999), and O'Connell (1999).

Fostering Support

It is also important to help the couple acknowledge the influence of the interrelated systems of societal discrimination with which they are faced. Interracial and intercultural lesbian couples must be encouraged to nurture each other and their relationships and to seek support outside themselves. This is particularly important in the midst of multiple systems that may not be offering support for them individually much less as couples. For lesbians living in more urban areas support may come through increased participation in the lesbian community or through support groups from their own cultures. Lesbians in more rural areas may have to seek support mainly from accepting family members and friends.

CONCLUSION

Writing this article has made me very aware of the dearth of research and scholarly work dedicated to interracial or intercultural lesbian (and gay) couples. Most authors, of course, mention the importance of race and ethnicity in their work. In fact, when I first wrote about preparing therapists to work with sexual orientation I realize that I only paid lip service to the variability of lesbians and lesbian relationships (Long, 1996). I wrote the article based on my own experiences with trainees and at that time, while I was very conscious of attending to issues such as race and class, it seemed that broad statements needed to be made simply to begin a dialogue. Others wrote about specific populations (African Americans, Asian Americans) but almost no one wrote specifically about intercultural or interracial lesbian couples. Recently, there are exceptions (e.g., Pearlman and Weston), but they are still rare.

I have noted that many of the works I used in my literature review for this article were published in 1996. In the years that have passed since then, important demographic shifts have occurred. Given that we are becoming a smaller global community and given the current population demographics of the United States, I believe that this topic will become more pronounced in the literature in the future. I would like to see research that is focused on the strengths and resiliencies of these couples and families rather than the previous focus on pathology and deficits. I would also support the use of qualitative research methods in capturing the experience of and giving voice to this nearly invisible (in the literature anyway) population. As stated previously, lesbians from different racial and ethnic backgrounds will increasingly form partnerships. Their mix of identities and the integration of their multiple layers of complexity will present us with challenges as therapists but will also teach us much about "the incredibly true adventures of two women in love."

REFERENCES

Ariel, J. & McPherson, D. W. (2000). Therapy with lesbian and gay parents and their children. *Journal of Marital and Family Therapy*, 26, 421-432.

Association of MultiEthnic Americans, Inc. (AMEA) Website, The Loving Decision Document. Retrieved February 17, 2002, from <*http://ameasite.org/loving.asp*>.

Austin, S. (2001). Race matters. *Radical Psychology*, 2. Retrieved January 12, 2002 from <*http://www.radpsy.yorku.ca/vol2-1/austin.htm*>.

Basham, K. K. (1999). Therapy with a lesbian couple: The art of balancing lenses. In J. Laird (Ed.), *Lesbians and lesbian families* (pp. 143-177). New York, NY: Columbia University Press.

Bernstein, A. C. (2000). Straight therapists working with lesbians and gays in family therapy. *Journal of Marital and Family Therapy*, 26, 443-454.

Falco, K. L. (1991). *Psychotherapy with lesbian clients*. New York, NY: Brunner-Mazel.

Fields, J. & Casper, L. M. (2001). America's families and living arrangements: March 2000. Current Population Reports, P20-537. Washington, DC: U.S. Census Bureau.

Frankenberg, R. (1993). *White women race matters: The social construction of whiteness*. Minneapolis, MN: University of Minnesota Press.

Franklin, J. H. (1966). *From slavery to freedom*. New York: Knopf.

Greene, B. (1994a). Ethnic-minority lesbians and gay men: Mental health and treatment issues. *Journal of Consulting and Clinical Psychology*, 62, 243-251.

Greene, B. (1994b). Lesbian women of color: Triple jeopardy. In L. Comas-Diaz & B. Greene (Eds.), *Women of color: Integrating ethnic and gender identities in psychotherapy* (pp. 389-427). New York, NY: Guilford Press.

Greene, B. & Boyd-Franklin, N. (1996a). African American lesbian couples: Ethnocultural considerations in psychotherapy. In M. Hill & E. D. Rothblum (Eds.), *Women & Therapy* (pp. 49-60). New York, NY: The Haworth Press, Inc.

Greene, B. & Boyd-Franklin, N. (1996b). African American lesbians: Issues in couples therapy. In J. Laird & R. J. Green (Eds.), *Lesbians and gays in couples and families: A handbook for therapists* (pp. 251-271). San Francisco: Jossey-Bass Publishers.

Hare-Mustin, R. T. (1987). The problem of gender in family therapy theory. *Family Process, 26*, 15-27.

Hurtado, A. (1989). Relating to privilege: Seduction and rejection in the subordination of white women and women of color. *Signs: Journal of Women in Culture and Society, 14*, 833-855.

Johnson, T.W. & Keren, M. S. (1998). The families of lesbian women and gay men. In Monica McGoldrick (Ed.) *Re-visioning family therapy: Race, culture, and gender in clinical practice.* (pp. 179-199). New York: The Guilford Press.

Laird, J. (1999). Gender and sexuality in lesbian relationships. In J. Laird (Ed.), *Lesbians and lesbian families* (pp. 47-89). New York, NY: Columbia University Press.

Laird, J. (2000). Gender in lesbian relationships: Cultural, feminist, and constructionist reflections. *Journal of Marital and Family Therapy, 26*, 455-467.

Liu, P. & Chan, C. S. (1996). Lesbian, gay, and bisexual Asian Americans and their families. In J. Laird & R. J. Green (Eds.), *Lesbians and gays in couples and families: A handbook for therapists* (pp. 137-152). San Francisco: Jossey-Bass Publishers.

Long, J. K. (1996). Working with lesbians, gays, and bisexuals: Addressing heterosexism in supervision. *Family Process, 35*, 377-368.

Lott-Whitehead, L. & Tully, C. T. (1999). The family lives of lesbian mothers. In J. Laird (Ed.), *Lesbians and lesbian families* (pp. 213-242). New York, NY: Columbia University Press.

Morningstar, B. (1999). Lesbian parents: Understanding developmental pathways. In J. Laird (Ed.), *Lesbians and lesbian families* (pp. 197-212). New York, NY: Columbia University Press.

Munzio, C. (1999). Lesbian co-parenting: On being/being with the invisible (m)other. In J. Laird (Ed.), *Lesbians and lesbian families* (pp. 180-196). New York, NY: Columbia University Press.

O'Connell, A. (1999). Voices from the heart: The developmental impact of a mother's lesbianism on her adolescent children. In J. Laird (Ed.), *Lesbians and lesbian families* (pp. 261-280). New York, NY: Columbia University Press.

Pearlman, S. F. (1996). Loving across race and class divides: Relational challenges and the interracial lesbian couple. In M. Hill & E. D. Rothblum (Eds.), *Couples therapy: Feminist perspectives* (pp. 25-35). New York, NY: The Haworth Press, Inc.

Pinderhughes, E. (1998). Black genealogy revisited: Restorying an African American family. In Monica McGoldrick (Ed.) *Re-visioning family therapy: Race, culture, and gender in clinical practice* (pp. 179-199). New York: The Guilford Press.

Population Reference Bureau. (2000, July). *Foreign Born Population.* Washington, DC: Author. Retrieved April 21, 2001 on the World Wide Web: <*http://www. ameristat.org/foreign_born_population/*>.

Rothblum, E. D., & Brehony, K. A. (Eds.). (1993). *Boston marriages: Romantic but asexual relationships among contemporary lesbians.* Amherst: The University of Massachusetts Press.

Stacey, J. (1996). *In the name of the family: Rethinking family values in the postmodern age.* Boston: Beacon Press.

State of Alabama Website, 1901 Constitution, Section 102. Retrieved on February 17, 2002 from *<http://www.legislature.state.al.us/CodeOfAlabama/Constitution/1901/CA-245637.htm>*.

Streitermatter, R. (1998). *Empty without you: The intimate letters of Eleanor Roosevelt and Lorena Hickok*. New York: The Free Press.

U.S. Census Bureau Website. 2001 Publications. Retrieved on February 12, 2002. from *http://www.census.gov/prod/2001pubs/p20-537.pdf*.

Weston, K. (1996). *Render me, gender me: Lesbians talk sex, class, color, nations, studmuffins*. New York, NY: Columbia University Press.

Yutrzenka, B. (1995). Making the case for training in ethnic and cultural diversity in increasing treatment efficacy. *Journal of Consulting and Clinical Psychology, 63,* 197-206.

Latino Cross-Cultural
Same Sex Male Relationships:
Issues of Ethnicity, Race,
and Other Domains of Influence

Andres Nazario

SUMMARY. Utilizing six different gay couples this article illustrates salient issues relevant to Latino cross-cultural same-sex male relationships. It emphasizes issues of both similarities and differences in terms of ethnicity, race, class, language, and other domains of influence. It conveys the potential danger of conceptualizing Latinos as members of a same race group, or as a homogeneous group. Furthermore, it identifies some of the stresses affecting the development and maintenance of gay couples, and offers suggestions for a conceptual approach for dealing with this population. *[Article copies available for a fee from The Haworth Document Delivery Service: 1-800-HAWORTH. E-mail address: <docdelivery@haworthpress.com> Website: <http://www.HaworthPress.com> © 2003 by The Haworth Press, Inc. All rights reserved.]*

KEYWORDS. Latinos, cross-cultural, gay relationships, ethnicity, race, domains of influence

Andres Nazario, PhD, is affiliated with the Gainesville Family Institute, Center for Couples and Family Development Training Program, 1031 NW Street, Suite C-2, Gainesville, FL 32601.

[Haworth co-indexing entry note]: "Latino Cross-Cultural Same Sex Male Relationships: Issues of Ethnicity, Race, and Other Domains of Influence." Nazario, Andres. Co-published simultaneously in *Journal of Couple & Relationship Therapy* (The Haworth Press, Inc.) Vol. 2, No. 2/3, 2003, pp. 103-113; and: *Clinical Issues with Interracial Couples: Theories and Research* (ed: Volker Thomas, Terri A. Karis, and Joseph L. Wetchler) The Haworth Press, Inc., 2003, pp. 103-113. Single or multiple copies of this article are available for a fee from The Haworth Document Delivery Service [1-800-HAWORTH, 9:00 a.m. - 5:00 p.m. (EST). E-mail address: docdelivery@haworthpress.com].

http://www.haworthpress.com/store/product.asp?sku=J398
10.1300/J398v02n02_08

> *Culture does not just refer to the way in which persons of color are different from White people.* (Greene, 1997)

Simply stated, much of what we see, read, and hear in the media and society at large express a patriarchal, Anglo-Saxon, white, Christian, male, middle class, able and heterosexual view of the world. No wonder we are often unaware of the impact of oppressive systems in our clients, ourselves, and our professions. We are all susceptible to the pressures from the dominant culture. Often feminists find themselves caught in unexamined sexism; gay, lesbian and bisexual individuals often struggle with homophobic beliefs; and often heterosexual individuals struggle with heterosexist viewpoints and homophobic beliefs. Racism is ever present in our lives.

Race, gender, class, culture, ethnicity, age, sexual orientation, spirituality, and physical and mental ability are domains of influence organizing our existential meaning (Nazario, 1998; Early, Nazario, & Steier, 1994). These domains of influence impact everyone in this society–women and men, gays, lesbians, bisexuals and straights; children and adults; young and old; Asians, Blacks, Latino/as, Native Americans, and Whites; the poor, the rich and the middle class; professors and students, family therapists, and clients; all of us. These domains of influence provide the context in which we all live. They organize how we are included or excluded and how we participate in the dominant culture. Utilizing these concepts, this article will examine some salient issues of Latino cross-cultural same sex male couples.

A brief description of some of the more salient issues for gay men, and gay couples in general, as well as for Latinos specifically, will be provided before describing several cases of Latino cross-cultural same sex couples.

BEING GAY

As a minority group, gay men in general have to deal, beyond the coming out process, with issues of stigma and homophobia (Herek, 1998). They also have to deal with "minority stress," the sense of conflict or disharmony that exists between the gay individual an the dominant culture (Meyer & Dean, 1998). This is the context in which male couples develop their relationships. It is a context that devalues and discourages the formation and maintenance of same sex intimate relationships (Meyer & Dean, 1998). Meyer and Dean (1998) propose that gay men who are able to challenge heterosexist attitudes are more likely to develop satisfying intimate couples relationships. Heterosexism has been identified as central to any discussion with gay men in therapy, regardless of the presenting problem (Bepko & Johnson, 2000; Meyer & Dean 1998; Gonsiorek, 1985).

Results from several surveys of MFTs indicate that for the most part family therapists are not adequately trained, nor do they feel "good about their lack of competence" in treating same sex couples (Green, 2000, pg. 407). Bepko and Johnson (2000) have identified several internal and external factors impacting same sex couples. Internal factors refer to the issues that couples in general face when they struggle with interpersonal difficulties. These internal factors are the primary target of intervention in many couple's therapy approaches. In addition to the internal factors, significant external factors affect same sex couples' functioning. Bepko and Johnson have identified these as "(1) homophobia and heterosexism; (2) gender norms; (3) issues around coming out to others; and (4) social support from family of origin and family of choice" (Bepko & Johnson, 2000, pg. 409).

LATINOS IN THE USA

As a minority group in the United States, Latinos have to deal with numerous stressors. Although Latinos are often conceptualized by the dominant culture, and within our profession as a race, "there is no such thing as a Latino or Hispanic race . . . Latinos can be white, black, American Indian (or indigenous), Asian, mestizos . . . or any racial combination of these" (Falicov, 1998, pg. 93). Latinos comprise a mosaic of different peoples, cultures, customs and even languages. Latinos share their ancestry from the region that runs from Mexico to Tierra del Fuego, including some Caribbean islands. This region is characterized by its diversity rather than for its uniformity, despite similar colonial experiences (Nazario, 1998; Morales, 1992). (For a more in-depth description of Latino socio-political issues, see Falicov, 1998, and Nazario, 1998.)

Understanding Latino diversity is essential to the provision of competent services to this population. Current literature and popular beliefs that inform clinical practice with Latinos, the second largest and fastest growing minority group in the US, are often stereotypical and culturally biased. Consequently, many clinicians are hampered when treating Latinos. The term Latino is useful to politically coalesce an often disenfranchised and marginalized group of people in the United States. (For a discussion of the different terms used to identify this ethnic minority group, see Comas-Diaz, 2001.) But, Latinos in the United States do not form a homogeneous group (Nazario, 1998). Language fluency, level of adaptation and acculturation among other things may vary across Latino families and even within a single family. Falicov (1998) proposes a "multicultural ecosystemic comparative approach" (MECA) as a guide for psychotherapeutic practice with Latino/a families. She describes a theoretical framework for approaching Latinos therapeutically. Yet, it is impossible to assume that there is a theory or approach best suited for all Latinos as a group. As with any other marginalized people, there is always the danger of stereotyping in describing the characteristics of Latinos as an ethnic group. Yet, the concepts of respeto (respect), personalismo (personalism), familismo (familism), machismo and marianismo have been described as applicable to assist in the understanding of those growing up in Latino families (Bernal & Flores-Ortiz, 1988; Boyd-Franklin & Garcia-Preto, 1994; Falicov, 1982; Garcia-Preto, 1982; Morales, 1992; Nazario, 1998; Stevens, 1973; Vasquez, 1994), and can serve "as the basis for informed inquiry" (Vasquez, 1994).

LATINO AND GAY

Gay Latinos have to deal with the complexities of multiple identities and multiple oppressions (Reynolds & Pope, 1991). Gay Latinos in the United States may function within three separated yet sometimes overlapping communities: the gay and lesbian community, the Latino/a community; and the dominant culture. These three communities are often at odds with each other (Morales, 1992). Perhaps one of the most significant issues for many gay Latinos is the negotiation of family of origin relationships. Given the importance of the family within the Latino/a culture, and the negative attitudes of many Latino/as toward homosexuality, the process of coming out for Latinos can be very difficult, and many gay Latinos may opt not to disclose their sexual identity to their families. Machismo refers to the sense of responsibility that Latino men have about providing and caring for their families. Since gay men are seen as less of a man, or effeminate, they do not fit into the traditional sex roles of Latino/a society (Morales, 1996). Issues of sexuality and intimacy are compounded for gay Latinos when they decide to couple.

LATINO CROSS-CULTURAL SAME SEX MALE COUPLES

The following six clinical couples serve to illustrate the diversity of Gay Latinos in cross-cultural same sex relationships:

Gay Latinos in cross-cultural same sex relationships struggle with the same issues of all gay and lesbian relationships: heterosexism and homophobia. In addition, they encounter specific issues related to power and oppression according to their position vis á vis dominant culture and the position of their partners. The balance of power in the cross cultural same-sex gay relationship is best understood when all domains of influence are simultaneously explored. The following six cross-cultural same sex male couples illustrate the diversity of Latino identities in terms of race, ethnicity, religion, class, age, and nationality. In order to convey the importance of a stance of curiosity (Early, Nazario, & Steier, 1994) rather than the stance of expert who draws on theoretical knowledge about Latinos and/or gay, these couples are described using the self-descriptions provided by themselves. Conversations about the meaning attributed to domains of influence, heterosexuality and homophobia were part of the therapeutic conversations with all of these couples.

Teodoro and Michael

Teodoro is a graduate student in the USA. He is from the Yucatan Peninsula in Mexico, and describes himself as "mestizo." His mother is Mayan and his father is of Spanish descent. Teodoro is in a relationship with Michael–a non-student African-American. Michael works as a laboratory assistant at the same university that Teodoro attends. Teodoro does not describe himself as Latino, although he recognizes that in the USA he is classified as either Hispanic or Latino. He describes himself as "Yucateco" (from the Yucatan Peninsula) when speaking in Spanish, and as "Mexican" when in English. His plans are to return to Mexico with Michael once he graduates. Michael and Teodoro presented their difficulties as "not getting along well," and disagreement about time spent together. They have been a couple for about two years, and described themselves as "lovers." Teodoro's language of preference is Spanish and although he speaks English with Michael, he insists that Michael will have to learn Spanish to survive in Mexico. Michael is cut-off from his family of origin. He attributes his lack of contact with his family to their rejection of his sexual orientation. On the other hand, he has visited Teodoro's family in Mexico and finds himself welcomed as "a family member." Teodoro is a practicing Catholic and Michael is the son of a Baptist minister.

From a therapeutic perspective, salient issues for this couple were Teodoro's sense of privilege in relation to Michael as implied by his insistence that Michael needs to learn Spanish. Family of origin issues stood out for Michael, and the couple identified religious differences.

Reinaldo and Roig

Reinaldo presents himself as a 40-year-old White male from Mexico. He works for a multinational company in the USA. He comes from a very rich Mexican family of Polish ancestry. Reinaldo has lived in the USA for almost 20 years, but he maintains an apartment in Mexico, and goes to Mexico quite often. Reinaldo is a legal resident in the United States. Roig presents himself as a White male, 35 years old, born in Cuba and raised in Puerto Rico. He is a US citizen, and works as a real estate broker. Reinaldo and Roig had a marriage ceremony soon after they began to live together 10 years ago. They consider themselves married, although their commitment ceremony was not religious nor considered legal by the State. Parents and friends from both sides attended the ceremony. Both Reinaldo and Roig recognize their Latino identity as an important political statement. They are both bilingual and socialize primarily with other Latinos. In terms of religion, Reinaldo identifies himself as Jewish, and Roig believes in and practices Santeria. The presenting problems for this couple was a recent incident in which Reinaldo went to a gay bar by himself, got drunk and arrived home very late in a taxi, with bruises all over his body, and no recollection of the incident.

Salient issues for this couple revolved around issues of power related to income, class, and religion, as well as monogamy and sex outside the relationship.

Armando and Joe

Armando is a 55-year-old White male. He is Cuban born, and a US citizen. He describes himself racially as white, but as a man of color, culturally, in appreciation of his cultural roots. He is a health professional. He has been partnered with Joe for 25 years. Joe is a 50-year-old White male from New York. He is also a health professional. Armando came to the USA as a child. He was married to a woman once for six years, and has two children, already grown, from that union. Joe and Armando have supported each other through graduate school, taking turns to complete their degrees. They were in therapy once before, when Armando's children were teenagers and came to live with them. Joe and Armando maintain close contact with "their children." They presented for therapy after Joe disclosed a series of casual sexual contacts outside the relationship. Both Armando and Joe attend the Metropolitan Community Church. Armando is strongly identified as Latino, and Joe describes himself as an advocate of the culturally different.

Salient issues for this couple centered around power in relation to monogamy.

Timmy and Bruce

Timmy describes himself as a 32-year-old White male born in Puerto Rico of English parents. He considers himself Puerto Rican and recently moved to the mainland where he is working as a College instructor. He speaks English well, but he has a strong Spanish accent. He is married to Bruce, a 32-year-old white male from Tennessee, who lived in Puerto Rico at the time they met. They have been married for 7 years. They are both bilingual and go between Spanish and English in their conversations. Timmy was in a Catholic seminary until he met Bruce. Bruce describes himself as a Southern Baptist. Bruce has been unemployed for several months. Timmy requested services, initially stating that he was dissatisfied with the relationship. He was unhappy about Bruce not working, and about what he described as his desire for more independence.

Salient issues for this couple related to the power differential in relation to income, and difficulties negotiating religious differences.

Roberto and T.J.

Roberto describes himself as a 35-year-old Cuban born, sent as a small child to Madrid to live with his grandparents. His parents were hopeful that they could leave Cuba soon after him, but it took them 10 years to reunite with their son. Roberto came to the USA at age 21 when his parents were able to leave Cuba to come to Florida. He is an Spanish citizen, and a resident alien in the USA. His lover of 3 years, T.J., is a 62-year-old medical doctor with a very successful practice. T.J. was once married to a woman for three years. He has a 40-year-old son from that union. Over the years, T.J. has had several gay relationships, usually lasting from three to five years. His son has usually gotten along well with T.J.'s previous partners, but he is now upset with his father because of the age difference between Roberto and T.J. Roberto is fluent in English, although he speaks with an accent. He is attending a community college at the present time in hopes of obtaining a 2 year technical degree. He works part-time at his partner's office. They both describe themselves as atheists. T.J. requested therapy for the couple in an effort to break his pattern of dissatisfaction with his relationships that historically begins around the third year.

There were several salient issues for this couple including age differences, family of origin, discrepancy in education and income, and power related to Roberto's employment with his partner.

Vendabal and Jules

Vendabal is a 23-year-old Black male from Panama. He came to the US as an exchange high school student, and once he completed high school he decided to stay illegally. He is unable to obtain a legal work permit, and therefore works in a plant nursery where several illegal immigrants work. He is frightened of being identified as a gay man at work. His lover is Jules, a 25-year-old American born of an Italian father and Costa Rican mother. Jules does not speak Spanish.

Salient issues for this couple were illegal status and class differences.

AN OPPRESSION SENSITIVE APPROACH

The stories of these couples invite a stance of curiosity for exploration of domains of influence. What are the points of convergence and divergence for each couple? In what areas does each partner feel privileged and in what areas does he feel oppressed? How do they deal with their similarities and differences? What does each partner think about the race of the other; their nationality; or their ethnic identity? What role does income play in the division of power for the couple, and in their sense of class? How does the more privileged member respond to the sense of oppression of the other? For example, how does Bruce respond to the reaction that some members of the dominant culture may have about Timmy's accent? How does each member of the couple deal with heterosexism; with their families of origin; and with the dominant gay culture? What are the salient cultural issues for each member of the couple; and for their relationships with friends and the dominant culture? What role does nationality plays? What are the couple's strengths? How does spirituality influence their relationship?

Same sex couples, whether cross-cultural or not, seek therapy for a variety of difficulties. These are usually not very different from the difficulties brought to the attention of therapists in different-sex relationships and marriages. The primary difference is one of context. It is the context in which these difficulties occur that requires additional understanding, cultural awareness and sensitivity on the part of the therapist. The impact of racism, sexism, heterosexism, classism, ethnocentrism and other forms of oppression need to be explored when working with same sex male couples. Even more so, when one or both partners share an additional minority status, it is important to explore the impact of multiple oppressions on the couple. Bepko and Johnson (2000) emphasize that same sex couples have the expectation that therapists affirm their relationships, whether the therapist is gay, lesbian, or straight. This expectation also applies to Latino cross cultural gay couples.

Early, Nazario, and Steier (1994), and Nazario (1998) have proposed a therapeutic approach, Oppression Sensitive, appropriate for working with a variety of presenting problems and diverse populations. This approach considers race, gender, class, culture, ethnicity, age, sexual orientation, spirituality, and physical and mental ability as domains of influence organizing existential meanings for both clients and therapists. These domains influence our perceptions, attitudes and behaviors in society, and therefore our intimate relationships. These authors suggest that as therapists, we can not exclude ourselves from the therapeutic process, and must consider our own race, culture, age, gender, class, sexual orientation, ethnicity, and spirituality. Therapy with Latino cross cultural gay couples is an encounter between the subjective experiences of the therapist and the subjective experiences of each member of the couple, with domains of influence contextualizing the presenting problems. These presenting problems are dissolved by conversations that open space for new and more generative narratives to evolve. These conversations move back and forth from the political and socio-cultural to the personal (Johnson & Keren, 1996). Oppression Sensitive is health-oriented, gender-sensitive, and supports and affirms diversity in terms of ethnicity, race, cultural background, sexual orientation, age, ability and lifestyles (Early, Nazario & Steier, 1994). Oppression Sensitive is not a series of techniques, but a philosophical and political stance that provides a broad umbrella of social justice and power, as lenses for conversations with clients. Oppression Sensitive suggests that race, or culture or sexual orientation can not be isolated from other domains of influence when working with Latino cross-cultural gay couples.

REFERENCES

Bepko, C., & Johnson, T. (2000). Gay and Lesbian Couples in Therapy: Perspectives for the Contemporary Therapist. *Journal of Marital and Family Therapy, 26,* 409-419.

Bernal, G., & Flores Ortiz, Y. (1988). Latino Families in Therapy: Engagement and Evaluation. *Journal of Marital and Family Therapy, 8,* 357-365.

Boyd-Franklin, N., & Garcia-Preto, N. (1994). Family Therapy: The Cases of African-American and Hispanic Women. In L. Comas-Diaz & B. Greene (Eds.). *Women of Color: Integrating Ethnic and Gender Identity in Psychotherapy.* New York: The Guilford Press.

Comas-Diaz, L. (2001). Hispanics, Latinos, or Americanos: The Evolution of Identity. *Cultural Diversity and Ethnic Minority Psychology, 7,* 115, 120.

DiPlacido, J. (1998). Minority Stress Among Lesbians, Gay Men, and Bisexuals: A Consequence of Heterosexism, Homophobia, and Stigmatization. In G. M. Herek (Ed.). *Psychological perspectives on lesbian and gay issues: Vol. 4. Stigma and Sexual Orientation: Understanding prejudice against lesbians, gay men, and bisexuals.* Thousand Oaks, CA: Sage.

Early, G., Nazario, A., & Steier, H. (1994). Oppression Sensitive Family Therapy: A Health Affirming Model. American Orthopsychiatric Association. Washington, DC. 29 April.

Falicov, C. (1982). Mexican Families. In M. McGoldrick, J. K. Pearce, & J. Giordano (Eds.). *Ethnicity and Family Therapy.* New York: The Guilford Press.

Falicov, C. J. (1998). Latino Families in Therapy: A Guide to Multicultural Practice. New York: The Guilford Press.

Garcia-Preto, N. (1982). Puerto Rican Families. In M. McGoldrick, J. K. Pearce, & J. Giordano (Eds.). *Ethnicity and Family Therapy.* New York: The Guilford Press.

Gonsiorek, J. C. (Ed.). (1985). A guide to psychotherapy with gay and lesbian clients. Binghamton, NY: Harrington Park Press.

Green, R. J. (2000). Introduction to the Special Section: Lesbian, Gay, and Bisexual Issues in Family Therapy. *Journal of Marital and Family Therapy, 26,* 407-408.

Greene, B. (Ed.) (1997). Psychological perspectives on lesbian and gay issues: Vol. 3. Ethnic and Cultural Diversity Among Lesbians and Gay Men. Thousand Oaks, CA: Sage.

Hawkins, R. L. (1992). Therapy with the Male Couple. In S. H. Dworkin & F. J. Gutierrez (Eds.). *Counseling Gay Men and Lesbians: Journey to the End of the Rainbow.* Alexandria, VA: American Counseling Association.

Herek, G. M. (Ed.). (1998). Psychological perspectives on lesbian and gay issues: Vol. 4. Stigma and Sexual Orientation: Understanding prejudice against lesbians, gay men, and bisexuals. Thousand Oaks, CA: Sage.

Johnson, T. W., & Keren, M. S. (1996). Creating and Maintaining Boundaries in Male Couples. In J. Laird & Green, R-J. (Eds.). *Lesbians and Gays in Couples and Families: A Handbook for Therapists.* San Francisco: Jossey-Bass Publishers.

Meyer, I. H., & Dean, L. (1998). Internalized Homophobia, Intimacy, and Sexual Behavior Among Gay and Bisexual Men. In G. M. Herek (Ed.). *Psychological perspectives on lesbian and gay issues: Vol. 4. Stigma and Sexual Orientation: Understanding prejudice against lesbians, gay men, and bisexuals.* Thousand Oaks, CA: Sage.

Morales, E. (1996). Gender Roles Among Latino Gay and Bisexual Men: Implications for Family and Couple Relationships. In J. Laird & Green, R-J. (Eds.). *Lesbians and Gays in Couples and Families: A Handbook for Therapists*. San Francisco: Jossey-Bass Publishers.

Morales, E. S. (1992). Counseling Latino Gays and Latina Lesbians. In S. H. Dworkin & F. J. Gutierrez (Eds.) *Counseling Gay Men and Lesbians: Journey to the End of the Rainbow*. Alexandria, VA: American Counseling Association.

Nazario, A. (1998). Counseling Latina/o Families. In W. Parker, *Consciousness-Raising: A Primer for Multicultural Counseling*, 2nd Edition. Springfield, IL: Charles C. Thomas Publisher.

Reynolds, A. L., & Pope, R. L. (1991). The Complexity of Diversity: Exploring Multiple Oppressions. *Journal of Counseling and Development, 70*, 174-180.

Stevens, E. (1973). Marianismo: The Other Face of Machismo. In A. Pescatello (Ed.). *Female and Male in Latin America*. Pittsburgh: University of Pittsburgh Press.

Vasquez, M. J. T. (1994). Latinas. In L. Comas-Diaz & B. Greene (Eds.). *Women of Color: Integrating Ethnic and Gender Identity in Psychotherapy*. New York: The Guilford Press.

Assessment and Intervention
with Black-White Multiracial Couples

Carolyn Y. Tubbs
Paul C. Rosenblatt

SUMMARY. Effective therapy with Black-White multiracial couples begins with therapist work on self attitudes and with sensitive assessment of the ways racism and race may or may not be connected to a couple's problems. We suggest ways to begin to explore self attitudes and suggest basic assessment questions for work with Black-White couples. In addition, we point out important clinical issues that may come up for Black-White couples in the areas of social support/social network, parenting, and grief. *[Article copies available for a fee from The Haworth Document Delivery Service: 1-800-HAWORTH. E-mail address: <docdelivery@haworthpress.com> Website: <http://www.HaworthPress.com> © 2003 by The Haworth Press, Inc. All rights reserved.]*

Carolyn Y. Tubbs, PhD, is Postdoctoral Fellow, Family Research Consortium III, The Pennsylvania State University.

Paul C. Rosenblatt, PhD, is Professor, Family Social Science, University of Minnesota, 290 McNeal Hall, St. Paul, MN 55108.

Address correspondence to: Carolyn Y. Tubbs, PhD, The Pennsylvania State University, 601 Oswald Tower, University Park, PA 16802 (E-mail: cxt20@psu.edu).

[Haworth co-indexing entry note]: "Assessment and Intervention with Black-White Multiracial Couples." Tubbs, Carolyn, Y., and Paul C. Rosenblatt. Co-published simultaneously in *Journal of Couple & Relationship Therapy* (The Haworth Press, Inc.) Vol. 2, No. 2/3, 2003, pp. 115-129; and: *Clinical Issues with Interracial Couples: Theories and Research* (ed: Volker Thomas, Terri A. Karis, and Joseph L. Wetchler) The Haworth Press, Inc., 2003, pp. 115-129. Single or multiple copies of this article are available for a fee from The Haworth Document Delivery Service [1-800-HAWORTH, 9:00 a.m. - 5:00 p.m. (EST). E-mail address: docdelivery@haworthpress.com].

http://www.haworthpress.com/store/product.asp?sku=J398
10.1300/J398v02n02_09

KEYWORDS. Multiracial couples, interracial couples, therapist self attitudes, assessment, social support, social networks, parenting, grief

Since miscegenation laws were declared unconstitutional in 1967, interracial dating, partnering and marriage have been on the rise in the U.S. (Davidson, 1992; Qian, 1999). The removal of legal barriers to mixed-race marriage saw an almost 400% increase in interracial marriages from 310,000 to 1,161,000 from 1970 to 1990 (Qian, 1999). Amid this staggering growth in multiracial matrimony, marriages between White Americans and Black Americans lagged far behind White Americans' marriages to Latino and Asian Americans, even though the Black American population outnumbered Latino and Asian populations (Harrison & Bennet, 1995). Several explanations have been offered for this tendency for White Americans to maintain social distance from Black Americans including theories of social propinquity, irreconcilable cultural differences, and endogamous social norms (Gadberry & Dodder, 1993).

Despite the skewed trend toward maintaining social distance, interracial marriage between Black Americans and European Americans in the United States increased almost fourfold from 65,000 in 1970 to approximately 246,000 in 1992 ("interracial/multiracial coupling" would be the preferred phrase; however, published studies are primarily or entirely based on married couples) (Kouri & Lasswell, 1993; Rosenblatt, Karis & Powell, 1995). (The authors' preferred term for coupling between individuals of different racial backgrounds is "multiracial." However, for purposes of this paper, we use the term "multiracial" to refer to couples and "interracial" to refer to dating; multiracial seems appropriate when describing the racial composition of the couple. Interracial seems apropos for the activity of coupling across racial lines, but too narrow to capture the complex racial backgrounds represented by some couples.) Increased access to educational opportunities for Black Americans and the ensuing, inevitable interracial interactions have fueled this rise. Indeed, the best predictors of interracial dating are being young, a male of color, college educated and an individual (regardless of gender or race) who holds the belief that one's pool of potential mates can be enlarged by considering others outside one's own racial/ethnic group (Davis & Strube, 1993; Tucker & Kernan, 1995). When interracial dating and partnering occur, age, education, gender and ethnic group have been found to be important factors contributing to the willingness to cross racial barriers (St. Jean & Parker, 1995; Tucker & Kernan, 1995; Wilson & Jacobson, 1995).

The prevailing public attitude toward interracial partnering and marriage, especially those relationships involving Black and White partners, has yet to reveal the same level of acceptance afforded multiracial couples with an Asian or Latino partner married to a White partner. Although now less overt and patent, many Black-White multiracial couples still report incidents of subtle negative behavior aimed at them, especially at the Black partner. Many Whites still hold negative attitudes toward Black-White couples and this attitude may manifest in behavior that is unconscious and unintentional, sometimes called conformist racism (Rosenblatt, Karis & Powell, 1995). Overall, Blacks more readily accept Black-White relationships, but Black women are more likely to express negative attitudes toward Black-White interracial relationships than White women (Todd et al., 1992). It remains to be seen whether this expression of negative attitude is an issue of cultural differences in communication or greater tolerance among White women (McGoldrick, 1993). Indeed, research by Zebroski (1999) found that perceived expressions of support or opposition to Black-White marriages were based on a complex interaction of the race and gender of the respondent (Black and White, male and female), with the race and gender of the individual in the Black-White multiracial couple. Hence, White men were perceived by Black-White couples to be most opposed to their relationship, followed by Black women. Regardless, Black-White couples expect to experience negative reactions from members of their own racial groups, as well as individuals from other racial groups.

The notion that Black-White interracial marriages are unstable has not been empirically supported. Persisting notions of the inherent biological incompatibility of the races, as well as the belief that individuals involved in interracial relationships are psychologically flawed, has fueled the myth of instability in Black-White multiracial relationships. According to studies on the effect of cultural variables on multiracial relationships, the relational dynamics in interracial and same-race couples are similar (Aldridge, 1978; Shibazaki & Brennan, 1998). Black woman-White man couples indicated higher marital satisfaction than same race couples and Black man-White woman couples (Chan & Smith, 1998). Indeed, several studies suggest that the quality of multiracial relationships is more profoundly affected by social pressure than by racial/ethnic differences (Chan & Smith, 1998; Shibazaki & Brennan, 1998).

To the best of our knowledge, the literature on clinical populations fails to indicate a higher prevalence rate for Black-White couples than same race couples. One can infer that their presentation for therapy is no higher than same race couples, or that multiracial couples may avoid therapy to avoid further stigmatization of their relationship. Still, given demographic trends, clinicians can expect encounters with interracial couples. What are some of the potential issues that might affect a clinician's judgment when working with Black-White couples? What should a clinician do when a Black-White multiracial couple presents to her office? Should she immediately refer to a clinician more experienced in "issues of diversity"? Should she act from a position of colorblindness because "each couple is unique"? We will address these questions throughout this paper as we identify issues important to clinicians work with multiracial couples.

CLINICAL PREPARATION

Given the changing racial and ethnic composition of the U.S. as well as the expanded Black middle class and the reduced racial segregation of schooling at all levels, the probability that clinicians will encounter multiracial couples has increased. With a focus on Black-White multiracial couples, we next examine some of the self-of-the-therapist issues that may have remained unchallenged in clinicians' training.

Self of the Therapist

Self-of-the-therapist work in reference to Black-White couples requires that the clinician honestly and openly examine her feelings (with herself and a trusted colleague or supervisor) about Black-White couples. It would be an error for clinicians to assume that their comfort with other types of multiracial relationships would generalize to Black-White relationships because of the pervasive dehumanization of and discrimination against African Americans in the U.S. This statement is true not only for white clinicians, but for clinicians of color, too, especially African American clinicians. Although clinicians may have a racially and ethnically diverse group of friends, acceptance of diversity in friendship does not necessarily extend to acceptance of diversity in married couples (St. Jean & Parker, 1995). The clinician should not assume that she has fully dealt with issues of miscegenation or interracial coupling. White parents who adopt Black children often articulate their pain at the harsh realization that their children's earlier acceptance as White children's playmates changed during adolescence when the prospects of pregnancy and partnering become more salient.

Most family therapy graduate programs require that students engage in family of origin work prior to or concurrent with clinical work. To the field's credit, family of origin work focuses on the generational, developmental, relational, and ethical legacies transmitted to trainees. Therefore, much time is spent examining family beliefs and identities, structure, transitions, and coping and adjustment strategies. However, unpacking the family genome often focuses on a microsocial context, with occasional attention to macrosocial processes if they proved catastrophic (e.g., the Depression, Vietnam War). Practically, this means that family of origin work often occurs devoid of examinations of ubiquitous in-group/out-group processes, most notably race relations (McGoldrick, 1993). Many therapists have done little to examine the implicit and explicit messages their parents, grandparents, and other immediate family members have shared about White people or Black people (this is true for clinicians of all racial and ethnic backgrounds). For example, families may discourage open racism, but may give children mixed messages about the intellectual abilities or morality of African Americans, or implicit mandates against the acceptability of dating or coupling with African Americans or those who do. Conversely, other families may unfairly portray European Americans generally as racists and persecutors, or as the only racial group capable of producing morally upright and productive citizens. Incorporating a cultural genogram with emphases on one's own perceptions of Blacks and Whites, as well as one's perceptions of Black-White interracial relationships (as opposed to all interracial relationships) would initiate the process of dealing with powerful, yet potentially socially undesirable and unexamined, responses (Boyd-Franklin, 1993; Hardy & Laszloffy, 1995; McGoldrick, 1993).

We suggest that clinicians ask themselves the following questions with regard to examining their attitudes about Black-White, multiracial relationships. The questions provide an introduction to some of the self of the therapist issues in reference to Black-White couples and can be used in conjunction with Hardy and Laszloffy's cultural genogram (1995):

a. What perception do you hold of White women who date or marry Black men?
b. What perception do you hold of Black women who date or marry White men?

   c. What perception do you hold of White men who date or marry Black women?

   d. What perception do you hold of Black men who date or marry White women?

   e. Do you believe that racism is an important issue in the lives of Blacks in the U.S.? How or in what ways? If not, why not?

   f. What are your thoughts and feelings about multiracial couples?

   g. Are there aspects of your beliefs about or attitudes/behaviors towards Blacks or Whites that might be considered by somebody to be racist? If so, which are most difficult for you to admit to yourself, or to others, and to change?

Common to the experience of the authors is the sense of disappointment and surprise that many scholars of color express over the unspoken and often covert racial biases expressed by highly educated White colleagues and clinicians. These scholars of color express incredulity over the incongruence between public lip-service to cultural sensitivity and compliance with diversity criteria, and private resentment and disingenuous approaches toward diversity issues. This incongruence is present when disparaging comments are made about the qualifications of scholars of color or about the emphasis on targeted searches for scholars acquainted with issues of racial and ethnic diversity, and when clients of color have been hastily diagnosed as pathological while the benefit of the doubt has been extended to European American clients. These attitudes witnessed by clinicians of color are almost sure to be perceived by clients seeking help from such White professionals. Therefore, White clinicians should not assume that because they believe their racial attitudes are open to diversity that others, especially their clients, will see them as they see themselves. This is one reason why it is important for therapists, particularly White therapists, to make attitudes and feelings toward diversity an important part of self-of-therapist work.

ASSESSMENT AND INTERVENTION

Initial Assessment

One of the questions posed earlier in this paper was, "What should a clinician do when a Black-White multiracial couple presents to her office?" We believe that the majority of the issues affecting Black-White couples are not different from those affecting same race couples, so clinicians should not automatically assume that racial or cultural issues are any more significant than they are in same race couples (Aldridge, 1978; Shibazaki & Brennan, 1998). Still, one cannot assume that racial or cultural issues are irrelevant or insignificant. We recommend erring on the side of caution by allowing the couple to initially define the extent to which racial/cultural issues are part of, or linked to, the presenting problem.

As part of the conventional assessment process, clinicians should listen for any overt statements or references to race or racism by one or both partners. Even though the presenting problem may be framed as dyadic and interpersonal, it may be occurring within the context of overt or subtle racism. If the partners disagree about the influence of race or racism on an issue, this is an important piece of clinical information about couple dynamics and beliefs and the varying influences and impacts of race on their lives; and thereby may call for additional exploration. What at one moment might be attributed to gender or class differences, may at another be understood as a racial (or "cultural") difference. If a partner seems to deny, second-guess or ignore negative (or seemingly neutral or positive) racial comments and gestures expressed by the other, perhaps in order to avoid emotional distress that might detract from the positives of their relationship, that too would be something to explore further.

Clinicians should also be alert for reference to class differences during the initial assessment period. We include class as an important assessment variable, because the interaction of race and class defines the nature and meaning of the couple's interactions with one another and their social location, individually and collectively. Sometimes, the socioeconomic disparities that are appropriately attributed to class in same race couples are too easily attributed to race in Black-White couples. Clinicians should be sensitive in attempting to discern, or helping the couple to discern, whether contributing elements are race- or class-related, or both, because one member of the couple may interpret the clinician's haste to be color- or classblind as patronizing or as an attempt to trivialize the perceived (racial or socioeconomic) concern. For example, notions about the appropriate expressions of emotion, particularly negative emotion, might be viewed as class-based by one partner and racially-based by the other, especially if they identify themselves as being different in socioeconomic background. This suggestion is particularly true for Black male-White female couples. Chan and Smith (1995) suggest that lower levels of marital satisfaction in Black male-White female couples may be due to the socioeconomic background and potentially truncated financial prospects of the Black male partner. Although speculative, a systemic interpretation of Chan and Smith's work would suggest that low levels of satisfaction may be the outcome of frustration fueled by the White female's unwilling forfeiture of the choice of staying at home or working and the Black male's perception of the impact of racism on his career advancement.

If the issue of race has not been raised during the initial assessment, the clinician should not feel hesitant to raise the issue with the couple at a later time. Asking about the couple's perception of the impact of race on the issues on the table indicates the clinician's sensitivity and thoroughness in assessment. It also sets the stage for the couple to bring up the impact of race in the future if it seems relevant to the couple and their concerns. If the couple denies that race or racism has any impact on their problems, the clinician should accept this assertion, yet remain curious about racial influences that the couple may have learned to ignore (Boyd-Franklin, 1993; McGoldrick, 1993).

The couple's description of the relationship's beginning and progress toward marriage may include significant clinical material, especially given cultural stereotypes that pathologize interracial partnering. Couples may be acting (or reacting) to internalized notions that reflect negative cultural stereotypes which assume that their relationships are based on unconscious or unexpressed forms of exhibitionism, sexual curiosity, low self-esteem, familial rebellion, or gold digging (Davidson, 1992). As such, the clinician should be aware of their sensitivity to her responses to their story, as well as the nature of her clarifying and follow-up questions. In addition, information about relationship formation and maintenance provide the clinician with vital information about areas of social support and marginalization since there is a high probability that their definition as a couple disenfranchised them, individually and collectively, from those groups that provided various forms of support.

We have suggested that the initial clinical assessment include probes for a number of different matters that are linked to a couple being a Black-White multiracial couple. The following seem to us to represent the minimum of what should be assessed:

   a. Does the White partner fail to understand or choose to ignore the impact of racism on the Black partner's perceptions or decisions (or vice versa)?
   b. Does either partner fail to educate the other about the impact of racism on his/her perceptions or decisions?

   c. How do the partners articulate or refer to racism's impact on their children?

   d. Openly inquire about the potential impact of race and racism on the presenting problem if the couple does not mention it.

   e. Openly inquire about the potential impact of class on the presenting problem if the couple does not mention it.

   f. Evaluate the strength of the couple's social network and sources of social support, especially if there are indications of partner violence.

With respect to the question of referring to clinicians more experienced in issues of diversity ("Should she immediately refer to a clinician more experienced in 'issues of diversity'"?), each clinician will have to honestly assess her comfort with multiracial couples based on self-assessment and interaction with a clinical supervisor. The suggestions in the self-of-the-therapist section will assist with her self-assessment. If the clinician provides herself with the opportunity to examine that which has been potentially unexamined, she will feel less compelled to immediately refer multiracial couples because of fears about unacknowledged racism (however, she might refer for other reasons).

Target Intervention Areas

The remainder of this paper will focus on three key issues that surface for Black-White multiracial couples. They are social support, parenting, and grief (Kouri & Lasswell, 1993; Phoenix & Owen, 1996; Rosenblatt, Karis & Powell, 1995; Rosenblatt & Tubbs, 1998). In and of themselves, these issues are integral aspects of most families' lives. They are not idiosyncratic to Black-White couples. However, given the unique sociohistorical context of Black-White relationships in the U.S., these issues take on unique relevance. While some Black-White couples may indicate that these areas are not important to them, these are key issues that may be especially challenging to many Black-White couples.

Social Network/Social Support

Questions about the formation and maintenance of the couple relationship will provide vital information about the couple's sources of social support. Identifying supportive individuals or groups provides the clinician with possible resources for intervention inside and outside the couple's respective families. Few supportive individuals within the family may signal unresolved issues in one or both families of origin that existed prior to the relationship and that may have been exacerbated by the relationship. Assisting couples in re-connecting with important network members may be a crucial goal in reconnecting them with one another.

In addition, normative transitions may become crises or causes for maladaptive behaviors because the couple may fear ongoing rejection or criticism from family or friends who may have voiced concerns about the interracial relationship. Justifiably, multiracial couples often feel apprehensive about sharing their relationship concerns with family and friends because race too quickly becomes a part of the family member's or friend's explanation rather than considerations of normal relationship stress or development. Some family and friends may have difficulty viewing the normative transitions in the multiracial couple's relationship as similar to those that they are currently experiencing or have experienced in the past. The birth of the couple's first child may be one such crisis. A typically joyous occasion can highlight unresolved grief issues related to family disengagement (Rosenblatt & Tubbs, 1998). Asserting one's independence to choose a spouse of whom one's family disapproves may mean one's child is not connected with grandparents and extended family. Too, the couple may, in their individual ways, need to grieve the absence of family members at ritual events when family identity is reinforced (e.g., births, deaths, celebrations).

Some couples may struggle with gaining a good sense of normative behaviors from various friendship and professional networks. Will their causal acquaintance, colleagues or supervisors discriminate against them for being part of a multiracial couple? Comments or behaviors that are inconspicuous or irrelevant when one is not known to have a racially-different partner may take on a new meaning when one knows that others know one has a racially different partner (McGoldrick & Giordano, 1996). Helping the partners to sort, for themselves, behaviors (from others) that either or both deem inappropriate may be crucial to the couple addressing their presenting problem. The clinician should be aware of concerns over having to abandon aspects of friendship or professional networks because of rejection.

One other issue related to social support warrants mention. Domestic violence is more likely to occur in couples in which social support is relatively weak (Barnett, Martinez & Keyson, 1996). Anecdotal evidence suggests that women in interracial relationships may be less likely to report domestic violence to friends and family. If relationships are already strained because of disapproval about the interracial relationship, women may fear that reporting domestic violence will lead friends and families to interpret the violence as resulting from the relationship being interracial. Too, law enforcement officers and other helpers may be more likely to dismiss the need for intervention in interracial couples, especially lower socioeconomic status couples because of stereotypes about the irrational behavior of poor Whites and Blacks, the place and prevalence of violence in low income households, and racist trivializing of Black-White couple concerns.

Parenting

Although Black-White couples often indicate that they have successfully overcome the interpersonal or social difficulties associated with their marriage, many express much less certainty about their children doing the same (Phoenix & Owen, 1996; Rosenblatt, Karis & Powell, 1995). Some parents of multiracial children express ongoing concern about their children facing extrafamilial pressure to define themselves as Black or White. Multiracial children may be placed in a quandary over which aspect of themselves or their parents' heritage to reject or render invisible, either in general, or in particular situations. This conundrum also exists for multiracial children when others decide to label them without considering how they would self-identify. Parents' views about their children's rights to self-identify are often moot partly because much of what happens to a child with regard to identity is out of parental sight or control. And given the historical Black-White racial politics of the U.S., regardless of how their children might choose to self-identify, for most children the default prescriptive identity is Black. Having said this, however, both parents should be encouraged to articulate their views and values, to the child and others, regarding the child's right to self-identity and how others identify their child.

For some White partners, especially mothers, the inherent unfairness of their children being denied the privileges of being White and being forced to endure the devastating effects of racism is extremely painful. The pain is exacerbated by the contrast between the White parents' ability to retain many aspects of their White privilege and their limited ability to transmit this privilege to their children. Of course, it might be twice as devastating to realize that the sense of loss for one's children supports a social hierarchy that imputes privilege to the White partner and assumes inferiority to the Black partner based on race. Watching one's children experience and grapple with various forms of racism signals a violation of the relative safety of the accepted, multiracial and private family unit by potentially hostile, societal ideologies. For some couples, one partner's (regardless of race) tendency to trivialize or deny the import of the issue while the other (partner) does not complicates the issue.

Grief

Any couple therapy may need to be, in part, work with grief, and therapy with multiracial couples is no exception (Rosenblatt & Tubbs, 1998). One or both partners may at times be dealing with grief over the effects of racism on self, partner, child, or others, with identity losses resulting from being in an interracial relationship, or with the loss of family support for their relationship. They may be dealing with grief over the discrepancy between what America is and what it might be, with grief over the failures of community support, or with any of 10,000 other losses connected to being in an interracial relationship. Although the folk model of grief prevalent in the U.S. assumes that people can and should get over their grief, for many kinds of losses grief will continue or will repeatedly return (Rosenblatt, 1996). The task of the therapist is then not to make grief go away but to acknowledge the possibility that one or both partners are grieving and perhaps help one or both partners to get in touch with grief feelings. Beyond that, working on grief issues might involve helping the partners to find words for their losses, helping them respect and accept their differences in feelings, and helping them to address the ways that grief may undermine any aspect of the marital relationship–from paying attention to sexuality.

Colorblind or Not?

Should the clinician assume that all Black-White, multi-racial couples are the same, or should she "act colorblind" and assume that each Black-White, multiracial couple is unique? As the reader may have already guessed, we, like many other researchers and clinicians addressing issues of diversity, advocate for aspects of both positions. There is a core set of concerns that seem common to most Black-White couples about which the clinician should be sensitive, i.e., racism aimed at the Black partner, being marginalized in public settings, parental concerns about the racial identity of their children, and the impact of White privilege on the couple. However, the extent of the impact of these issues and their consequences should never be assumed for any Black-White multiracial couple. The configuration of impact and consequences will be unique for each couple, as well as the other issues that constitute their presenting problem. The assessment process allows the clinician to take the broad parameters of common issues not only as reasonable starting places for clinical exploration, but also to fill in the details unique to each couple.

DISCUSSION AND CONCLUSION

We have outlined three key areas in which, no matter what else a couple presents as problems, there may be links to the couple being multiracial. These are social network/social support, parenting, and grief. Exploring these areas and helping the couple work with them may give the couple personal and relationship tools to deal with many other problems. It may also be the case that a couple does not experience problems in any of these areas, or does not want to acknowledge or address problems in any of these areas.

In the U.S., marriage and marital therapy are alike in that neither can escape the daunting complexities, frustrations, ignorances, illusions, and harm arising from American racism. It would be a rare Black-White couple who said that they not only wanted to have a good marital relationship but that they also wanted to use their relationship to illuminate and undermine racism. And yet no couple can achieve isolation from the racist system, so couples are not only impacted by racism but also are, in various ways, in every situation where they are present, impacting racism by what they do or say. Similarly, it is a rare therapist who would say that beyond being a competent therapist, she wanted to use her professional skills to battle racism and its effects. And yet in every session, a therapist is connecting in one way or another with racism and its consequences, in self, in clients, and in the larger society. While Black-White couples make it easier for the therapist to think about matters of racism and to address them in self and in clients, racism may haunt any session with any client. In the end, therapists who intend to address matters of race and racism will find that the tools to explore the links of racism and race to client problems are as diverse as clients and client situations. Still, we believe that with any client–for example, a privileged White couple struggling with marital power issues, an immigrant couple struggling to find their way in America, or a couple trying to manage their finances wisely–matters of racism and race are potentially linked to their problems in important ways.

REFERENCES

Aldridge, D. P. (1978). Interracial marriages: Empirical and theoretical considerations. *Journal of Black Studies, 8,* 355-368.

Barnett, O. W., Martinez, T. E., & Keyson, M. (1996). The relationship between violence, social support, and self-blame in battered women. *Journal of Interpersonal Violence, 11,* 221-233.

Boyd-Franklin, N. (1993). Race, class and poverty. In F. Walsh (Ed.), *Normal family processes* (2nd ed., pp. 361-376). New York: Guilford.

Chan, A. Y., & Smith, K. R. (1995). Perceptions of marital satisfaction of black-white intermarriage. In C. K. Jacobson (Ed.), *American families: Issues in race and ethnicity* (pp. 369-386). New York, NY: Garland.

Davidson, J. R. (1992). Theories of Black-White interracial marriage: A clinical perspective. *Journal of Multicultural Counseling & Development, 20*, 150-157.

Davis, L. E., & Strube, M. J. (1993). An assessment of romantic commitment among Black and White dating couples. *Journal of Applied Social Psychology, 23*, 212-225.

Gadberry, J. H., & Dodder, R. A. (1993). Educational homogamy in interracial marriages: An update. *Journal of Social Behavior & Personality, 8*, 155-163.

Hardy, K. V., & Laszloffy, T. A. (1995). The cultural genogram: Key to training culturally competent family therapists. *Journal of Marital & Family Therapy, 21*, 227-237.

Harrison, R. J., & Bennet, C. (1995). Racial and ethnic diversity. In R. Farley (Ed.), *State of the union: America in the 1990s* (pp. 141-210). New York: Russell Sage Foundation.

Kouri, K. M., & Lasswell, M. (1993). Black-White marriages: Social changes and intergenerational mobility. *Marriage & Family Review, 19 (3/4)*, 241-255.

McGoldrick, M. (1993). Ethnicity, cultural diversity and normality. In F. Walsh (Ed.), *Normal family processes* (2nd ed., pp. 377-404). New York: Guilford.

McGoldrick, M., & Giordano, J. (1996). Overview: Ethnicity and family therapy. In M. McGoldrick, J. Giordano, & J. K. Pearce, *Ethnicity and family therapy* (2nd ed., pp. 1-27). New York: Guilford.

Phoenix, A., & Owen, C. (1996). From miscegenation to hybridity: Mixed relationships and mixed parentage in profile. In B. Bernstein & J. Brannen (Eds.), *Children, research and policy: Essays for Barbara Tizard* (pp. 111-135). Washington, DC: Taylor & Francis.

Qian, Z. (1999). Who intermarries? Education, nativity, region, and interracial marriage, 1980 and 1990. *Journal of Comparative Family Studies, 30*, 579-597.

Rosenblatt, P. C. (1996). Grief that does not end. In D. Klass, P. R. Silverman, & S. L. Nickman (Eds.), *Continuing bonds: New understandings of grief* (pp. 45-58). Washington, DC: Taylor & Francis.

Rosenblatt, P. C., Karis, T. A., & Powell, R. D. (1995). *Multiracial couples: Black and white voices*. Thousand Oaks, CA: Sage.

Rosenblatt, P. C., & Tubbs, C. Y. (1998). Loss in the experience of multiracial couples. In J. H. Harvey (Ed.), *Perspectives on loss: A sourcebook* (pp. 125-135). Philadelphia, PA: Brunner/Mazel.

Shibazaki, K., & Brennan, K. A. (1998). When birds of different feathers flock together: A preliminary comparison of intra-ethnic and inter-ethnic dating relationships. *Journal of Social and Personal Relationships, 15*, 248-256.

St. Jean, Y., & Parker, R. E. (1995). Disapproval of interracial unions: The case of Black females. In C. K. Jacobson (Ed.), *American families: Issues in race and ethnicity* (pp. 341-351). New York: Garland.

Todd, J., McKinney, J. L., Harris, R., Chadderton, R., & Small, L. (1992). Attitudes toward interracial dating: Effects of age, sex, and race. *Journal of Multicultural Counseling and Development, 20*, 202-208.

Tucker, M. B. & Mitchell-Kernan, C. (1995). Social structural and psychological correlates of interethnic dating. *Journal of Social and Personal Relationships, 12,* 341-361.

Wilson, D. S., & Jacobson, C. K. (1995). White attitudes toward Black and White interracial marriage. In C. K. Jacobson (Ed.), *American families: Issues in race and ethnicity* (pp. 353-367). New York: Garland.

Zebroski, S. A. (1999). Black-white intermarriages: The racial and gender dynamics of support and opposition. *Journal of Black Studies, 30,* 123-132.

Intercultural Therapy with Latino Immigrants and White Partners: Crossing Borders Coupling

Gonzalo Bacigalupe

SUMMARY. Interethnic and interracial marriages of Latinos and White Americans are on the rise and will continue to reshape the identities of individuals, couples, families, and communities. Clinicians working with these intercultural couples find no systematic training to address what is becoming a significant segment of our society. Couple therapists, however, cannot be culturally competent and effective based solely on knowledge of some dimensions of a couple's cultural backgrounds. Using clinical and theoretical ideas, the author defines clinical work with these couples as an explicit intercultural exchange. Our task as clinicians requires a rethinking of our conversations with these couples. It involves a

Gonzalo Bacigalupe, EdD, is Assistant Professor and Director of the Family Therapy Program, Graduate College of Education, University of Massachusetts Boston.

Address correspondence to: Gonzalo Bacigalupe, EdD, Family Therapy Program, Graduate College of Education, University of Massachusetts Boston, 100 Morrissey Boulevard, Boston, MA 02125-3393 (E-mail: <gonzalo.bacigalupe@umb.edu>; Website: <http://omega.cc.umb.edu/~gonzalo>).

The author thanks Jodie Kliman for editorial contributions and conceptual ideas and Tara Donnelly, graduate research assistant, who searched the library and the World Wide Web for literature.

The author offers special thanks to those who have shared their stories in therapy and through consultations with colleagues.

[Haworth co-indexing entry note]: "Intercultural Therapy with Latino Immigrants and White Partners: Crossing Borders Coupling." Bacigalupe, Gonzalo. Co-published simultaneously in *Journal of Couple & Relationship Therapy* (The Haworth Press, Inc.) Vol. 2, No. 2/3, 2003, pp. 131-149; and: *Clinical Issues with Interracial Couples: Theories and Research* (ed: Volker Thomas, Terri A. Karis, and Joseph L. Wetchler) The Haworth Press, Inc., 2003, pp. 131-149. Single or multiple copies of this article are available for a fee from The Haworth Document Delivery Service [1-800-HAWORTH, 9:00 a.m. - 5:00 p.m. (EST). E-mail address: docdelivery@haworthpress.com].

caring therapeutic approach that is sustained on relational and systemic levels, and intercultural conversational skills inspired by clinical and other literatures that are explicitly dedicated to work with cultural difference and the "other." *[Article copies available for a fee from The Haworth Document Delivery Service: 1-800-HAWORTH. E-mail address: <docdelivery@haworthpress.com> Website: <http://www.HaworthPress.com> © 2003 by The Haworth Press, Inc. All rights reserved.]*

KEYWORDS. Intercultural therapy, immigrants, bicultural couples, therapeutic conversation

All couple therapy can be construed as an intercultural encounter–a conversational domain in which cultural assumptions organize both clinical work and the couple's expectations and stories. This paper explores various epistemological and clinical approaches that include intercultural frameworks for relational therapy.[1] The paper uses the author's research on the stories of bicultural/bilingual therapists working with couples and families, using clinical vignettes in which cultural dilemmas are themes in the therapeutic conversation. Major issues and an inclusive set of metaphors that are useful for therapists to consider when working with these couples are also presented. Like the intercultural couples described in this paper, linking form and content, the author acknowledges and embraces a writing style that merges Latino and White intellectual traditions. This paper is informed by a literature review and a synthesis of clinical work with couples; its inspiration is grounded in experiences that are often inhibited in academic journals. Just as therapists need to be able to "read" biculturally to effectively engage with bicultural couples, this paper calls for a bicultural reading, an effort that may require *hablar los dos*. "Speaking both" involves linguistic as well as meaning making skills and is lived as a natural process for children of immigrants who grow up bilingual (Zentella, 1997).

The most recent census data (Guzman, 2001; Ramirez, 2000) suggest that more than one of nine families have *at least one member* who is self-designated as Latino/a. These revealing statistics are dissonant with the lack of understanding that Latinos/as encounter in their communities and in society at large when they engage with partners from the dominant racial group. Interethnic families are growing in number but neither theoretical nor empirical investigations seem to follow that trend (Lindahl & Malik, 1999; Negy & Snyder, 2000). Over 70% of interracial heterosexual marriages involve Anglos married to Latinos/as or to Asian Americans, yet such partnerships constitute only about 3% of all marriages in the United States (Gaines & Liu, 1997). These numbers may be changing, however, as Latinos/as marry across race and ethnicities at a higher rate than any other group (Falicov, 2001). Rodriguez (1996, in Cabrera, 2000) found that 31% of U.S.-born middle-class Latinos and 34% of U.S.-born Latinas marry non-Latinos. Interracial couples constitute a discriminated against ethnic and racial group and like other non-dominant groups, therapists and researchers have given them little attention.

Psychosocial research on international and/or immigrant couples and on intercultural marriages (Gleckman & Streicher, 1990; Lehrman, 1967; Levkovitch, 1990) emphasizes the potential risks of partnering cross-culturally. Contextual variations (Falicov, 1998; Kearl & Murguia, 1985) and resilience mechanisms (Garcia-Preto & McGoldrick, 1984; Johnson, 1995) have, however, been invisible. Negy and Snyder (2000) compared Mexican American and non-Hispanic White American interethnic couples with monoethnic Mexican and White American couples. They concluded that the levels of relationship satisfaction in the interethnic couples are similar to the White couples in contexts in which Mexican-Americans are not a minority group. Root (2001) has written that conflicts within interracial marriages are more likely to arise from cultural, gender, class, social, and personal differences than from racial ones.

No systematic research, other than that conducted by Negy and Snyder (2000) has been published in the family therapy field about this couple configuration. Clinicians serving this population therefore can only find guidance by drawing on the research and theorizing of related disciplines' studies of intercultural phenomena. My clinical work with interracial couples is often inspired by the writings of feminist Latinas who critically explore the lives of immigrant families in the U.S., and how to give voice to the experiences of those living at the cultural borders (Anzaldua, 1990). My work with intercultural couples explicitly acknowledges the complexities of clinical dynamics and of couples, incorporating the tools of a critical, reflexive, and postmodern researcher (Clifford & Marcus, 1986; Hymes, 1996; Lather, 1991; Merchant & Willis, 2001; Smith, 1999; Van Maanen, 1988). All therapies are cultural encounters, although working with intercultural couples requires more than just recognizing difference in the individual and couple domains. It involves reflecting on how differences relate to larger social contexts, which are defined by histories of inequity and colonialism. Some of the increase in interethnic and interracial marriages, for example, is based less on a romantic view of relationships than on the economic needs of immigrants who marry U.S. residents for the documents that allow them to stay in this country (J. Inclan, personal communication, April 28, 2001).

This paper refers to Latino/a immigrants in committed relationships with non-Hispanic White partners who have consulted a therapist, and explores dimensions that affect partners' identities in the course of therapy. It does not attempt to be inclusive of all interethnic couples, nor of all potential issues that present in therapy. Nor does it exhaustively review the literature about Hispanic families to develop a set of guidelines for "what therapists should be prepared to do" (Bean, Perry, & Bedell, 2001) that applies exclusively to the case of Latino families. My approach is a collaborative one in which I integrate research ideas into therapeutic conversations with couples. Frequently I find myself telling couples in therapy[2] and supervisees that something they say, or something we have a conversation about, deserves further documenting and sharing with others through writing (Bacigalupe, 1996). This paper is written in that spirit.

CULTURE AND INTERCULTURAL THERAPY

When couples are explicit about their cultural backgrounds, a therapist can draw on the most basic form of intercultural sensitivity. Even in this situation, a knowledgeable, competent therapist is not merely someone who has achieved some sort of "cultural literacy" (Dyche & Zayas, 1995). In addition, Dyche and Zayas (1995, p. 389) have suggested, "cultural naiveté and respectful curiosity are given equal importance to knowledge and skill." Working competently with an interracial couple requires more than learning about one or two cultures; such learning often obscures the heterogeneous nature of human systems. "Insider" knowledge of the family's specific culture of origin may be less important than the therapist's personal experience of a "transcultural differentiation process" (Khisty, 2001, p. 23). Therapists' awareness of her/his own cultural history as much as understanding of intercultural communication issues is central in this differentiation process.

Less obvious forms of intercultural work evolve from therapists' and clients' reactions to each other's values and core beliefs (Bot, 1990; Gorkin, 1986; Harvey, 1993; Sue, Arredondo, & McDavis, 1992), or from entering the unique worldview of our patients (Rigazio-DiGilio & Ivey,

1995). This form of cultural exploration implies a personal knowledge of the therapist's own cultural background (Hardy & Laszloffy, 1995; Lappin, 1983; Pinderhughes, 1989) and the evolving nature of such story vis-à-vis the couple's stories. At a more subtle level, an intercultural conversation may reflect a gentle form of colonialism (Bacigalupe, 1998; Cheyfitz, 1991). In the latter, the couple is deprived of open and transparent access to the therapist's assumptions, even as they seem to participate in a learning experience with the therapist. A postcolonial therapeutic sensibility recognizes the intersecting play of multiple positions and categories that frame our lives (Marks & Leslie, 2000).

Representing Latinos/as as a homogeneous group is problematic considering the multiple and intersecting nationalities, races, languages, immigration histories, social class positions that distinguish Latino and White identities (Baca Zinn, 1995; Casas & Pytluk, 1995; Comas-Diaz, 2001; Falicov, 2001). Yes, Latino and White individual identities evolve. Race and ethnicity are not static variables with the infallible central role that some critiques of multicultural approaches have suggested. Recognizing their definitional ambiguity creates a space to fully experience our clients as distinct and unique (Gordon, 1996; Tobin, 1986). An ambiguous sense of culture can be very useful clinically, since it offers a venue for reflective engagement. Although a therapist needs to be cautious about defining identity on the basis of a specific social marker, race matters in family life:

> Race makers do count in the way people perceive and interact with others, the way "racialized" persons construct and negotiate their own identities in everyday public life and in immediate, nuclear and extended family relations, and in the ways that it can reshape relationships among interracial couples and families. (Luke & Carrington, 2000, p. 5)

Like an ethnographer, a relational therapist learns about each individual's and couple's indigenous (emic) categories of experience in addition to those that are non-indigenous (etic) and imposed. Although a collaborative therapist is particularly interested in emic categories of experience, exploring imposed meanings systems is important since they also shape the couple's experiences (Terri Karis, personal communication, September 5, 2001). An etic stance is often based on prevalent western cultural meaning systems that are insufficient to create a collaborative conversation in couple therapy. As narrative theory proposes (Ricoeur, 1981), the telling shapes the identity of the teller; thus, meaning evolves as the couple and the therapist reflect upon their own understandings. As in any intercultural exchange, couples and therapists negotiate meaning in a social context. In this case, clients are positioned into a social context for interaction with someone who is interested (or not) in how they communicate. Just as couples are continuously being transformed by the intercultural relationship, the therapeutic system is a transforming entity. Couples are not fixed entities or unchanging essences colliding with a fixed, stable, and unchanging culture (Laird, 1998). Concepts such as transcultural differentiation (Khisty, 2001) or fluid identities (Hoffman, 1998) help us understand the interactive changes in which intercultural couples participate. Clinicians can explore these changes as couples embrace aspects of each culture: the ones they join, the ones they want to know, and the one(s) they collaboratively create. Interactional patterns may illustrate this process. Some couples, spontaneously or as a response to a question I have made, describe "acting White" or "responding like an immigrant" as ways of naming changes in the way they react to each other.

Empathy and respect, research evidence suggests, is at the core of effective clinical work (Duncan, Miller, & Hubble, 1998; Duncan, Solovey, & Rusk, 1992). Similarly, a respectful and empathic stance is basic of therapeutic cross-cultural sensitivity (Jordan, 2000). For relational or systemic therapists, openness and curiosity intersect to create a stance that ensures a trustworthy engagement in light of intercultural differences, both within couples and between therapist and clients. Obvious cultural differences may arise in situations in which privilege and oppression are present, as is often the case when recent immigrants partner with residents or citizens. In a meta-analysis of 33 studies of cross-national marriage, three main types of couple arrangement were found: "war bride/colonizer, educated Western and non-Western, and educated Western-Western"; these couples also reflected "the culture of the country in which they reside, unless there is strong commitment to the foreign partner's culture" (Cottrell, 1990, p. 151). If the dominant culture predominates in how the couple construes their relationship, the therapist will need to carefully unpack the privileges that this predominance provides to one of the members in the relationship. The therapeutic process, in this case, would include what feminist therapy proposals call for to directly address issues of power and agency (Byrne & McCarthy, 1999; Seu & Heenan, 2000).

INTERCULTURAL COUPLE ISSUES IN COUPLES THERAPY

Who you date and who you marry are among the most personal decisions a person can make, yet strangely enough, nothing elicits such an outcry as when we date outside our cultural, ethnic or racial groups. Suddenly the private boundaries disappear and our personal lives are fair game for strangers and family alike. (Cabrera, 2000, p. 1281)

Plurality of Language and Languages

Conversations about language use lead to labels that may foster a deficit model or an opportunity for learning and engagement. Couples' negotiations about the use of English and/or Spanish often reveal a core dimension of their relationship that therapists need to carefully and respectfully explore. For both members of the couple to share code switching–the back and forth usage of Spanish and English depending upon an evolving communicational context–is not always embedded in an interracial couple's relationships unless it was already an accepted element at the time the couple met. Investigating the history of language switching or lack thereof provides venues for the couple to discover themselves anew, which may be terrifying and/or exhilarating to one or both partners. Who is more fluent, and in what contexts? Who accepts the challenge of learning a new language and for what purpose? In what languages do discussions and conflict resolution occur? In what language(s) is love made? What sort of mix or integrative approach does the couple take regarding the shared language? How does the couple reproduce or innovate on dominant and subordinated language structures? What social structures are created, maintained, and/or reflected in the use of one, two, or a combination of languages at home? How are decisions made about the preferred languages of children at home? When adopting children, what language issues are brought forth?

Eloisa,[3] a Venezuelan, a student counselor at a community college, is married to Charles, a Caucasian professor at an Ivy League college. Prior to their marriage and Eloisa's immigration to the US, Eloisa had a long love relationship with a compatriot. Eloisa and Charles came to therapy because of flashbacks Eloisa had been having about the previous relationship for several months and her difficulties describing these flashbacks to their family physician, who does not speak Spanish. The primary language spoken at home is English and only a few of Eloisa's acquaintances speak Spanish. The couple struggled with how to manage the care of their 11-year-old daughter, as Eloisa is pursuing a new career that requires further education. Charles does not speak Spanish, although he is fluent in French. Eloisa's grandmother from a rural town in Ecuador raised Eloisa after her parents had died when she was a toddler. Charles' parents, with whom he maintains little contact, live in another state. They had an upper middle class well-educated background. The couple met a couple of years after Eloisa had graduated from a state college and Charles had completed his doctorate at a private institution.

Eloisa set up the first appointment, in which Charles' initial question to the therapist was about the therapist's education. Charles was surprised by the therapist's initial "culturally sensitive" question about which language they would prefer for the session. Eloisa started to cry almost immediately. An attachment injury (Johnson, Makinen, & Millikin, 2001) was patently demonstrated in the initial session, but the couple quickly moved into a discussion about Eloisa's flashbacks. Charles reaffirmed his support for her recovery but declared that his presence might not be necessary for treatment. To engage Charles, I explored how he defined "being supportive" and the connection that existed between this meaning and his upbringing as a White upper-middle-class man. My questions addressed the flashback and their reactions, their constructions of why they were occurring, and their behaviors before and after. In sum, I attempted to capture their knowledge and how it had been insufficient to resolve their actual concerns. They talked with love about their daughter but disagreed about the work that Charles was dedicating towards her care.

After establishing a sense of shared trust in the couple therapy work, we spent the next few meetings exploring the content of the flashbacks. Eloisa talked about some of the violence she witnessed as an adolescent. Her story switched to Spanish as she talked about the details of her upbringing. Charles seems "to understand" some of the content but was unable to actually contain some of the emotional aspects that surfaced as Eloisa told her childhood traumatic stories. Charles was often motionless or responded with short sentences that seemed unconnected to the emotional tone of Eloisa's story. Not engaging in Spanish seemed to protect Charles from having to deal with Eloisa's emotional needs. Since the telling of the story is as important as the content, I reassured Eloisa and asked her to tell what she felt comfortable sharing. This simple instruction clearly surprised Charles, who later tried a similar approach at home when Eloisa attempted to mutter a piece of her traumatic experience. Now, she felt less inadequate when pieces of the story emerge in Spanish when they are together. It is as if talking about this issue had provided her with the permission to reclaim Spanish as her language when she is in pain. Anger at having "forgotten" this story was mixed with anger and sadness about the trade-offs made in the relationship because Charles has not attempted to learn Spanish. In one of the sessions, we concluded that Charles' lack of Spanish proficiency had hindered their development as a couple and might symbolize a missing part in their relationship, that which allows for traumatic events to be shared and worked through in the intimacy of their telling. This lack of intimacy also translated into sexual difficulties, which the couple shared later on in the therapy work. Charles started to learn Spanish and recognized that his knowledge of French could support his capacity to hear Eloisa's Spanish if she was "willing to withstand his English 'accent.' " Being willing to share the same difficulty that Eloisa often confronts impacted positively the couple relationship. Working on this aspect of their relationship was easier now that the language deficit and proficiencies could be playfully discovered in their own relationship.

Understanding Self and Family

Latino family researchers (Padilla, 1995; Sotomayor, 1991; Zambrana, 1995) and clinicians (Espin, 1997; Falicov, 1998; Shapiro, 1996) have written extensively about Latinos' familism as a core identity dimension. A central and constitutive identity element for Latinos and Latinas is family. The past, present, and future are mediated by an allegiance to family, a symbolic and real presence in the lives of couples. This identity dimension suggests that when conflict arises, a major issue complicating their resolution is the powerful effects of deep-rooted cultural assumptions about who I am as person in the world. For White partners–more specifically, those who don't come from the collectivist cultures of the Mediterranean and Middle East or East European Jews–it may be difficult to understand and accept their partners' deep concern with their families' economic and emotional welfare even when this concern questions the stability of the couple relationship. Taking care of extended family members who are far away may be a primordial ethical and moral undertaking for the Latino partner. At the beginning of relationship, the Caucasian partner may construe this allegiance as congruent with her/his own culture's privileging of the couple over kin; when conflict arises, however, this priority may become the target of disqualification and attack. The dominant culture's emphasis on individualism and the Latino cultural emphasis on familism (collectivism) may come into conflict within the couple relationship. At the beginning of the relationship, the Latino partner may have construed this tendency towards individual development as empowering; but when conflict develops or becomes acute, and emotional upheaval increases, the Latino partner's construction may change.

A Latina client, Maya, told me about her relationship with an older woman, a well-known Caucasian writer, with whom Maya lived while writing her doctoral dissertation. Living with Julie provided Maya with emotional and pragmatic support to complete her graduate degree. After having accepted a faculty position at a college in the Northeast, they broke off the relationship when Julie was not willing to move to the Midwest. Years later, while Maya was pursuing her academic career and developing a stable relationship with a businesswoman, she still resented Julie's stance, even while feeling guilty about the break up. In therapy, Maya explored how that relationship had been entrapping, even though it allowed her the freedom to explore a relationship with a woman without being rejected for living openly as a lesbian. She was able to strengthen her sexual identity but, in her perspective, could not maintain a strong connection with her family in Latin America. To prevent a repetition of similar patterns in her present relationship, the therapy benefited from innovative ways of constructing self, autonomy, and connection. Helping each construct a renewed sense of self while also reconnecting with their extended families required my thinking beyond the myths of independence that are typical of family therapy and psychological theories (DiNicola, 1996; Luepnitz, 1988). Therapy helped when a focused balancing of self and family was introduced into the couple's conversation, aimed at resolving their conflicts and appreciating their strengths and abilities.

Creating Intimacy and Trust: It's Not Just About Acculturation

Acculturation is a popular concept in the analysis of immigrants' relations with the dominant culture; it is most often assumed to be the goal for individuals and families. Even critical analyses of multicultural family counseling myths accept assimilation as a family goal, although not necessarily one "evenly distributed among all family members" (Montalvo & Gutierrez, 1990, pp. 36-37). Adaptation (which is almost synonymous with success in this country) seems to require obliteration of what may be central to the identity of someone partnered with a person who belongs to the dominant group. Acculturation and assimilation are not the only desired outcomes for immigrants entering transcultural couple relationships, nor do they imply a healthier outcome. First, acculturation as a clinical goal is problematic, as it suggests an a priori standard to be achieved and a subtext signifying what constitutes a dysfunctional pattern. Second, even if we accepted acculturation as a pattern that immigrants go through, the concept has little descriptive power;

individuals who come with their partners to therapy can be at very different levels of cultural assimilation. Some assimilate and adopt the values of the dominant culture. Others develop a bicultural identity, negotiating both the values of mainstream culture and their culture of origin. A third group continues to embrace the values of their own culture of origin alone. Still others may reject both sets of cultural values. Moreover, many immigrants develop combinations of positions, which evolve and mutate as they develop a commitment to a partner or transform their relationships.

Cultural homelessness, Vivero and Jenkins' (1999) term for experiences and feelings reported by some multicultural and multiracial individuals, also applies to intercultural couples and offer a powerful metaphor for these couples in therapy. Intercultural couples may have a heightened sense of marginality arising "from cross-cultural tensions within the ethnically mixed family and between the family and its culturally different environment, especially due to geographic moves" (Vivero & Jenkins, 1999, p. 6). Joining with a couple that experiences this sense of isolation is difficult, but recognizing this construction of the relationship can transform each partner's lack of trust about the other's social location.

Assumptions arising from partners' respective experiences with those who have real or perceived privilege can be more powerful than constructions about masculinity (Bacigalupe, 2000) or womanhood (Flores-Ortiz, 2000). Latinos/as may disqualify and fear their White partner's privilege at the same time that they desire that influence for themselves. Therapists must be sensitive to the meanings and the practices that sustain unequal arrangements. How is meaning conveyed in the case of couples in which there are unavoidable differences sustained by cultural histories? Partners who have less privilege are often placed in rigid arrangements with implicit or taken-for-granted truths that rule their relationships with the more privileged.

Francisco, a recent Mexican immigrant in his early forties who works at a restaurant, recently married Sharon, the White mother of two teenagers. His boss told Francisco that not speaking English hurt his chances of working more closely with his customers and reduced the probability of earning good tips. Only after marrying Sharon had he been able to start working with legal immigration documents. Lacking language skills and having to send a large portion of his salary to his family in Mexico, decreased his chances of generating savings, or working fewer hours so that he could further his education. Sharon and Francisco did not speak much to each other and were referred to couple therapy after

Sharon had completed a mandated parenting group after an investigation for child neglect. When asked about how they had met and fallen in love, they, in their respective native languages, shared that it was in an urban hospital waiting room where they first saw each other and started to talk. The couple told their story without suggesting any romantic interlude to their relationship or the emotional tone characteristic of couples describing their courtship. When asked how they fell in love, they both revealed that they were "not really in love," that they married quickly to resolve Francisco's undocumented status, and that they never had a courtship period "like couples who give flowers to each other." In this exchange, expectations about how Francisco could remain in the U.S. created the context not only for failure, but also for how true love could not develop.

ALTERNATIVE METAPHORS
FOR COUPLES THERAPY CONVERSATIONS

Therapy with couples in which one of the partners can easily be defined as the "other" by the dominant culture requires an ethnographic listening stance. This listening is not detached, but a personally committed endeavor of choosing to share expertise while learning constantly about the complexities that such couples construe and face. Engaging with these couples involves both reflecting on the taken for granted and inquiring about the unknown. Traveling through conversation with the couple requires not only a therapeutic stance but also a continuous translation of clinical skills into a moving, ever-evolving cultural context. Simple interventions may work at times but do not allow one to learn with the couple how to honor the complexities of living in unknown territories. Tourist metaphors do not work to describe such work, since effective intercultural conversations and real dialogue require true engagement, not just traveling through.

Crossing Borderlands

The following are some metaphors and questions I find useful in working with intercultural couples in therapy, and they may be useful to all therapists working with couples in multicultural social contexts. How does your relationship resemble traveling to unknown lands? Does it resemble your immigration journey? How do you experience yourself as the traveler and/or the host? What were the difficulties settling into this new territory? What are your reactions when someone/something invalidates your beliefs? How do larger social and cultural problems find a space in your relationship? How would you compare your values with the values that sustained each of your parents? How do your extended family values find a place with your own values? What aspects of the relationship feel like nowhere zones? What dimensions of the relationship appear to you as secure ports? What do I, as a therapist, need to know to stay attuned to your values? What ideas would be fine to discuss and reevaluate? Asking Sharon and Francisco some of these questions helped them to redefine romantic love and put into a context that did not disqualify the basis of their caring relationship.

Couples as Nations

The following questions have a militaristic tone, foreign to what couples expect in a therapeutic conversation about couple relationships. The questions, however, may allow for couples to acknowledge deep fears and wounds that are not necessarily related to their relationship histories. When did the continent start to crumble? Did you quickly develop neutral zones? How does your relationship resemble a larger political and/or national conflict? Having experienced your partner as an enemy during times of high conflict, how have you engaged collaboratively with him/her later? What territories have you explored, conquered (or lost), and which ones are you not willing to give up? As commander-in-chief of your respective countries, what do you use against each other during full-force battle? If one of you were the political prisoner and the other the jailer, how would you free the prisoner, or as a prisoner, how would you escape? What would be required of a neutral bystander? What would a therapist need to know to survive without injuries? When Eloisa and Charles were asked some of these questions, their interest moved them into developing "language neutral zones." As they reported, the task involved developing truce periods while also becoming aware of the need for each other's language to have a space in their conversation and to develop a shared language for intimacy.

Couples Multi-Tasking

Added to the potential stresses of having to negotiate two or more culture of origin value sets, couples living in this country are confronted with the exhausting requirements of "balancing family and work" (Bacigalupe, in press; Fraenkel, 2000). It is useful to incorporate this dimension into work with couples who care for children or elder adults. How do larger economic/social/political dimensions frame your difficulties? How has your sex life changed as your income increased or decreased? How do metaphors from the culture find a place in your minds and expectations (e.g., accounting, acquiring, branding, consumer satisfaction, fast change, interest, multi-tasking, teamwork, venture)? How would your relationship work in a rural (or urban, suburban, international, etc.) context? How does satisfaction in your couple relationship relate to success as an employee, worker, professional, or businessperson? When did you stop thinking about these expectations? Early on, as couples and I find difficult to schedule therapy sessions, I ask many of these questions to validate their experience and to place it in the context of conflicting demands that compound the struggles of growing in bicultural relationships.

INTERCULTURAL COUPLE THERAPY: A FINAL COMMENT

An intercultural couple therapist is a translator who invites collaboration (Baduna, 1998; Lyle & Gehart, 2000); invites conversations about "cultural" stories, and is attentive to multiple cultural vistas (Barbetta, Edelstein, & Gaspari, 1998); accepts initial ambiguities, acknowledges, validates, and normalizes couples' differences and complementarities (Perel, 2000); and poses not-knowing as an ethical, collaborative stance of deep respect for the other (Larner, 1994). Therapeutic conversation, however, can also be a subtle, or gentle, form of colonialism that evolves from a reproduction of oppressive structural social patterns. The therapist herself can also be part of this reproductive stance; her expert position can simply disallow conversations that require critiquing the authority, including her own.

System or relational ideas are useful elements in making these conversations respectful and inviting grounds. These clinical practices include honoring the importance of context and process, the use of genograms, particularly historical and cultural oriented genograms, future and reflexive questions, reflecting teams, the practice of meaning making through stories and the deconstruction of narratives and discourses. Shared knowing requires a therapist who is attentive to the continuous implications of his/her privileged position. Such a therapist creates a zone of safety (Byrne & McCarthy, 1988) and often checks how therapy is honoring others' reality without fearing to share her/his own thoughts. The tools for caring in an intercultural conversation are multiple and integrating in the practice of relational therapists is a must for those working with couples struggling to create loving relationships while crossing national, racial, class, and cultural borders.

NOTES

1. Relational therapy is the term I use rather than systemic because I find it a theoretically more inclusive term and prefer its emphasis on relationship, while the systemic therapy framework includes relationship only as one aspect, rather than as a constitutive therapeutic element. My use of the term acknowledges the systemic and post-systemic/postmodern traditions in our field. It does not invoke the specific description of the Stone's Center's particular therapeutic stance (Jordan, Kaplan, Miller, Stiver, & Surrey, 1991).

2. How we name those we serve as clinicians is bound by social and institutional meanings, which are not neutral (Sluzki, 2000). As of this writing, none of the names clinicians use to name the ones seeking help adequately represents who they are or will be. The terms "patient," "client," or "consumer" do not seem ethically appropriate, and even less when referring to interracial couples. I will call these, orphan of a single relational term, people in therapy or couples in therapy.

3. All names and identification information has been disguised for the purpose of telling aspects of my supervisees' or clients' stories.

REFERENCES

Anzaldua, G. (Ed.). (1990). *Making face, making soul=Haciendo caras: Creative and critical perspectives by feminists of color.* San Francisco, CA: An Aunt Lute Foundation Book.

Baca Zinn, M. (1995). Social science theorizing for Latino families in the age of diversity. In R. Zambrana (Ed.), *Understanding Latino families: Scholarship, policy and practice* (pp. 177-189). Thousand Oaks, CA: Sage.

Bacigalupe, G. (1996). Writing in therapy: A participatory approach. *Journal of Family Therapy, 18*(4), 361-375.

Bacigalupe, G. (1998). Cross-cultural systemic therapy training and consultation: A postcolonial view. *Journal of Systemic Therapies, 17*(1), 31-44.

Bacigalupe, G. (2000). El Latino: Transgressing the macho. In M. T. Flores & G. C. Carey (Eds.), *Family therapy with Hispanics: Toward appreciating diversity* (pp. 29-57). Boston, MA: Allyn and Bacon.

Bacigalupe, G. (in press). Is balancing family and work a sustainable metaphor? *Journal of Feminist Family Therapy.*

Baduna, D. T. (1998). What can family therapists can learn from literary translators? *Journal of Systemic Therapies, 17*(1), 4-17.

Barbetta, P., Edelstein, C., & Gaspari, G. (1998). Intercultural communication on immigration. Narratives and meta-narratives fostering dialogue. *Human Systems: The Journal of Systemic Consultation & Management, 9*(3-4), 253-263.

Bean, R. A., Perry, B. J., & Bedell, T. M. (2001). Developing culturally competent marriage and family therapists: Guidelines for working with Hispanic families. *Journal of Marital & Family Therapy, 27*(1), 43-54.

Bot, H. (1990). Transference and countertransference in cross-cultural therapies. *The Psychotherapy Patient, 7*(1-2), 85-103.

Byrne, N. O. R., & McCarthy, I. C. (1988). Moving statutes: Re-questioning ambivalence through ambiguous discourse. *The Irish Journal of Psychology, 9*, 173-182.

Byrne, N. O. R., & McCarthy, I. C. (1999). Feminism, politics and power in therapeutic discourse: Fragments from the Fifth Province. In I. Parker (Ed.), *Deconstructing psychotherapy* (pp. 86-102). London: Sage.

Cabrera, Y. (2000, Issue Date). Interethnic couples engage controversy, growth. *Knight-Ridder/Tribune News Service*, pp. K1281.

Casas, J. M., & Pytluk, S. D. (1995). Hispanic identity development: Implications for research and practice. In J. G. Ponterotto & J. M. Casas & L. A. Suzuki & C. M. Alexander (Eds.), *Handbook of multicultural counseling* (pp. 155-180). Thousand Oaks, CA: Sage.

Cheyfitz, E. (1991). *The poetics of imperialism: Translation and colonization from the tempest to Tarzan*. Oxford: Oxford University.

Clifford, J., & Marcus, G. E. (Eds.). (1986). *Writing culture: The poetics and politics of ethnography*. Berkeley, CA: University of California Press.

Comas-Diaz, L. (2001). Hispanics, Latinos, or Americanos: The evolution of identity. *Cultural Diversity & Ethnic Minority Psychology, 7*(2), 115-120.

Cottrell, A. B. (1990). Cross-national marriages: A review of the literature. *Journal of Comparative Family Studies, 21*(2), 151-169.

DiNicola, V. (1996). *A stranger in the family: Culture, families, and therapy*. New York, NY: W.W. Norton.

Duncan, B. L., Miller, S. D., & Hubble, M. A. (1998). Is the customer always right? *Family Therapy Networker, March/April*, 81-90, 95-96.

Duncan, B. L., Solovey, A. D., & Rusk, G. S. (1992). *Changing the rules: A client-directed approach to therapy*. New York, NY: The Guilford Press.

Dyche, L., & Zayas, L. H. (1995). The value of curiosity and naivete for the cross-cultural psychotherapist. *Family Process, 34*(4), 389-399.

Espin, O. M. (1997). *Latina realities: Essays of healing, migration and sexuality* (First ed.). Boulder, CO: Westview Press.

Falicov, C. J. (1998). *Latino families in therapy: A guide for multicultural practice*. New York, NY: The Guilford Press.

Falicov, C. J. (2001, April 28). *Counseling the couple: Can (and should) marriage be saved?* Paper presented at the What's marriage got to do with it? Rethinking debates over research, practice and policy, Fordham University, New York, NY.

Flores-Ortiz, Y. G. (2000). La mujer Latina: From margin to center. In M. T. Flores & G. Carey (Eds.), *Family therapy with Hispanics: Toward appreciating diversity* (pp. 59-76). Boston, MA: Allyn and Bacon.

Fraenkel, P. (2000). Clocks, calendars, and couples: Time and the rhythms of relationships. In P. Papp (Ed.), *Couples on the fault lane: New directions for therapists* (pp. 63-103). New York, NY: The Guilford Press.

Gaines, S. O., & Liu, J. H. (1997). Romanticism and interpersonal resource exchange among interethnic couples. In S. O. Gaines (Ed.), *Culture, ethnicity and personal relationship processes* (pp. 91-118). New York, NY: Routledge.

Garcia-Preto, N., & McGoldrick, M. (1984). Ethnic intermarriage: Implications for therapy. *Family Process, 23*, 347-364.

Gleckman, A. D., & Streicher, P. J. (1990). The potential for difficulties with Jewish intermarriage: Interventions and implications for the mental health counselor. *Journal of Mental Health Counseling, 12*(4), 480-494.

Gordon, P. (1996). A fear of difference? Some reservations about intercultural therapy and counselling. *Psychodynamic Counselling, 2*(2), 195-208.

Gorkin, M. (1986). Countertransference in cross-cultural psychotherapy: The example of Jewish therapist and Arab patient. *Psychiatry, 49*(1), 69-79.

Guzman, B. (2001). *The Hispanic population:* (Census 2000 Brief C2KBR/01-3). Washington, DC.

Hardy, K. V., & Laszloffy, T. A. (1995). The cultural genogram: Key to training culturally competent family therapists. *Journal of Marital and Family Therapy, 21*(3), 227-237.

Harvey, M. A. (1993). Cross cultural psychotherapy with deaf persons: A hearing, White, middle class, middle aged, non-gay, Jewish, male, therapist's perspective. *Journal of the American Deafness and Rehabilitation Association, 26*(4), 43-55.

Hoffman, D. M. (1998). A therapeutic moment? Identity, self, and culture in the anthropology of education. *Anthropology and Education Quarterly, 29*(3), 324-346.

Hymes, D. (1996). *Ethnography, linguistics, narrative inequality: Toward an understanding of voice.* Bristol, PA: Taylor & Francis.

Johnson, A. C. (1995). Resiliency mechanisms in culturally diverse families. *The Family Journal: Counseling and Therapy for Couples and Families, 3*(4), 316-324.

Johnson, S. M., Makinen, J. A., & Millikin, J. W. (2001). Attachment injuries in couple relationships: A new perspective on impasses in couples therapy. *Journal of Marital & Family Therapy, 27*(2), 145-155.

Jordan, J. (2000). The role of mutual empathy in relational/cultural therapy. *Journal of Clinical Psychology, 56*(8), 1005-1018.

Jordan, J. V., Kaplan, A. G., Miller, J. B., Stiver, I. P., & Surrey, J. L. (1991). *Women's growth in connection: Writings from the Stone Center.* New York, NY: The Guilford Press.

Kearl, M. C., & Murguia, E. (1985). Age differences of spouses in Mexican American intermarriage: Exploring the cost of minority assimilation. *Social Science Quarterly, 66,* 453-460.

Khisty, K. (2001). Transcultural differentiation: A model for therapy with ethno-culturally diverse families. *Australian & New Zealand Journal of Family Therapy, 22*(1), 17-24.

Laird, J. (1998). Theorizing culture: Narrative ideas and practice principles. In M. McGoldrick (Ed.), *Re-visioning family therapy: Race, culture, and gender in clinical practice* (pp. 20-36). New York: The Guilford Press.

Lappin, J. (1983). On becoming a culturally conscious family therapist. In C. Falicov (Ed.), *Cultural perspectives in family therapy* (pp. 122-147). Rockville, MD: Aspen Publications.

Larner, G. (1994). Para-modern family therapy: Deconstructing post-modernism. *Australian & New Zealand Journal of Family Therapy, 15*(1), 11-16.

Lather, P. (1991). *Getting smart: Feminist research and pedagogy with/in the postmodern.* New York: Routledge.

Lehrman, S. R. (1967). Psychopathology in mixed marriages. *Psychoanalytic Quarterly, 38*, (67-82).

Levkovitch, V. P. (1990). Marital relationships in binational families. *The Soviet Journal of Psychology, 11*, 26-37.

Lindahl, K. M., & Malik, N. M. (1999). Marital conflict, family processes, and boys' externalizing behavior in Hispanic American and European American families. *Journal of Clinical Child Psychology, 28*(1), 12-24.

Luepnitz, D. A. (1988). *The family interpreted: Feminist theory in clinical practice.* New York, NY: Basic Books Inc.

Luke, C., & Carrington, V. (2000). Race matters. *Journal of Intercultural Studies, 21*(1), 5.

Lyle, R. R., & Gehart, D. R. (2000). The narrative of ethics and the ethics of narrative: The implications of Ricoeur's narrative model for family therapy. *Journal of Systemic Therapies, 19*(4), 73-89.

Marks, S. R., & Leslie, L. A. (2000). Family diversity and intersecting categories: Toward a richer approach to multiple roles. In D. H. Demo & K. R. Allen & M. A. Fine (Eds.), *Handbook of family diversity* (pp. 402-423). New York: Oxford University Press.

Merchant, B. M., & Willis, A. I. (Eds.). (2001). *Multiple and intersecting identities in qualitative research.* Mahwah, NJ: Lawrence Erlbaum.

Montalvo, B., & Gutierrez, M. J. (1990). Nine assumptions for work with ethnic minority families. In G. W. Saba & B. M. Karrer & K. V. Hardy (Eds.), *Minorities and family therapy* (pp. 35-52). New York: The Haworth Press, Inc.

Negy, C., & Snyder, D. K. (2000). Relationship satisfaction of Mexican American and non-Hispanic White American interethnic couples: Issues of acculturation and clinical intervention. *Journal of Marital and Family Therapy, 26*(3), 293-304.

Padilla, A. M. (Ed.). (1995). *Hispanic psychology: Critical issues in theory and research.* Newbury Park, CA: Sage Publications.

Perel, E. (2000). A tourist's view of marriage–cross-cultural challenges, choices, and implications for therapy. In P. Papp (Ed.), *Couples on the fault lane: New directions for therapists* (pp. 178-204). New York, NY: The Guilford Press.

Pinderhughes, E. (1989). *Understanding race, ethnicity and power.* New York, NY: The Free Press.

Ramirez, R. R. (2000). *The Hispanic population in the United States: Population characteristics* (Current Population Reports P20-527). Washington, DC: U.S. Census Bureau.

Ricoeur, P. (1981). *Hermeneutics and the human sciences: Essays on language, action and interpretation.* Cambridge: Cambridge University Press.

Rigazio-DiGilio, S. A., & Ivey, A. E. (1995). Individual and family issues in intercultural therapy: A culturally centered perspective. *Canadian Journal of Counselling, 29*(3), 244-261.

Root, M. P. P. (2001). *Love's revolution: Interracial marriage.* Philadelphia, PA: Temple University Press.

Seu, I. B., & Heenan, C. M. (Eds.). (2000). *Feminism & psychotherapy: Reflections on contemporary theories and practices.* London, UK: Sage.

Shapiro, E. R. (1996). Exile and professional identity: On going back to Cuba. *Cultural Diversity and Mental Health, 2*(1).

Sluzki, C. E. (2000). Patients, clients, consumers: The politics of words. *Families, Systems & Health, 18*(3), 347-352.

Smith, L. T. (1999). *Decolonizing methodologies: Research and indigenous people.* London, UK: Zed Books Ltd.

Sotomayor, M. (Ed.). (1991). *Empowering Hispanic families: A critical issue for the '90s.* Milwaukee, WI: Family Service America.

Sue, S., Arredondo, P., & McDavis, R. J. (1992). Multicultural counseling competencies and standards: A call to the profession. *Journal of Counseling & Development, 70,* 477-486.

Tobin, J. J. (1986). (Counter)transference and failure in intercultural therapy. *Ethos, 14*(2), 120-143.

Van Maanen, J. (1988). *Tales of the field: On writing ethnography.* Chicago, IL: The University of Chicago Press.

Vivero, V. N., & Jenkins, S. R. (1999). Existential hazards of the multicultural individual: Defining and understanding "cultural homelessness." *Cultural Diversity and Ethnic Minority Psychology, 5*(1), 6-26.

Zambrana, R. E. (Ed.). (1995). *Understanding Latino families: Scholarship, policy, and practice.* Newbury Park, CA: Sage Publications.

Zentella, A. C. (1997). *Growing up bilingual.* Malden, MA: Blackwell.

Asian American Intermarriage:
A Socio-Political Construction
and a Treatment Dilemma

MaryAnna Domokos-Cheng Ham

SUMMARY. This paper describes the therapeutic process of an interracial couple: an Asian American woman and a White American man. The intent of this therapy was to broaden the conversational space and encourage the couple to explore the effects of cultural beliefs and practices on their relationship. The therapist introduced two approaches for evoking the couple's interest in sharing narratives about their individual and couple racial identity. One approach was to have the couple interview their partner's "internalized other." The other approach used two research studies to stimulate conversation about outmarriage with Asian Americans. This case study offers an account of two different ways individual narratives and shared conversational space can be expanded. *[Article copies available for a fee from The Haworth Document Delivery Service: 1-800-HAWORTH. E-mail address: <docdelivery@haworthpress.com> Website: <http://www.HaworthPress.com> © 2003 by The Haworth Press, Inc. All rights reserved.]*

MaryAnna Domokos-Cheng Ham, EdD, is affiliated with the Family Therapy Track, Department of Counseling and School Psychology, Graduate College of Education, University of Massachusetts Boston.

Address correspondence to: MaryAnna Domokos-Cheng Ham, Graduate College of Education, University of Massachusetts Boston, 100 Morrissey Boulevard, Boston, MA 02125-3393 (E-mail maryanna.ham@umb.edu).

The author appreciates the wise counsel and support of Barbara and Cass Turner in preparing a demonstration videotape of the methods described in this paper.

The author thanks her Asian American clients who shared their lives with her.

Portions of this case were presented at the 53rd annual conference of the American Association of Marriage and Family Therapy in Baltimore, MD, November 2-5, 1995.

[Haworth co-indexing entry note]: "Asian American Intermarriage: A Socio-Political Construction and a Treatment Dilemma." Ham, MaryAnna Domokos-Cheng. Co-published simultaneously in *Journal of Couple & Relationship Therapy* (The Haworth Press, Inc.) Vol. 2, No. 2/3, 2003, pp. 151-162; and: *Clinical Issues with Interracial Couples: Theories and Research* (ed: Volker Thomas, Terri A. Karis, and Joseph L. Wetchler) The Haworth Press, Inc., 2003, pp. 151-162. Single or multiple copies of this article are available for a fee from The Haworth Document Delivery Service [1-800-HAWORTH, 9:00 a.m. - 5:00 p.m. (EST). E-mail address: docdelivery@haworthpress.com].

KEYWORDS. Asian Americans, couples, racial identity, interracial couples

It is a matter of finding a voice or style that does not violate one's several components of identity. In part, it is a process of assuming a pluralist, multidimensional, or multifaceted concept of self. (Michael Fischer, 1986, p. 196)

Family therapists can learn a great deal from demographic and research data. I find this statement reassuring whenever I am confronted with clinical situations that are puzzling to me. Even though I anticipate uncertainty in the therapeutic process, I cannot disclaim the presence of my own tension when I first discover in a session that clients' truths are contradictory with my own intuitive sense of a situation, or my own understanding about a body of knowledge. My tension settles into curiosity as clients begin to narrate the complexities of their own lives. Together we create yet another perspective of their situation. I contribute my experiences and learned knowledge; they offer their own lived perspectives.

This paper recounts a process that began with a lived perspective, an account of tensions experienced by an Asian American woman and an Irish American man in their interracial coupleship. The process continued with my contribution as a therapist focused primarily on the effects of cultural beliefs and practices on relational interactions (Tomm, 1998). Initially I was participating with the couple as we all became informed about their current situation through a therapeutic conversation about their life story (Anderson & Goolishian, 1988). Our conversation included a discussion around a group of reflexive questions (Tomm, 1987, 1998) that I asked as a way to identify and to explore their experiences in an interracial couple. They were intrigued with the ideas that had emerged from our conversation. To their newly developed ideas I added information that I had acquired from two studies I recently had read: a demographic study that examined the trends in Asian American racial/ethnic intermarriage by comparing census data from 1980 to 1990; and an empirical study that assesses a model developed by linking two perspectives for explaining the determinants of intermarriage. Our discussion of these studies provided additional ways the couple could view their relationship and accelerated the outcome of their therapy.

A LIVED EXPERIENCE

N., an ABC (American born Chinese), was seeking individual therapy because she wanted to leave her marriage with her European American husband. When she called to request individual therapy, I suggested that she and her husband, R., come together for couple therapy. Although N. was somewhat reluctant to ask her husband to join her in therapy, he was grateful she had invited him, and so together they began therapy.

The first several sessions provided an opportunity for N. and her husband to discover their relationship: to learn how the other experienced it and to explain how s/he experienced it. The goals of the couple therapy were uncertain: N. wanted to leave the relationship; R. wanted her to remain in the marriage. Each had a distinctly different description of their courtship and their marriage. They had been sweethearts in a high school located in a predominantly White community. The high school reflected the profile of the community. N. had gone to school with students of the community throughout her childhood and adolescence. She strongly identified with the prevailing values and culture of her White friends. N. was popular in her high school where she was the only Asian American person among a handful of ethnic minority students. R. recalled falling in love with her because of her "exotic" looks and her uncritical cheerful manner. N. characterized R. as her picture of the "perfect" American guy: blondish hair, blue eyes, and a "jock"-football player who liked her.

After graduation from high school they dated while he attended a college close to his home and she worked as an office worker. As soon as he graduated from college they married. After three years of marriage, N. made a decision to enter college. She attended a school with an ethnically diverse student population, where approximately six percent of the students were Asian American. During her first year at this college, N. took several courses offered by the Asian American studies program. At the end of her first year of college she felt that throughout her childhood she had betrayed her Asian heritage. Her marriage to R. just emphasized to her this betrayal. After a second year of college she told R. she could not stay married to him and then sought therapy. R. was baffled by N.'s identity conflict. He thought N.'s stress was the result of her hectic schedule, of going to school full-time while working part-time and keeping up their apartment.

In this early stage of therapy, N. and R. were both intent on telling their own stories and determined to have the other understand and accept the narrative information from his or her own perspective. Throughout this stage I was hearing two individuals tell two isolated stories. When I reflected my experience as a listener back to them, they understood because they had felt they were living unconnected lives. I suggested we create a way to link their narratives and offered a method of interviewing where they could explore how the narrative of the other person had influenced each of their own (Tomm, 1992; Tomm, 1998). In addition I encouraged both to share previous and present experiences that contributed to their individual racial identity development (Kerwin & Ponteroto, 1995). By exploring out loud their own racial identity development while their partner listened had the potential of expanding their own narratives to include their partner's (Anderson, 1997). At the time of therapy, N. was struggling to accept her own Asian heritage by seeking affirmation of her Asian identity from others (Kich, 1992). N. explained her feelings of confusion and conflict, and her need to choose sides: Would she identify herself as Asian American with values of her family of origin or as White American with values of her husband and childhood friends? Her racial ambivalence had left her feeling as if she had limited choices: either to live and follow the values of Asian Americans or to live and follow the values of White Americans. R., on the other hand, had not considered racial identity as an issue that intruded upon his own sense of self. However, his marriage to an Asian woman brought him to the awareness of race and culture. Although his parents were supportive of the interracial couple, R. took note that they actually ignored N.'s race and culture by always claiming N. to be "just N.," a unique personality.

EXPANDING THE NARRATIVE

In the second stage of therapy I suggested to N. and R. that we try to link their life stories by placing them within a social context. I mentioned using therapeutic methods for creating a link for their narratives. These methods had evolved from the understanding that families are embedded in a larger culture and are profoundly affected by it (Anderson, 1997; Anderson & Goolishian, 1991; Gergen, 1991; Hoffman, 1992; McGoldrick & Giordano, 1996; Tomm, 1998; Waldegrave, 1990; White & Epston, 1990). I was curious whether these therapeutic methods (Tomm, 1992, 1998; White & Epston, 1990), which acknowledge the flexibility of "the self" and its development as a social construction (Gergen, 1990), could help N. and R. expand the meanings they gave to their marriage.

To encourage the couple to expand their narratives I used a method of "internalized other" interviewing (Tomm, 1992, 1998). This method calls for one person to use her or his knowledge of the other and to speak from the other's position. One person is able to create internal images and dialogue of another from the knowledge s/he gains through the social interactions they have shared context. For one person to know the interior experiences of another is for the person to recognize that descriptions of reality always imply interactions (Maturana, 1978). As an introduction to the internalized-other interview (Tomm, 1992), I encouraged both R. and N. to bring to mind interactions and experiences with others whom they had integrated as part their own knowledge of themselves. A few examples of statements they made were, "We remember our parents saying things to us that we ourselves say now"; "Sometimes I notice that I sound just like my mother."

After this introductory conversation, I gave the following instructions to the couple: First, Partner A will begin and will be curious about what the "internalized other," Partner B, has to say. Partner A will not make judgments or offer interpretations about the responses of partner B. Partner B will step into the position of an "internalized other," such as a sibling, a mother , a father, and will speak in the voice of 'the other.' The conversation will be between Partner A and the 'internalized other' of Partner B. I suggested to N. and R. that they have conversations with four different "internalized others": with members from their family of origin, with peers from their adolescent years, with current peers in their social communities, and with the children they might have together in the future. I then continued to say, "To engage in a conversation with your partner's 'internalized other,' you might ask some simple question that begins, 'I am very interested in knowing how it feels for you when I ask the following question.' " For each conversation, they both had an opportunity to play the role of her/his "internalized other." After the conclusion of each role play, we talked about what they each had learned from the exercise and specifically from the questions.

The following questions are examples for each of the four conversations with "internalized others."

Conversations with your "internalized memory" of members of your family of origin; answer "as if" you were your mother or father.

- What did you imagine other members of the family would feel when we announced our plans to get married?
- After announcing our marriage what comments from family members do you remember as important?
- What stands out in your memory about our wedding ceremony?

N. spoke as her father who was proud to have his daughter marry "a regular guy, an American." N. remembered that her father was concerned that she fit into mainstream culture. On numerous occasions he told her,

"If you want to make your way into the culture, you need to find ways to be similar to them" (American girls). N. recalled her father's words on her wedding day, "You look just like an American." Her wedding, she said was "just like it should have been," like her White friends said it should be.

R., in the voice of his mother, was cautious about his enthusiasm about the marriage. He remembered that his mother was relieved that N. spoke English without an accent and was attractively dressed. As R. said, "She looks like the other girls except for her black hair and different shaped eyes."

Conversations with your "internalized memory" of your peers when you were in high school; answer "as if" you were a teenage or young adult friend.

- What did you imagine friends would say when they found out that the person you were marrying was racially different from you?
- How did you feel about asking your new wife/husband to go to parties your friends were having?

N. spoke as her best friend in high school. She felt complete support for her marriage from her friend. Her other high school friends thought highly of R. because of his status in high school and considered N. lucky to be marrying him.

R. spoke in the voice of his newly made friend from work. Unlike R.'s high school buddies, the work friend did not encourage R. to bring N. to work parties. Although he was always polite to N. when he was alone with N. and R., he discouraged a couple friendship between himself and his wife, and N. and R. by turning down dinner invitations that R. initiated. R. learned from conversations that his work friend's father fought in Viet Nam.

Conversations with your "internalized memory" of your assumption about what "society" might believe; answer "as if" you were a member of the prevailing society.

- Walking together on a main city street, what would people on the street think of us?
- How would we expect to be treated by a desk clerk who was checking us into a hotel?

N., in the voice of a makeup counter store clerk, conveyed discomfort in serving an Asian person. N. imagined that the clerk was embarrassed to ask her what kind of makeup she wanted, "I wonder how Asians use eye makeup when they have hardly any eyelids."

R., speaking in the voice of a hotel clerk, conveyed a sense of envy and admiration that R. had such a good looking wife. "If she's good looking then who cares if she's Asian."

Conversations with your "internalized imagination" of your future children: answer "as if" you were your daughter or your son.

- What do you remember learning from your grandparents?
- What experiences with your grandparents do you remember best?
- How did you feel when you were at "family gatherings" with your grandparents, cousins, and other relatives?

N., in the voice of her imagined daughter, had conflicted feelings and attitudes about her mother's heritage. "I like to visit my mother's parents because they do things in a special way, like the red envelope with money in it that I get on Chinese New Year, but they're hard to understand." "My Chinese grandfather thinks I'm really lucky to be an American." "My father's parents seem too polite. I don't really feel close to them because I'm not sure they really like me."

R., from the perspective of his imagined son, felt confident that both sets of grandparents loved and cherished him. He was indifferent about his mother's heritage, yet he enjoyed visiting his maternal grandparents and was mildly interested in their traditions.

The conversations of N. and R., with their "community of internalized others" (Tomm, 1998), reflected a social constructionist position in having conversations with "internalized others," we bring forth knowledge already within ourselves that we have learned from our family of origin, and from social and cultural influences and expectations (Gergin, 1990; Tomm, 1992). N. and R., in their conversations with "internalized others," discovered that the voices of many people and institutions influenced the meanings they gave to events and behaviors, and affected their construction of themselves.

From the four conversations N. and R. heard the amplified voices of their "internalized community." N. heard even more loudly a call to experience her Asian heritage and identity, while R. continued to be convinced that "Americans are Americans." "Why does she have to do this Asian thing?" he asked.

RESEARCHERS AS CONVERSATIONAL PARTNERS

"Why does she have to do this Asian thing?" R. explained that he wanted to challenge N.'s belief about her need to identify herself as

Asian American. I considered his challenge to be an invitation to expand the conversational space: His question served the purpose of expanding small chambers into a large cavern, as dynamite demolishing a wall separating one chamber from another. To this conversation I wanted to contribute the voices of researchers who were studying the very issue N. and R. were living and investigating in their lives: an interracial marriage. I suggested to N. and R. that they read the abstract and scan the text of two research articles that I had recently found relevant to their situation. I proposed that we discuss them in our therapy session. They were willing to "try to read them" even if they did not fully understand the articles.

The first article, "Trends in Asian American racial/ethnic intermarriage: A comparison of 1980 and 1990 census data" (Lee & Fernandez, 1998) describes a demographic study and offers interpretations of the census data. The main findings from the comparison of census data show that: "(i) the overall out-marriage rate has declined between 1980 and 1990 by 10%; (ii) Asian America inter-ethnic marriage (that is, marriages between two Asian Americans of different Asian ethnicities) has increased, doubling from 11% in 1980 to 21% in 1990; and (iii) marital distance between Asian Americans and other racial and ethnic groups has widened and is an indicator that social distance between Asian Americans and Whites, Blacks, and Hispanics has widened over the last decade" (Lee & Fernandez, 1998, p. 323, 337).

The second article, "Structural and assimilationist explanations of Asian American intermarriage" (Hwang, Saenz, & Aguirre, 1997), reports a study that made efforts to synthesize two intermarriage perspectives: one explaining intermarriage at the micro level using individual attributes such as cultural and socioeconomic status traits; the other explaining it at the macro level using aggregated community characteristics such as the size of the Asian group, the availability of potential partners in Asian groups, the social and spatial proximity between the Asian and the White, Black and/or Hispanic groups (Hwang, Saenz, & Aguirre, 1997). The results of the study suggested that individual and community variables affect Asian intermarriage (Hwang, Saenz, & Aguirre, 1997).

In our conversation about these articles the researchers were an imagined presence. Both N. and R. argued with the researchers. They doubted some of the researchers' hypotheses and they agreed with others. Both the articles generated curiosity about the determinants, the social meaning, and the factors influencing an individual's attraction for someone of another race, and heightened their interest in interracial marriage, and in their own marriage.

What made the articles useful in the therapy was not the statistical analysis or the facts, but how N. and R made meaning of specific facts, selecting and remembering those that were considered relevant to their relationship. I asked them the question, "As you read the articles what information do you remember, and what points in the researchers' discussion seemed to describe your relationship?" N. and R. agreed that both articles informed them about the historical context of Asian American intermarriage. They had previously not known the effects of the Chinese Exclusion Act of 1882 on Asian marriage patterns, the impact of anti-miscegenation laws on the choice of marriage partner, or the influence of the U.S. Immigration and Naturalization Law of 1995 (Lee & Fernandez, 1998).

N. felt that the Lee and Fernandez (1998) paper best described her feelings about her marriage with R. "As the Asian American population grows, the effect of increased group size on intermarriage is expected to become evident. . . . Members of small populations are much more likely to out-marry because their chances of meeting potential spouses from (their own group) are lower than meeting individuals from other groups (with larger numbers)" (Lee & Fernandez, 1998, p. 325). N. pointed out that throughout her childhood she and her sister were the only Asians in their schools. In high school she had to "become white" culturally and socially, or just be a loner. She had no chance of meeting potential marriage partners who were Asian because there were none in her social environment. However, in college where the Asian American population was substantial, she had the opportunity to date Asian American men who could become her marriage partner. As noted by Hwang, Saenz and Aguirre (1997), a larger group affords its members more opportunities for within-group contact than does a smaller group, thus the availability of potential partners in the Asian community highly affects whether an Asian American might consider out-group marriage.

R. felt the most affinity with the perspective of Hwang, Saenz and Aguirre (1997). He showed us a statement from their article that gave meaning to his relationship with N.: "Immigrants often possess cultural traits and socioeconomic status that distinguish them from members of the host society. Their distinctive cultural and status traits initially would hinder intimate interactions between immigrants and members of the host society. More intimate relations, however, are expected to occur when immigrants gradually overcome cultural and structural barriers that block their full membership in the host society; acculturated and structurally assimilated Asians would be more likely to intermarry than their less acculturated and structurally assimilated counterparts" (Hwang, Saenz & Aguirre, 1997, p. 759). R. carried the belief that N. was American, not Chinese American, "She talks just like we do, she dresses the same, and acts just like one of us."

AN ENLARGED SPACE

The research-based conversation the three of us had was pivotal to the outcome of the couple therapy. Both N. and R. felt exhilarated by the conversational therapy and were curious to see if they could create a relationship that would include both of their perspectives. From therapy they learned to ask more questions rather than to settle for premature answers. They wondered if together they could develop a set of shared beliefs, values, and rules of behavior they could both accept. Would it be possible for them to include in their shared mainstream American values another set of cultural values? N. and R. left therapy believing they could co-create a couple relationship.

THE VOICE OF SOCIAL IDENTITY

About a year after N. and R. decided to leave therapy, and three months after the termination N. called me to say that she had just separated from R. Although she loved him and continued to be his friend, she felt the conflicts within her "internalized community" had become external and thus apparent to her in daily life. She felt more strongly than ever that her primary identity was as an Asian American and that her life mission was to preserve that identity in others as well as in herself. One year after she and R. had separated she called to inform me that she had graduated from college and had began working with the Asian American community as a counselor in a community agency located in the local Chinatown. She reported that in her marriage to R., in their therapy together, she learned a great deal about herself. By expanding their conversational space both had gained respect for the other's perspective and for their different interpretations of the same events. N. stated that she felt ready to leave R. only after she was able to "internalize" his social narrative as part of her own, yet separate hers from his. At this point she then felt she had choices to expand her own social narrative: to amplify the voices of her cultural heritage or to reconfigure cultural voices by modulating them into a new song. Her choice was to hear more clearly the voices from the past and to carry the inviolate song into the future.

R. never called me after the therapy had ended and so I was unaware of his thoughts and feelings about N. leaving the marriage. N. reported in her second conversation with me, one year after her separation from R., that he was perplexed by her intense focus on her Asian heritage and identity, and by her rejection of him she had also rejected her identity as an American. I can only imagine his hurt and confusion about losing a woman whom he thought he knew but was, instead, a multidimensional context.

Throughout the therapy with this couple I was aware that my own racial and ethnic identity influenced the therapeutic space. As a biracial person, I have been aware of the factors that affected my parents' interracial relationship. Perhaps the historical-societal context of their marriage was the greatest contributor to the demise of their relationship. My Hungarian mother and Chinese father, as an interracial couple living in California during World War II, were confronted with governmental legislated prejudice against Asian Americans, more specifically the internment of Japanese Americans in relocation camps and the State of California's legal restriction of interracial marriage (Spickard, 1989). My own marriage to a European American has been a journey where many stereotypes had to be dispelled for it to continue and for us to create a new narrative for our relationship. Our children have continued our expanding narrative; they are living their own interpretation of our evolving interracial relationship. Was I an unbiased therapist? My answer is that I was not neutral. Moreover, I contributed to the therapy narrative my own experience as a biracial person in an interracial marriage by using selected strands of transparency. In my reflections about this couple work I feel that I learned the lesson that "it (is) possible to be open about what you were doing without lessening your influence (as a therapist)" (Hoffman, 2002, p. 14).

REFERENCES

Anderson, H. (1997). *Conversation, language, and possibilities: A postmodern approach to therapy.* New York: BasicBooks.

Anderson, H. & Goolishian, H. (1988). Human systems as linguistic systems: Evolving ideas about the implications for theory and practice. *Family Process, 27,* 371-393.

Anderson, H. & Goolishian, H. (1991). Revisiting history. *Australian-New Zealand Journal of Family Therapy*, 12, iii.

Fischer, M. M. J. (1986). Ethnicity and the post-modern arts of memory. In J. Clifford & G. E. Marcus (Eds.), *Writing culture: The poetics and politics of ethnography* (pp. 184-233). Berkeley, CA: University of California Press.

Gergen, K. J. (1990). Social understanding and the inscription of self. In J. W. Stigler, R. A. Shweder, & G. Herdt (Eds.), *Cultural psychology: Essays on comparative human development* (pp. 569-606). New York: Cambridge University Press.

Gergen, K. J. (1991). *The saturated self.* New York: BasicBooks.

Hoffman, L. (1992). A reflexive stance for family therapy. In S. McNamee & K. J. Gergen (Eds.), *Therapy as social construction* (pp. 7-24). Newbury Park, CA: Sage.

Hoffman, L. (2002). *Family therapy: An intimate history.* New York: W.W. Norton.

Hwang, S. S., Saenz, R., & Aguirre, B. E. (1997). Structural and assimilationist explanations of Asian American intermarriage. *Journal of Marriage and the Family*, 59, 758-772.

Kerwin, C. & Ponterotto, J. (1995). Biracial identity development: Theory and research. In J. Ponterotto, J. Casas, L. Suzuki, & C. Alexander (Eds.), *Handbook of multicultural counseling* (pp. 199-217). Thousand Oaks, CA: Sage.

Kich, G. (1992). The developmental process of asserting a biracial, bicultural identity. In M. Root (Ed.), *Racially mixed people in America* (pp. 304-317). Newbury Park, CA: Sage.

Lee, S. M. & Fernandez, M. (1998). Trends in Asian American racial/ethnic intermarriage: A comparison of 1980 and 1990 census data. *Sociological Perspectives*, 41, 323-342.

McGoldrick, M. & Giordano, J. (1996). Overview: Ethnicity and family therapy. In M. McGoldrick, J. Giordano, & J. K. Pearce (Eds.), *Ethnicity and family therapy* (pp.1-27). New York: The Guilford Press.

Spickard, P. R. (1989). *Mixed blood: Intermarriage and ethnic identity in twentieth-century America.* Madison: University of Wisconsin Press.

Tomm, K. (1987). Interventive interviewing: Part II. Reflexive questioning as a means to enable self-healing, *Family Process*, 26, 167-184.

Tomm, K. (1992, October). Interviewing the "internalized other." Presentation at the annual conference of the American Association for Marriage and Family Therapy, Miami Beach, Florida.

Tomm, K. (1998). A question of perspective. *Journal of Marital and Family Therapy*, 4, 409-413.

Waldegrave, C. (1990). Social justice and family therapy. *Dulwich Centre Newsletter*, 1.

White, M. & Epston, D. (1990). *Narrative means to therapeutic ends.* New York: Norton.

Therapists' Perspectives
on Working with Interracial Couples

Shruti S. Poulsen

SUMMARY. This paper is based on interviews with seven marriage and
family therapists (AAMFT Clinical Members) on their experiences of
providing therapy to interracial couples in the course of their private practices. The interviews were conducted by the author as part of a masters thesis project. Interracial couples may frequently present for therapy with a
variety of generic couples' issues and concerns. However, therapists often
find that underlying these more generic concerns are issues related to the
ethnic, racial, and cultural differences that the partners bring to the relationship. This paper focuses on the historical context of intermarriage,
specific concerns and issues that interracial couples experience in their relationships, and on the experiences of therapists providing therapeutic services to this diverse and challenging client population. *[Article copies
available for a fee from The Haworth Document Delivery Service: 1-800-HAWORTH.
E-mail address: <docdelivery@haworthpress.com> Website: <http://www.Haworth
Press.com> © 2003 by The Haworth Press, Inc. All rights reserved.]*

Shruti S. Poulsen, MA, is affiliated with the Department of Child Development and
Family Studies, Purdue University.

Address correspondence to: Shruti S. Poulsen, MA, Department of Child Development and Family Studies, Purdue University, 1269 Fowler House, West Lafayette, IN
47907-1269 (E-mail: poulsen4@aol.com).

The author would like to thank Harry Berman, PhD, of the University of Illinois at
Springfield for his help and support as Chair of the author's masters thesis committee.

The author would also like to acknowledge Margaret Keiley, PhD, and Volker
Thomas, PhD, of Purdue University for their support and encouragement in developing
this paper.

[Haworth co-indexing entry note]: "Therapists' Perspectives on Working with Interracial Couples."
Poulsen, Shruti S. Co-published simultaneously in *Journal of Couple & Relationship Therapy* (The Haworth
Press, Inc.) Vol. 2, No. 2/3, 2003, pp. 163-177; and: *Clinical Issues with Interracial Couples: Theories and
Research* (ed: Volker Thomas, Terri A. Karis, and Joseph L. Wetchler) The Haworth Press, Inc., 2003, pp.
163-177. Single or multiple copies of this article are available for a fee from The Haworth Document Delivery
Service [1-800-HAWORTH, 9:00 a.m. - 5:00 p.m. (EST). E-mail address: docdelivery@haworthpress.com].

http://www.haworthpress.com/store/product.asp?sku=J398
10.1300/J398v02n02_12

KEYWORDS. Interracial, intermarriage, therapy, relationship

INTERRACIAL COUPLES IN THE UNITED STATES: AN OVERVIEW

Interracial relationships in the United States have a long history, but only recently have they been the focus of research interest (Adams, 1973; Baptiste, 1984; Ho, 1990). Until the landmark case of Loving vs. Virginia (1967) when the United States Supreme Court questioned the constitutionality of statutes barring marriage for people from different racial backgrounds, intermarriages were still illegal in seventeen states (Tucker & Mitchell-Kernan, 1990; Zinn, 1980).

In 1970, interracial marriages represented .7 percent of all marriages. By 1992 this number had increased to 2.2 percent (Qian, 1999). This small but steady increase over the last few decades indicates that marriage across racial, ethnic and cultural lines will continue to be an option that couples choose (Cretser & Leon, 1982; Wilson, 1984).

Historically, the multicultural movement has existed since the late 1800s. In Chicago, the Manassah Society for black-white couples supported this movement from 1830 to 1932 ("Multiracial People," 1993). The multicultural movement began to make a significant impact in 1978 with the creation of Interracial Intercultural Pride Inc. in San Francisco ("Multiracial People," 1993). Despite these support networks for interracial couples and families, intermarriage continues to face social intolerance by couples' families and mainstream society. Even as recently as 1983, intolerance towards intermarriage was evident when the Texas Civil Liberties Union called for the removal of three justices of the peace who refused to perform interracial marriages (Ho, 1990).

Increasingly, changes in American demographics are leading to contact of young people across racial and cultural lines in schools and colleges, through employment, and through better-integrated communities. This, coupled with the greater opportunity for travel and exposure to diverse peoples and cultures, has led to an increasing awareness of interracial relationships (Kitano, 1984). For the purpose of this paper, the term interracial relationship will include heterosexual intimate partners whose race and ethnicity differ from each other (Ho, 1990).

Issues for Interracial Couples

All couples face inter- and intrapersonal challenges in their intimate relationships. Interracial couples experience similar relational issues and concerns that same-race couples do, but with added complexity due to differences in their racial, cultural, or ethnic backgrounds (Motoyoshi, 1990). Frequently the complexities of interracial relationships are portrayed in the research literature as problematic, pathological, and leading to relationship instability (Cerroni-Long, 1984; Fu, Tora, & Kendall, 2001; McGoldrick & Preto, 1984). However, research is increasingly also focusing on interracial relationships from a strength-based perspective in an attempt to understand the creative, proactive, and unique ways in which these couples engage in their relationships with their partners and with others (Davidson, 1992; Gaines, 1997; Negy & Snyder, 2000; Root, 2001). It is beyond the scope of this paper to review in depth the complexities of interracial relationships. The following section of this paper will provide a brief overview of some of the challenges and opportunities that interracial couples may experience in their relationship.

Social support. Though social attitudes towards interracial unions are changing, some segments of society still view such unions as something of an anomaly–a "gray area" that does not readily fit into the racial stratification system (Motoyoshi, 1990). Interracial couples, and especially black-white couples cannot ignore the impact of racial tensions and divisions in U.S. society (Brown, 1987). One mechanism interracial couples may use to deal with such ecological challenges is to intentionally isolate themselves from their own communities in an attempt to establish independence from their group's racism and intolerance (Pope, 1986; Ho, 1990; Solsberry, 1995). While interracial couples may at times feel isolated, they may also attempt to disconnect from individuals rather than entire communities that they experience as racist, and thus develop communities of their own choosing that are supportive and tolerant of their relationship (Hill & Thomas, 2000).

Family of origin. For interracial couples, a once satisfying and supportive relationship with extended family, may become subject to dramatic changes after the intermarriage (Ho, 1990). Interracial couples frequently have to deal with disapproval from extended family members, which in turn might lead couples to disconnect from these individuals (Fu, 2000). Though family disapproval may diminish over time and especially with the birth of children, couples may also develop relationships with others outside their family of origin to strengthen their social and kinship networks and to gain additional support (Fu, 2000; Gaines et al., 1999).

Development and the lifespan. Same-race couples and interracial couples experience the developmental stages of early marriage, parenthood and early childhood, middle childhood, adolescence, launching young adult children, pre-retirement, retirement, and old age over the course of their marital life (Erikson, 1950; Ho, 1990). For interracial couples, the transitions from stage to stage may be prone to cultural conflicts because these transitions are frequently times when identification in the form of rituals and symbols becomes more evident (Falicov, 1995; Ho, 1990). With each life-stage transition, the couple's racial and cultural identities may come into question if they are unable to turn to familiar mechanisms of adjustment such as cultural rituals because of their position in the interracial relationship (Falicov, 1995).

Parenting biracial children. Childrearing practices are deeply rooted in cultural contexts, and finding middle ground on this issue can be challenging (Ho, 1990). Interracial couples may experience tension and disagreement over childrearing practices, which in turn may negatively affect their relationship satisfaction.

Another aspect of parenting biracial children is the issue of developing a cultural and racial identity (McRoy & Freeman, 1986; Xie & Goyette, 1997). Parents of biracial children experience the additional challenge of helping their child negotiate the complexities of racial identification while at the same time dealing with normative adolescent developmental issues such as autonomy versus dependence, sexuality, self-identity, and peer groups (Gibbs, 1987; Gibbs & Moskowitz-Sweet, 1991).

Rationale for study. Interracial couples experience a variety of challenges and opportunities for growth and development in their intimate and social relationships. This study was developed to: (1) Understand how therapists perceive and deal with the issues and concerns that interracial couplepresent in therapy, and (2) Understand therapists' experience in providing therapy to these couples.

METHODS

The following section of this paper is based on interviews with seven therapists from Midwestern, metropolitan areas. The names and addresses of 140 therapists were drawn from AAMFT's 1992 *Register of Marriage and Family Therapy Providers*. The seven therapists in this study were recruited through an initial screening letter to determine if they had provided therapy to interracial couples, and if they would be available for an interview. Of the 140 letters sent, 28 were returned to sender due to expired forwarding orders. Another 41 therapists returned the initial screening form indicating they were unavailable for interviews due to insufficient experience with interracial couples or because they were no longer in clinical practice. No responses were received from the remaining 64 therapists.

Demographics of the therapists. All seven of the therapists interviewed were clinical members of AAMFT and three of the therapists were also AAMFT approved supervisors. Their years of experience as marriage and family therapists ranged from twelve to thirty years. Six of the therapists were in private practice. Of these six therapists, five were also full-time, tenured faculty at large, midwestern universities. The seventh therapist was employed as an administrator, supervisor, and clinician at a community social service agency. Five of the therapists were female and two were male. Of the female therapists, two were African-American. Five therapists reported their racial background as Caucasian of European descent. Two female therapists, one African-American and the other Caucasian, reported that they themselves were in interracial marriages.

Procedure. The interviews with each therapist consisted of one to two hour long, face-to-face sessions during which they were asked to talk about their experiences providing therapy to interracial couples. All but one therapist agreed to allow the interview to be audiotaped. Interviews were organized around several questions this author presented to the therapists. Examples of some of these questions are:

- Among the interracial couples that you see or have seen, what has been the presenting problem?
- What is your initial reaction to interracial couples and families in their first session? Do you form an initial hypothesis based on the intake information they provide?
- Are there any specific family therapy techniques that you have found particularly effective? What are these and in what ways do you find them useful?
- What do you believe about interracial marriages?

The questions that therapists were asked were meant to elicit information and recollections in three areas:

1. Therapists' reports of clients' presenting problems,
2. Therapists' perceptions of clients' issues, concerns, and relationship, and
3. Therapists' overall experiences providing marriage and family therapy to interracial couples.

Data analysis included listening to the audiotapes several times, transcribing the interviews, and coding therapists' answers for specific responses to the specific questions asked. In addition, interviews were analyzed for overarching themes and for therapists' personal reflections and retrospective recollections of their overall experiences of providing therapy to interracial couples.

Researcher background. This author's academic and professional interest in interracial relationships stems from her own personal experience of being a partner in an interracial relationship for over seventeen years. The author was born in India and has lived the majority of her life as an immigrant not only in the United States, but also in several countries across the world. Her spouse is Caucasian-American of European descent, and they are raising two biracial adolescents. As a marriage and family therapist who has also personally experienced the benefits of couple's therapy, this author is particularly interested in learning about the issue of interracial couples in therapy and how therapists experience these unique couples in therapy. Although this author's lived experiences have led her to believe that interracial couples deal with many of the same relationship and family issues and concerns that all couples deal with, she also believes that differences in culture, ethnicity, and race may present unique challenges and opportunities for interracial couples.

RESULTS AND DISCUSSION

The most common racial combination among the couples seen by the therapists were African-American and Caucasian couples. Some of the other couple combinations included Asian (East Indian or Chinese) and Caucasian, Hispanic and Caucasian, and one Asian and African-American couple. All the couples seen in therapy were heterosexual. Three therapists had seen as few as two to four couples in their twenty years of clinical practice. Three therapists had seen between eight to fourteen couples in approximately twenty to twenty-five years of clinical practice, while only one therapist had seen as many as fifty interracial couples in her twelve years of clinical experience. None of the therapists interviewed represented themselves as specializing in or having expertise in providing therapy specifically to interracial couples.

Therapists' perceptions of interracial couples' issues. Therapists reported that all the couples they had seen for therapy came to them for help with "generic" marital conflict issues. Among the issues that couples presented in therapy were conflict over expectations or belief systems, parenting issues, infidelity, alcoholism, lack of communication, sexual dysfunction, domestic violence, and coping with in-laws and extended family. For instance, one therapist working with a couple on issues of domestic violence reported:

> Some of the couples that came in, I think, would have very similar issues to non-interracial couples; it was just the same male authoritarian, dominant pattern versus codependency female pattern. . . . It was very rigid. . . . So in some ways, they were similar to any other couples. Sometimes the assumptions, the rigidity of . . . I don't know whether to call it of culture or of the family of origin.

Although therapists did not want to discount the possibility that the couples' racial, cultural, and ethnic backgrounds would also have an effect on the relationship and functioning, they reported that most interracial couples they had provided therapy to generally presented with similar problems as same-race couples.

Social support. When asked whether interracial couples face any special concerns, the therapists reported that they believed that there might be greater potential for concerns because of social perceptions of, and intolerance towards such unions. Therapists tended to include the issue of racial and ethnic differences in their own assessment of the clients' presenting problems while they also wrestled with their own values and beliefs about interracial relationships.

> Well, you know, I think of myself as being a liberal person but I guess I was looking at them as 'yes, this has to be stressful' . . . there's certainly problems that they are probably going to be facing socially, and their children, socially.

As this quote reflects, therapists acknowledged that their own internalized biases were interwoven with their desire to be sensitive to their clients' experiences when considering the influence of social support on an intimate relationship.

Family of origin issues. Therapists also reported on concerns that interracial couples might face as a result of lack of family support. Some of these concerns may be related to the extent to which their families of origin identify with their culture and the impact this may have on the couple. This was illustrated by one therapist's response:

If it starts out negative, where one family doesn't approve. The family that I saw–the wife was Jewish (Caucasian) and the husband was black. And so there were a lot of ethnic problems there because you know, they're both in a way, minority groups. So they both had strong issues or feelings about the marriage. It seemed like the black family in this case accepted her more than the Jewish family was accepting him.

Developmental and life cycle issues. Developmental issues within a couple's marital and family life were also cited as a concern. One therapist indicated that with one partner's increased education and exposure to her heritage over her life span, marital tensions also increased as a result of this person's "sudden" (as perceived by her partner) involvement and interest in her ethnic heritage.

Where suddenly someone becomes extraordinarily ethnic, starting wearing ethnic costumes. I was working with one couple here, black-white couple, in which she became very militant and began wearing African costume. She was coming into a sense of ownership of her heritage. Not quite a "roots" issue. Although I think, the more she became educated within the university setting, she became more polarized around differences.

This therapist, although attempting to acknowledge the impact of developmental events on the client's sense of identity and her relationship, may indeed not fully understand the client's reality. This quote may reflect some of the therapist's own internalized cultural biases of how differences and ethnicity are perceived to be located in the individual rather than in the relationship. However, it is important to note that although identity development is a process undertaken in adolescence, cultural identity development may indeed continue to be influenced by significant events over the lifespan and with increased maturity (Erikson, 1950; Okun, 1996).

Parenting biracial children. Although not all the therapists had actual experience providing therapy to the whole family system, they reported on several issues that interracial couples might have to cope with pertaining to parenting of biracial children. Some of the concerns that couples face are those that their biracial children might also face; for example, the lack of extended family support for the parents' interracial relationship. In addition to family attitudes towards the relationship, the parents' own level of adjustment and acceptance of their interracial relationship may have an impact on the children's racial self-concept and identity. For instance, according to one therapist:

> When you do have children, you have to give the kids a sense of identity, and I think that that's a big issue, especially as they get older; who are they, because they identify with one race or the other, or are they kind of a mixture of both and acknowledging that?

> . . . only thing that would be an issue is to make sure it's not a loy-alty thing, so that if you think the white race is better, or the black race is better, then who are you loyal to?

While it is generally normative for all adolescents to deal with identity formation and the influence of social pressures, issues such as differences in skin coloring and racism within their own family and in society, not feeling like they fit in anywhere, and difficulty identifying with either parent may be areas of potential concern for biracial children (Erikson, 1950; Gibbs, 1987). One therapist reported that some interracial couples he had worked with were aware of the potential for such concerns in raising biracial children and that this may have lead them to take a rather unique approach with this issue.

> I have met biracial [interracial] couples who have decided to adopt rather than biologically parent children . . . well, rather than create confusion by being half-black, half-white, we will adopt black children . . . or, I met one couple, she was white, he was black, they adopted Asian [children].

Interestingly, it seems that interracial couples who chose this particular avenue may have felt more able to deal with the complexities that can arise in raising transracially adopted children (Hollingsworth, 1997; Taylor & Thornton, 1996) than in raising biracial children.

Therapists' experience and responses. In addition to questions on the issues and concerns that interracial couples present in therapy, therapists were also asked to think about their own reactions and responses to their interracial clients.

> Curiosity. Because I think each time you have to . . . you really have to do a lot of circular questioning like you would any other

family. But with an interracial couple or family you even have to do more; you'd have to understand how they're working.

Therapists' reactions tended to be curiosity and interest in finding out more about the couple's backgrounds and experiences, and wanting to be sensitive and respectful to their clients' realities. Therapists may have also believed that coming from a non-expert stance with interracial couples was one way they could provide space for the couples' own narratives while at the same time increasing their understanding and appreciation of the complex nature of these relationships.

In developing an initial hypothesis for working with the couple, therapists reported that they considered the racial backgrounds of the individuals involved. Therapists' initial reactions included a desire to explore issues of racial and ethnic differences in the couple's relationship.

> I would ask them, do you believe that your ethnic-cultural-racial identity has anything to do with this problem? . . . depending on how they would respond to that, I would ask them to clarify . . . how they think that contributes to or helps minimize the problems they're experiencing.

This therapist overtly addressed the issue of the clients' racial and ethnic differences and at the same time left space for the possibility that these issues did not only contribute to problems in the relationship but might even help minimize some of these problems.

Five of the seven therapists interviewed were clinicians and teachers in academic settings. Therefore their overall response to the concept of interracial relationships was positive and seemed to lack the racial intolerance or prejudice that couples might face in mainstream society.

> . . . I don't believe there are impediments that *have* to be impediments, but it's your assumptions and your beliefs about those differences and how permeable they are, or how rigid they are . . . if you are comfortable with differences and have seen adults in your life handle differences, or if you have not, then you really struggle.

Overall, therapists tried to maintain a sense of curiosity and openness to learning about the lived experiences of interracial clients in order to be more effective in their therapy and to better understand their clients' reality.

Marriage and family therapy techniques. Therapists were asked specifically about marriage and family therapy techniques and any personally creative techniques they might have used in their work with interracial couples. One therapist's perspective appropriately summed up the general consensus among the therapists on the issue of techniques:

> My understanding of techniques is that it's something you use until the real therapist comes along . . . when you feel more comfortable with people, you don't use techniques. I mean, you might use them as a "sit down, would you like some coffee?," that's a technique to make people comfortable, "let's do a genogram," but what you're getting at is information that will help you carry on a conversation.

The belief that techniques were less central to successful work with interracial couples than therapist attitudes and beliefs, was expressed in this statement:

> What we need to do is examine how we think about and conduct marital therapy [rather than focus on specific techniques, there is a need for professionals to address how their roles and attitudes as therapists affect interracial couple clients]–is [techniques] that sufficient to deal with issues related to race?

The therapists in this study seemed to agree that for clinicians to successfully provide support to interracial couples it would be crucial that therapists understand the historical, social, and psychological context in which these relationships are based. The therapists in this study also indicated a need for flexibility in their ways of conceptualizing interracial relationships, and a willingness to remain genuinely open to their clients' narratives rather than focusing on therapy techniques.

The use of creativity was not necessarily unique to therapists' work with just interracial couples, but therapists did find creativity to be an effective tool in their work with these couples. Some examples of the creative use of techniques included assigning "homework" such as watching appropriate movies or recommending reading to clients to help them become more culturally aware of their partner's background. For example, movies like "Jungle Fever" or "Mississippi Masala" might be suggested to encourage dialogue on racial and cultural stereotyping and their impact on relationships. Reading fiction such as *White Teeth* (Smith, 2000) might also provide couples with a way to understand the complexities, richness, and experiences of interracial relationships and family life.

One therapist reported that the use of a creative technique such as family sculpting could be beneficial for couples dealing with issues such as displays of affection. For interracial couples public displays of affection may be negatively interpreted or pathologized by mainstream society (Gaines, 1997), while in private they may struggle with cultural differences in issues of proximity and expression of affection (Strong, Devault, Sayad, & Cohen, 2001).

> . . . again I can use this with and have used it with same-race couples . . . is that of the affection issues, physical displays of affection. Sometimes I do the sculpting kinds of things, to get a sense of what they [the couple] want from each other as far as physical displays of affection and that kind of thing. Because again, in different cultures, closeness and distance issues in physical space . . . to help them communicate that better, because it's hard to say it in words . . .

Another therapist's use of personal creativity involved suggesting different ways for the couple to think about themselves and their relationship:

> Asking them to think of themselves as if they were not an interracial couple, but they still have to come up with a solution . . . as if there were not those differences there. Forgiving them for a while to have to defend those positions . . . if they only have the loyalties to one another to worry about for the next fifteen minutes, then they don't have to justify this position to any family member . . . what then will they do?

Providing therapy in creative and flexible ways rather than adhering rigidly to specific therapeutic techniques may contribute to a successful and supportive relationship with interracial clients and may also challenge clients to think about their relationship and issues in different ways.

CONCLUSION

Interracial couples experience challenges and difficulties in their intimate relationship, and may seek therapy just as same-race couples do. Therapists who have experience providing therapy to interracial couples may be a valuable source of insight and information on ways in which to successfully support and work with these couples, and this study is a brief exploration of this insight and information. Limitations to this study include the small sample size and the focus on just the therapists' experiences. Another limitation to the study is that the race and gender of the therapists were not included as part of the data analysis. In retrospect, this author believes that including those two variables in the analysis would have provided important contextual information and depth to the study. However, the interviews with the therapists provide a brief glimpse into the complexities and challenges of interracial relationships, and providing therapeutic services to these couples.

An area of future study is further exploration of the lived experiences of interracial couples and their experiences participating in marriage and family therapy. Researchers are beginning to study interracial couples from a strengths-based perspective and to explore how these relationships can be a source of resilience and tolerance at personal and social levels (Root, 2001; Rosenblatt, Karis, & Powell, 1995). However, more research in these areas would provide a much needed updated perspective to the traditionally pathologizing and problem-based literature on interracial relationships. Finally, an area for further study is that of developing a better understanding of the similarities and differences between specific racial combinations such Asian and Caucasian or African-American and their levels of relationship functioning. All of these suggested areas of study could potentially add to the overall understanding and knowledge for clinicians providing services to an increasingly diverse client population.

REFERENCES

Adams, P.L. (1973). Counseling with interracial couples and their children in the south. In I.R. Stuart & L.E. Abt (Eds.), *Interracial marriages: Expectations and realities* (pp. 63-79). New York: Grossman Publishers.

Baptiste, D.A. (1984). Marriage and family therapy with racially/culturally intermarried stepfamilies: Issues and guidelines. *Family Relations, 33*, 373-380.

Brown, J.A. (1987). Casework contacts with black-white couples. *The Journal of Contemporary Social Work, 68*, 24-29.

Cerroni-Long, E.L. (1984). Marrying out: Socio-cultural and psychological implications of intermarriage. *Journal of Comparative Family Studies, 16(1)*, 25-46.

Cretser, G.A. & Leon, J.J. (1982). Intermarriage in the U.S.: An overview of theory and research. In G.A. Cretser & J.J. Leon (Eds.), *Intermarriage in the United States* (pp. 3-15). New York: The Haworth Press, Inc.

Davidson, J.R. (1992). Theories about Black-White interracial marriage: A clinical perspective. *Journal of Multicultural Counseling and Development, 20,* 150-157.

Erikson, E. (1950). *Childhood and society.* New York: Norton.

Falicov, C.J. (1995). Cross-cultural marriages. In N.S. Jacobson & A.S. Gurman (Eds.), *Clinical handbook of couple therapy* (pp. 231-246). New York: The Guilford Press.

Fu, X. (2000). An interracial study of marital disruption in Hawaii: 1983 to 1996. *Journal of Divorce & Remarriage, 32(3/4),* 73-92.

Fu, X., Tora, J., & Kendall, H. (2001). Marital happiness and inter-racial marriage: A study in a multi-ethnic community in Hawaii. *Journal of Comparative Family Studies, 32(1),* 47-60.

Gaines, S.O. (1997). Communalism and the reciprocity of affection and respect among interethnic married couples. *Journal of Black Studies, 27(3),* 352-364.

Gaines, S.O., Granrose, C.S., Rios, D.I., Garcia, B.F., Youn, M.S., Farris, K.R., & Bledsoe, K.L. (1999). Patterns of attachment and responses to accommodative dilemmas among interethnic/interracial couples. *Journal of Social and Personal Relationships, 16(2),* 275-285.

Gibbs, J.T. (1987). Identity and marginality: Issues in the treatment of biracial adolescents. *American Journal of Orthopsychiatry, 57,* 265-278.

Gibbs, J.T. & Moskowitz-Sweet, G. (1991). Clinical and cultural issues in the treatment of biracial and bicultural adolescents. *The Journal of Contemporary Human Services, 72,* 579-589.

Hill, M.R. & Thomas, V. (2000). Strategies for racial identity development: Narratives of Black and White women in interracial partner relationships. *Family Relations: Interdisciplinary Journal of Applied Family Studies, 49(2),* 193-200.

Ho, M.K. (1990). *Intermarried couples in therapy.* Springfield, IL: Charles C. Thomas.

Hollingsworth, L.D. (1997). Effect of transracial/transethnic adoption on children's racial and ethnic identity and self-esteem: A meta-analytic review. *Marriage & Family Review, 25(1/2),* 99-130.

Kitano, H.H., Yeung, W.T., Chai, L., & Hatanaka, H. (1984). Asian-American interracial marriage. *Journal of Marriage and the Family, 46,* 179-190.

McGoldrick, M. & Preto, N.G. (1984). Ethnic intermarriage: Implications for therapy. *Family Process, 23(3),* 347-364.

McRoy, R.G. & Freeman, E. (1986). Racial identity issues among mixed-race children. *Social Work in Education, 8,* 164-174.

Motoyoshi, M.M. (1990). The experience of mixed-race people: Some thoughts and theories. *The Journal of Ethnic Studies, 18,* 77-89.

Multiracial People want a single name that fits (1993, May). *Chicago Tribune,* p. 1.

Negy, C. & Snyder, D.K. (2000). Relationship satisfaction of Mexican American and non-Hispanic White American interethnic couples: Issues of acculturation and clinical intervention. *Journal of Marital and Family Therapy, 26(3),* 293-204.

Pope, B.R. (1986). Black in interracial relationships: Psychological and therapeutic issues. *Journal of Multicultural Counseling and Development, 14,* 10-16.

Qian, B.F. (1996). Who intermarries? Education, nativity, region, and interracial marriage, 1980-1990. *Journal of Comparative Family Studies, 30(4),* 579-597.

Root, M. (2001). *Love's revolution: Interracial marriage.* Philadelphia: Temple University.

Rosenblatt, P.C., Karis, T.A., & Powell, R.D. (1995). *Multiracial couples: Black and White voices.* Thousand Oaks, CA: Sage.

Smith, Z. (2000). *White Teeth.* New York: Random House.

Solsberry, P.W. (1995). Interracial couples in the United States of America: Implications for mental health counseling. *Journal of Mental Health Counseling, 16(3),* 304-317.

Strong, B., Devault, C., Sayad, B., & Cohen, T. (2001). *The Marriage and Family Experience (8th ed).* California: Wadsworth/Thompson Learning Inc.

Taylor, R.J. & Thornton, M.C. (1996). Child welfare and transracial adoption. *Journal of Black Psychology, 22(2),* 282-291.

Tucker, M.B. & Mitchell-Kernan, C. (1990). New trends in black American interracial marriage: The social structural context. *Journal of Marriage and the Family, 52,* 209-218.

Wilson, B.F. (1984). Marriage's melting pot. *American Demographics, 6,* 34-45.

Xie, Y. & Goyette, K. (1997). The racial identification of biracial children with one Asian parent: Evidence from the 1990 Census. *Social Forces, 76(2),* 547-570.

Zinn, H. (1980). *A people's history of the United States* (pp. 54-55). New York: Harper & Row.

Index

Acculturation
  in intercultural therapy with Latino
      immigrants and white partners,
      140-142
  perceived levels of, in Latino/a and
      white marriages, 52
  from white majority group to
      Latino/a minority group, in
      Latino/a and white marriages,
      52
Aguirre, B.E., 159
"Alpha bias," 95
Antagonism, by family of origin,
      toward interracial and intercultural
      lesbian couples, 93
Ariel, J., 98
Arrendondo, P., 69
Asian American couples, research-
      based conversation with, 157-160
Asian American intermarriage, 151-162
  therapeutic methods for, 154-157

Bacigalupe, G., 2, 131
Bepko, 105, 111
Berg, R.R., 42
"Beta bias," 95
Bias(es)
  "alpha," 95
      avoidance of, by interracial and
          intercultural lesbian couples, 96
  "beta," 95
Biracial children, parenting of, for
      interracial couples, 166
  study of, 170-171
Black men, with white women, race
      impact on, 23-40. See also Interracial

relationships, white women with black
      men, race impact on
Black-white multiracial couples
  assessment and intervention with,
      115-129
  clinical preparation for, 118-120
      self of the therapist, 118-120
  discussion, 127
  grief, 126
  initial assessment, 120-123
      class differences, 121-122
      race, 122
  parenting, 125-126
  social network/social support,
      123-125
  target intervention areas, 123
  domestic violence in, 124-125
  public attitude toward, 117
"Border patrolling," 38
Boston marriages, 89
Boyd-Franklin, N., 92,93,94

Celebrations, non-Muslim, in
      multicultural Muslim
      couples' relationships, 62-63
Census data, on interracial couples, 88-89
Chai, L., 76
Chan, A.Y., 79,121
Chan, C.S., 95
Child rearing
  in interracial relationships, 78
  in multicultural Muslim couples'
      relationships, 64-66
Children
  biracial, parenting of, for interracial
      couples, 166

study of, 170-171
influence of, on Latino/a and white
    marriages, 49-50
in multicultural Muslim couples'
    relationships, 64-66
Chinese Exclusion Act of 1882, 159
Christian-Muslim couples, 57-71. *See
    also* Muslim couples, multicultural
Civil Rights Movement, 88
Class
    differences of, in assessment and
        intervention with black-white
        multiracial couples, 121-122
    sensitivity to, for interracial and
        intercultural lesbian couples,
        96-97
Clinician(s). *See also* Therapist(s)
    family-of-origin work of, 119
    role in assessment and intervention
        with black-white multiracial
        couples, 115-129
        clinical preparation for, 118-120
            self of therapist, 118-120
        cultural genogram in, 119-120
        discussion, 127
        grief, 126
        initial assessment, 120-123
            class differences, 121-122
            race, 122
        parenting, 125-126
        social network/social support,
            123-125
        target intervention areas, 123
Communication issues, in interracial
    relationships, 77-78
Community(ies)
    in Latino cross-cultural same sex
        male relationships, 106
    lesbian, limited connection to, by
        interracial and intercultural
        lesbian couples, 93-94
Community issues, in multicultural
    Muslim couples' relationships,
    61-62
Consciousness, double, 15-16

Conversation, research-based, with
    Asian American couples, 157-160
Couples therapy
    conversations in, alternative
        metaphors for, 142-144. *See
        also* Intercultural therapy,
        with Latino immigrants and
        white partners, alternative
        metaphors for
    with Latino immigrants and white
        partners, 131-149. *See also*
        Intercultural therapy, with
        Latino immigrants and white
        partners
Crohn, J., 24
Cross-cultural relationships, same sex
    male, Latino, 103-113. *See also*
        Same sex male relationships,
        Latino cross-cultural
Cultural expansion, by interracial and
    intercultural lesbian couples, 95
Cultural genogram, 119-120
Cultural homelessness, 141
Culture
    intercultural therapy and, 134-136
    new, adjustment to, by interracial
        and intercultural lesbian
        couples, 93

Daneshpour, M., 2, 57
Dating, interracial, predictors of, 116
Davidson, J.R., 68
Dean, L., 104
Developmental issues, for interracial
    couples, 165-166
    study of, 170
Developmental Research Sequence, 46
Discourse, dominant, defined, 4
Discrimination, defined, 6
Domestic violence, in black-white
    multiracial couples, 124-125
Dominant discourses, defined, 4
Double consciousness, 15-16

Dress codes, Islamic, in multicultural
    Muslim couples' relationships, 63-64
Dual awareness, of race impact on
    interracial relationships, 35-37
Duality, 15
DuBois, 15
Dyadic double consciousness, 15-16
Dyche, L., 134

Early, G., 111
Ellis, H., 89
Empathy, in intercultural therapy, 136
Ethnicity, 16-17

Faderman, 89
Falicov, C.J., 106
Family
    extended, contact with, changing
        racial meanings and, 33-35
    influence of, in assessment and
        intervention with black-white
        multiracial couples, 124
    perceived reactions from, to
        Latino/a and white marriages,
        50-52
    role of, in multicultural Muslim
        couples' relationships, 68-69
    understanding of, in intercultural
        therapy with Latino
        immigrants and white
        partners, 139-140
Family of origin
    antagonism by, toward interracial
        and intercultural lesbian
        couples, 93
    in interracial couples, 165
        study of, 169-170
    in Latino cross-cultural same sex
        male relationships, 106
Family of origin work, in black-white
    multiracial couples' intervention, 119
Family opposition, to interracial
    relationships, 76

Family sphere, public sphere *vs.*, in
    interracial relationships, drawing line
    between, 28-29
Family therapy, for interracial couples,
    techniques of, study of, 172-174
Female relationships, same sex,
    interracial and intercultural, 85-101.
        See also Lesbian couples,
        interracial and intercultural
Fernandez, M., 159
Frankenberg, R., 26,27,90
Friend(s)
    influence of, in assessment and
        intervention with black-white
        multiracial couples, 124
    perceived reactions from, to
        Latino/a and white marriages,
        50-52
Friendships
    in multicultural Muslim couples'
        relationships, 63
    romantic, 89

Gay relationships
    female, interracial and intercultural,
        85-101. *See also* Lesbian couples,
        interracial and intercultural
    male, Latino cross-cultural, 103-113.
        See also Same sex male
        relationships, Latino
        cross-cultural
Gender
    in interracial and intercultural
        lesbian couples, 97
    mixed reactions on basis of, to
        Latino/a and white marriages,
        50-52
    in multicultural Muslim couples'
        relationships, 66-67
Genogram, cultural, 119-120
Geography, social, interracial
    relationships in Hawaii and, 74-75
Giordano, J., 67
Gottman, J.M., 17
Greene, B., 92,93,94

Grief, in assessment and intervention
    with black-white multiracial
    couples, 126
Grounded theory approach, 7

Ham, M.D-C., 2, 151
Hardy, K.V., 119
Hare-Mustin, R.T., 95
Hatanaka, H., 76
Hawaii
    immigration history of, 75
    interracial relationships in, issues,
        benefits, and therapeutic
        interventions for, 73-83. *See
        also* Interracial relationships,
        in Hawaii, issues, benefits,
        and therapeutic interventions
        for
    racial groups in, 74-75
    residents of, unification of, 75
Heterogamy, 4
Heterosexism, 104-105
Ho, M.K., 78
Holidays, non-Muslim, in multicultural
    Muslim couples' relationships, 62-63
Homelessness, cultural, 141
Homogamy. *See also* Interracial
    couples, responses of, to racism and
        partner differences
    dominant discourse of, 4-5
    interracial couples' experiences of, 7-8
Hwang, S.S., 159
HyperRESEARCH, 7

Ibrahim, F.A., 69
Immigrant(s), Latino, and white
    partners, intercultural therapy with,
        131-149. *See also*
        Intercultural therapy, with
        Latino immigrants and white
        partners
Inside the Mixed Marriage, 53
Intercultural couples, lesbian, 85-101.
    See also Lesbian couples,
        interracial and intercultural

Intercultural therapy
    culture and, 134-136
    empathy in, 136
    indigenous (emic) categories of
        experience and, 135-136
    with Latino immigrants and white
        partners, 131-149
    alternative metaphors for, 142-144
        couples as nations, 143
        couples multi-tasking, 143-144
        crossing borderlands, 142-143
    intercultural couple issues in,
        136-142
        acculturation, 140-142
        creating intimacy and trust,
            140-142
        plurality of language and
            languages, 137-139
        understanding self and
            family, 139-140
    overview of, 132-134
    narrative theory in, 135-136
    non-indigenous (etic) categories of
        experience and, 135-136
    respect in, 136
Interethnic couples. *See also*
    Interracial couples; Interracial
        relationships
    experiences of, study of, 41-55. *See
        also* Latino/a and white
        marriages, experiences of,
        study of
Intermarriage, Asian American,
    151-162. *See also* Asian American
        intermarriage
"Internalized other" interviewing,
    154-155
Interracial Couple Questionnaire, 80
Interracial couples. *See also* Interracial
    relationships; Multiracial couples
    Asian American, 151-162. *See also*
        Asian American
        intermarriage
    clinical issues with, introduction to,
        1-2

historical perspective on, 164
homogamy's effect on, 7-8
issues for, 164-166
  development and lifespan, 165-166
  family of origin, 165
  parenting biracial children, 166
  social support, 165
  therapists' perceptions of, study
    of, 168-169
lesbian, 85-101. *See also* Lesbian
    couples, interracial and
    intercultural
responses of, to racism and partner
    differences, 3-21
  implications for therapy, 16-18
  introduction to, 4
  strategies of, 8-14
    deprioritizing racial
        differences, 11-14
    disassociating from one
        another, 9-10
    "fighting fire with fire," 9
    "making a special effort," 9
    not discussing negative public
        reactions, 10-11
    restricting itinerary, 10
  study of
    discussion, 14-16
    dyadic double consciousness,
        15-16
    grounded theory approach to
        analysis, 7
    HyperRESEARCH in, 7
    method, 6-7
    procedure, 6-7
    sample, 6
    survival strategies, 14-15
  study of, 166-174
    future studies in, 175
    limitations of, 175
    methods for, 166-168
      procedure, 167-168
      researcher background, 168
      therapists' demographics, 167
    rationale for, 166

results and discussion of,
    168-174
  development and life cycle
    issues, 170
  family of origin issues,
    169-170
  marriage and family therapy
    techniques, 172-174
  parenting biracial children,
    170-171
  social support, 169
  therapists' experience and
    responses, 171-172
  therapists' perceptions of
    interracial
    couples' issues,
    168-169
support groups for, 80
therapists' perspectives on
    working with, 163-177
in United States, overview of, 164-166
Interracial dating, predictors of, 116
Interracial Intercultural Pride Inc., 164
Interracial marriages
  approval rate of, 5
  consequences of, personal and
    systemic, 18
  incidence of, 164
  prevalence of, 42,116
Interracial relationship prejudice,
    interracial and intercultural
    lesbian couples and, 91-92
Interracial relationships. *See also*
    Interracial couples
  benefits of, 78-79
  black-white, stereotypes about, 27-28
  in Hawaii
  benefits of, 78-79
  immigration history and, 75
  issues for, 75-78
    child rearing, 78
    communication issues, 77-78
    family opposition, 76
    language barrier, 77-78
    sexuality, 78
    societal intolerance, 76-77

promotion of, history of, 75
social geography and, 74-75
therapeutic interventions for, 79-80
unification of Hawaii residents
    and, 75
unique setting for, 74-75
historical background of, 14, 88
issues for, 75-78
    child rearing, 78
    communication issues, 77-78
    family opposition, 76
    language barrier, 77-78
    sexuality, 78
    societal intolerance, 76-77
therapeutic interventions for, 79-80
white women with black men
    private family sphere *vs.* public
        sphere, drawing line between,
        28-29
    race as situationally and
        relationally constructed for, 29-30
    race impact on, 23-40
        dual awareness of, 35-37
        how race does not matter for,
            claim of, 27-30
        how race matters for, 30-35
        contact with extended family
            members and, 33-35
        stereotypes impacting rela-
            tionships, 30-33
        stereotypes impacting
            women's
            self-identity, 30-33
    overview of, 24
    study of
        data analysis, 25-26
        data collection, 25-26
        participants, 25
        research methodology, 25-26
        therapeutic implications of, 37-39
    stereotypes about, 27-28
Interviewing, "internalized other," 154-155
Intimacy, creation of, in intercultural
    therapy with Latino immigrants and
    white partners, 140-142

Islam, in multicultural Muslim
    couples' relationships, 61

Jenkins, S.R., 141
Johnson, M., 26
Johnson, T., 105,111
Johnson, W.K., 53
"Jungle Fever," 173

Karis, T.A., 1,2,23,53
Kearl, M.C., 42
Killian, K.D., 2, 3
Kitano, H.H., 76

Laird, J., 97
Lakoff, G., 26
Language, plurality of, in intercultural
    therapy with Latino immigrants and
        white partners, 137-139
Language barrier, in interracial
    relationships, 77-78
Laszloffy, T.A., 119
Latino(s), in United States, 105-106
Latino cross-cultural relationships,
    same sex male, 103-113. *See also*
        Same sex male relationships,
        Latino cross-cultural
Latino immigrants, and white partners,
    intercultural therapy with, 131-149.
        See also Intercultural therapy,
        with Latino immigrants and
        white partners
Latino/a and white marriages
    experiences of
        study of, 41-55
            clinical implications of, 53-54
            discussion of, 52-54
            findings of, 46-52
            acculturation from white
                majority group to
                Latino/a minority
                group, 52

additional societal pressures,
49
children's influence, 49-50
experiences and perceptions
of being in a
marriage with
someone from a
different racial
and/or ethnic group,
47-50
idealized perception of
"other," 47-48
mixed reactions on basis of
ethnic background
and gender, 50-52
perceived levels of
acculturation and
multiculturalism, 52
perceived reactions from
family, friends and
social institutions,
50-52
similar outlook on life, 48-49
limitations of, 54
methods, 43-46
data analysis, 46
interview protocol, 45-46
participants, 44-45
researcher, 43-44
purpose of, 43
themes of, 53
prevalence of, 42
rates of, 132-133
Lee, S.M., 159
Lesbian community, limited
connection to, by interracial and
intercultural lesbian couples,
93-94
Lesbian couples
history of, 89-90
interracial and intercultural, 85-101
challenges for, 91-94
adjustment to new culture, 93
antagonism by family of origin,
93

interracial relationship
prejudice, 91-92
limited connection to lesbian
community, 93-94
managing multiple
differences, 91
historical context of, 87-90
increase in number of,
evidence of, 88-89
interracial relationships
history, 88
increase in number of, evidence
of, 88-89
story related to, 86-87
strengths of, 94-95
cultural expansion, 95
heightened awareness of
destructiveness of
racism, 94-95
therapeutic considerations for, 95-98
avoiding alpha and beta bias,
95-96
avoiding stereotypes and
biases, 96
class sensitivity, 96-97
fostering support, 98
gender, 97
parenting, 97-98
Life cycle issues, for interracial
couples, 165-166
study of, 170
Liu, P., 95
Long, J., 2,85
Lott-Whitehead, L., 98
Loving v. Commonwealth of Virginia, 42
Loving *vs.* Virginia, 164
Luke, C., 26

Male relationships, same sex, Latino
cross-cultural, 103-113. *See
also* Same sex male relationships,
Latino cross-cultural
Manassah Society, 164
Marriage(s)

Asian American, 151-162. *See also* Asian American intermarriage
Boston, 89
interracial
approval rate of, 5
consequences of, personal and systemic, 18
incidence of, 164
prevalence of, 42, 116
Latino/a and white
experiences of, study of, 41-55. *See also* Latino/a and white marriages, experiences of, study of
rates of, 132-133
Marriage therapy, for interracial couples, techniques of, study of, 172-174
McDavis, R.J., 69
McGoldrock, M., 67
McPherson, D.W., 98
Men, black, with white women, race impact on, 23-40. *See also* Interracial relationships, white women with black men, race impact on
Mexican Americans, intermarriages of, 42. *See also* Latino/a and white marriages
Meyer, I.H., 104
"Mississippi Masala," 173
Morningstar, B., 98
"Multicultural ecosystemic comparative approach" (MECA), 106
Multicultural Muslim couples, 57-71. *See also* Muslim couples, multicultural
Multiculturalism, perceived levels of, in Latino/a and white marriages, 52
Multiracial Couples: Black and White Voices, 53
Multiracial couples, black-white, assessment and intervention with, 115-129. *See also* Black-white multiracial couples, assessment and intervention with

Multiracial families. *See also* Interracial relationships
white women in, 26-27
Murguia, E., 42
Muslim(s), presence in United States, 58
Muslim couples, multicultural, 57-71
areas of stress or tension for, 60
challenges of, 60-67
acceptable dress, 63-64
community issues, 61-62
friendship circles, 63
gender, 66-67
non-Muslim celebrations, 62-63
parenting and child rearing issues, 64-66
power, 66-67
religious compatibility, 61
social issues, 61-62
family members role in, 68-69
lives of, methodology, 58-59
myths and stereotypes related to, 68
similarities with other couples, 59-60
therapy with, approaches, interventions, and strategies for, 67-70
Muslim-Christian couples, 57-71. *See also* Muslim couples, multicultural
Muzio, C., 98

Narrative theory, in intercultural therapy, 135-136
Nazario, A., 2,103,111
Negy, C., 43, 133

O'Connell, A., 98
Okun, B.F., 69, 79
Oppression sensitive approach, to Latino cross-cultural same sex male relationships, 110-111

Padilla, A.M., 42

Parenting
   in assessment and intervention with
      black-white multiracial
      couples, 125-126
   of biracial children, for interracial
      couples, 166
      study of, 170-171
   in interracial and intercultural
      lesbian couples, 97-98
Parenting issues, in multicultural
      Muslim couples' relationships, 64-66
Partner differences, interracial couples
      responses to, 3-21. *See also* Interracial
      couples, responses of, to racism
      and partner differences
Pearce, J.K., 67
Pearlman, S.F., 89
Pinderhughes, E., 88
Pope, B.R., 76
Porterfield, E., 5
Poulsen, S.S., 2, 73, 163
Powell, R.D., 53
Power, in multicultural Muslim
      couples' relationships, 66-67
Prejudice, interracial relationship,
      interracial and intercultural lesbian
      couples and, 91-92
Public reaction, to interracial couples,
      3-21. *See also* Interracial couples,
      responses of, to racism and
      partner differences
Public sphere, private family sphere
      vs., in interracial relationships,
      drawing line between, 28-29

Race
   in assessment and intervention with
      black-white multiracial couples,
      122
   concept of, 29
   impact on white women with black
      men relationships, 23-40. *See
      also* Interracial relationships,

      white women with black
      men, race impact on
   as situationally and relationally
      constructed, 29-30
   social constructionist views of,
      29-30
Racial differences, deprioritizing, 11-14
Racism
   defined, 6
   destructiveness of, heightened
      awareness of, by interracial
      and intercultural lesbian
      couples, 94-95
   internalized, 92
   interracial couples responses to,
      3-21. *See also* Interracial
      couples, responses of, to
      racism and partner
      differences
   manifestations of, 5-6
*Register of Marriage and Family
      Therapy Providers*, 166
Religious compatibility, in
      multicultural Muslim couples'
      relationships, 61
Research-based conversation, with
      Asian American couples, 157-160
Researchers, as conversational
      partners, 157-160
Respect, in intercultural therapy, 136
Rodriguez, 133
Romantic friendships, 89
Roosevelt, E., 89
Root, M.P.P., 77, 133
Rosenblatt, P.C., 2,53,115

Saenz, R., 159
Salgado de Snyder, N., 42
Same sex couples, lesbian, interracial
      and intercultural, 85-101. *See also*
      Lesbian couples, interracial
      and intercultural
Same sex male relationships
   issues related to, 104-105

Latino cross-cultural, 103-113
    clinical examples of, 107-110
    communities of, 106
    gay issues related to, 104-105
    Latinos in United States, 105-106
    oppression sensitive approach
        to, 110-111
Schroeder, D.G., 69
Self, understanding of, in intercultural
    therapy with Latino immigrants and
    white partners, 139-140
Self-identity, women's, interracial
    relationships stereotypes impact on,
    30-33
Self-of-the-therapist work, in
    black-white multiracial couples'
    intervention, 118-120
Sexuality, in interracial relationships, 78
Smith, K.R., 121
Snyder, D.K., 43, 133
Social construction of whiteness, 90
Social constructionist views, of race, 29-30
Social geography, interracial
    relationships in Hawaii and, 74-75
Social institutions, perceived reactions
    from, to Latino/a and white
    marriages, 50-52
Social issues, in multicultural Muslim
    couples' relationships, 61-62
Social network, in assessment and
    intervention with black-white
    multiracial couples, 123-125
Social support
    in assessment and intervention with
        black-white multiracial
        couples, 123-125
    for interracial couples, 165
    study of, 169
Societal intolerance, of interracial
    relationships, 76-77
Solsberry, P.W., 69,79
Spradley, J., 46
Steier, H., 111
Stereotype(s)
    avoidance of, by interracial and
        intercultural lesbian couples, 96

of interracial couples
    impact on couples' relationships,
        30-33
    impact on women's self-identity,
        30-33
of multicultural Muslim couples, 68
Stone Center's Relational/Cultural
    (R/C) Theory, 26
"Structural and assimilationist
    explanations of Asian American
    intermarriage," 158
Sue, D.W., 69
Support, fostering of, in interracial and
    intercultural lesbian couples, 98
Support groups, for interracial couples, 80

Texas Civil Liberties Union, 164
"The Incredibly True Adventures of
    Two Girls in Love," 86
Therapeutic considerations, for
    interracial and intercultural lesbian
    couples, 95-98
Therapeutic conversation, with Latino
    immigrants and white partners,
        131-149. *See also*
        Intercultural therapy, with
        Latino immigrants and white
        partners
Therapeutic implications
    of interracial couples' responses to
        racism and partner differences,
        16-18
    of race impact on interracial
        relationships, 37-39
Therapeutic interventions
    for Asian American intermarriage,
        154-157
    with black-white multiracial couples,
        115-129. *See also* Multiracial
        couples
    for interracial relationships, 79-80
    for Latino cross-cultural same sex
        male relationships, 111
Therapist(s). *See also* Clinician(s)

experiences and responses of, in
interracial couples, study of,
171-172
intercultural therapy and, with Latino
immigrants and white partners,
131-149. *See also*
Intercultural therapy, with
Latino immigrants and white
partners
for Latino cross-cultural same sex
male relationships, 111
perspectives of, on working with
interracial couples, 163-177
role of
in interracial couples' responses
to racism and partner
differences, 16-18
in multicultural Muslim couples'
relationships, 67-70
Therapy
intercultural, with Latino immigrants
and white partners, 131-149.
See also Intercultural therapy,
with Latino immigrants and
white partners
for multicultural Muslim couples,
approaches, interventions,
and strategies for, 67-70
Thomas, V., 1
"Trends in Asian American
racial/ethnic intermarriage: A
comparison of 1980 and 1990
census data," 158
"Triple jeopardy," 92
Trust, creation of, in intercultural
therapy with Latino immigrants and
white partners, 140-142
Tubbs, C.Y., 2, 115
Tully, C.T., 98

United States, immigrants to, 89
United States Supreme Court, 164
U.S. Immigration and Naturalization
Law of 1995, 159

Usita, P.M., 2,73

Violence, domestic, in black-white
multiracial couples, 124-125
Vivero, V.N., 141

Warren, D.M., 53
Wetchler, J.L., 1
Wethington, E., 79
White and Latino/a marriages,
experiences of, study of, 41-55. *See
also* Latino/a and white
marriages, experiences of,
study of
White partners, Latino immigrants
and, intercultural couple
issues in, 131-149. *See also*
Intercultural therapy, with
Latino immigrants and white
partners
White Teeth, 173
White women
with black men, race impact on,
23-40. *See also* Interracial
relationships, white women
with black men, race impact on
in multiracial families, 26-27
racial identity shifts of, language
for, 26
White-black multiracial couples,
assessment and intervention with,
115-129. *See also*
Black-white multiracial
couples, assessment and
intervention with
White-Latino marriages, rates of, 132-133
Whiteness, social construction of, 90
Wieling, E., 2,41
Women
self-identity of, interracial
relationships stereotypes
impact on, 30-33
white, with black men, race impact
on, 23-40. *See also* Interracial
relationships, white women
with black men, race impact on

Yeung, W.T., 76

Zayas, L.H., 134
Zebroski, S.A., 117